THE ANTIQUARY'S BOOKS

THE HUNDRED
AND THE HUNDRED ROLLS

BURT FRANKLIN RESEARCH & SOURCE WORKS SERIES # 19

PLATE I

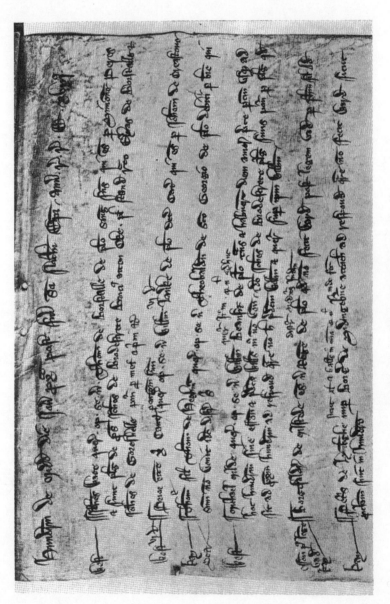

ROLL OF THE COURT OF MILTON HUNDRED

THE HUNDRED AND
THE HUNDRED ROLLS

AN OUTLINE OF LOCAL GOVERNMENT
IN MEDIEVAL ENGLAND

BY

HELEN M. CAM

WITH ELEVEN ILLUSTRATIONS AND TWO MAPS

BURT FRANKLIN RESEARCH & SOURCE WORKS SERIES # 19

BURT FRANKLIN

New York 25, N. Y.

Published by
BURT FRANKLIN
514 West 113th Street
New York 25, N. Y.

First Published in 1930
METHUEN & CO.

Printed in U.S.A. by
SENTRY PRESS, Inc.
New York 19, N. Y.

To

MY DEAR AND HONOURED TEACHER

MARGARET WADE LEYS

SOMETIME SENIOR STAFF LECTURER IN HISTORY AT THE

ROYAL HOLLOWAY COLLEGE

PREFACE

IN this book I have tried to do two things : to provide a guide to the study of the three great volumes of the *Rotuli Hundredorum* and *Placita Quo Warranto* printed early in the nineteenth century, and to give a sketch of the local governmental system at work in the reign of Edward I. Throughout my aim has been that of Richard Fitz Neal : to write *non subtilia sed utilia*. As an adequate bibliography, for instance, would have been unwieldy in the extreme, I have endeavoured to indicate in the foot-notes the most useful recent work on the subject, as well as a number of typical sources.

I should like here to thank all those who have helped in the making of this book. We are all the pupils of Maitland, of Vinogradoff, and of Tout. After them I would acknowledge my debt to the numberless army of workers in the Selden Society, the Victoria County History, and the many county societies into whose labours I have entered, and to my fellow-workers, notably Professor E. F. Jacob, Dr. W. A. Morris, and, above all, my friend Miss Mabel Mills, who has generously shared with me her unrivalled knowledge of the thirteenth-century Exchequer and has read the whole book in manuscript. For help in many small details I have to thank Dr. G. G. Coulton, Professor A. E. Levett, Mr. H. S. Bennett, Miss Latham, Mrs. Lobel, Miss F. M. Page, Miss L. J. Redstone, Mr. Robo, Mr. L. F. Salzman, and Miss M. A. Hennings, whose unpublished thesis on the sheriff was the starting point for much of my work. For the illustrations I owe thanks to the authorities of the Public Record Office and the British Museum for facilities, to Messrs. Monger and Marchant of Chancery Lane for photographing, and to the proprietors of the *Daily Sketch* and the Photocrom Co., Ltd., for leave to reproduce copyright photographs. I have to thank Mr. Hilary Jenkinson of the Public Record Office for invaluable help and advice from first to last, and my friend and colleague Miss M. G. Jones for her great kindness and care in reading the proofs.

Last and first of all my grateful acknowledgments are due to Girton College, who, amongst many other good gifts, has given me the means and the time to do the work here embodied.

H. M. C.

June 1930

CONTENTS

PART IV

THE SEQUEL TO THE INQUESTS OF 1274-5

LIST OF ILLUSTRATIONS, WITH NOTES

PLATE

I. ROLL OF THE COURT OF MILTON HUNDRED, KENT*

Frontispiece

P.R.O. Court Roll 1811–74.
The first six entries for the court held on Thursday December
8th 1289.
The pleas are of bloodshed, detention of chattels, debt, and
trespass; then two borshorlders are charged with not keeping
watch and ward ' as was proclaimed in the hundred '. The
notes above the line indicate the action to be taken : ' Let him
be distrained ', etc.

II. HEAD AND FOOT OF HUNDRED ROLL* . . .

Wilts H.R., No. 16 (printed R.H., II, 258, 259).
The original return for Elstub hundred, giving date (St.
Gregory's Day, March 12th 1275), names of commissioners, and
names of jurors and their returns to the first two articles.
At the foot are the tags for the twelve jurors' seals, one of
which is still on its ' rag '.

III. FOUR EXCHEQUER TALLIES* . . . . .

(1) From the sheriff of Cumberland (1285–98) *de debitis
pleurium*, i.e. for debts collected on the Exchequer Summons.
(2) From Osbert of Bereford, sheriff of Warwickshire and
Leicestershire (1273–5) for the arrears of the Twentieth.
(3) From the sheriff of Bedfordshire and Buckinghamshire
(1293–6) for minute particulars of serjeanties.
(4) From the bailiff of the liberty of the bishop of Ely
(Cambs.), who had the Summons of the Exchequer, *de debitis
pleurium*.
The different notches indicate pounds, shillings, pence, etc.
Towards the left end can be seen the place where the shorter tally
or foil, which the sheriff kept, was split off the stock, which the
Exchequer kept.

IV. THE COLLECTION OF WROTH SILVER, KNIGHTLOW
HUNDRED . . . .

' Wroth silver ', once wardsilver, is still paid every year at
Martinmas, at dawn, on Knightlow Hill, south-east of Coventry,
from the tenants of certain lands in the hundred to the Duke of
Buccleuch, the present lord of the hundred.
(*Photo : ' Daily Sketch '*)

*Photos : Monger and Marchant.

MAPS

INTRODUCTION

IN the history of English local government there is no
sudden breach of continuity such as the National Assembly
effected in France, to Burke's disgust, in 1790. The shire
of Alfred the Great, the county of William the Conqueror, is still
a working institution to-day ; the reforms of the nineteenth and
twentieth century, far from superseding it, have given it a new
lease of life, and the county member, the county court, and the
county council are all too familiar to rouse either curiosity or
sentiment. But it is another story when we come to the smaller
units of local government. The subdivisions of the shire that
we know to-day are not yet a century old ; and the district that
was as familiar to our administrators as it was to our mapmakers
from Hastings to Waterloo is now of interest only to the antiquarian and the historian. Superseded by the Poor Law Union
and the Urban and Rural District, the hundred has receded so
rapidly into the mists of the past that the first associations to be
called up by its name are likely to be those of remote antiquity—
of the Germany of Tacitus, the Gaul of Clovis or the England of
Edgar the Peaceable.

With the uncertainties of those far-off times we have here no
concern. No mists of romance or controversy obscure the history
of the hundred of the thirteenth century : it is possible to say
positively and definitely that every county of England was then
divided into districts, of varying size and shape, but capable of
being located with pretty close accuracy on a map ; and that
these districts, generally known as hundreds, but occasionally
going by the name of wapentakes or wards, formed an indispensable part of the system of local government. For taxation,
for justice, for police, for law, for military defence, the hundred
came into play. The sheriff administered the shire through the
bailiffs who held office in each hundred ; the king's justices

employed the hundred for the detection of crime ; the government clerks at headquarters kept their records of land tenure and of fiscal obligation under hundredal headings. Without an understanding of the hundred it is impossible to understand the working of the government of England in the early Middle Ages.

So much for the hundred : what were the Hundred Rolls ?

On 2nd August, 1274, Edward I landed in England, returning from that crusade which had proved fatal to his kinsman, the saintly King of France, and had nearly been fatal to himself. Four years before he had left a country exhausted by six years of civil war, but settling down to quiet and order under the rule of his father and the faithful counsellors who, from the 20th of November, 1272, were to have the sole responsibility for carrying on the government in Edward's name. Like Richard the Lionhearted, Edward could count on the services of a body of loyal and capable administrators ; unlike his great-uncle, Edward was prepared on his return instantly to take up the reins of government, and to exact from both high and low a strict account of their conduct in his absence. Before ten weeks were out he had issued orders for a searching inquiry into the usurpation of royal rights by the magnates and into the conduct of the officials who were carrying on the king's government up and down the country. Commissioners were sent to every shire charged, like the Domesday Commissioners of 1086, with a long series of questions, to be put to the juries of every hundred of every shire, and by March, 1275, they had brought back to Westminster the bundles of rolls, with the jurors' seals hanging from them, of which only a part are still in existence. In these rolls, then nicknamed the Ragman Rolls, but known to-day as the Hundred Rolls, was recorded a complete statement as to the administration of the counties ; and from them, incomplete though they now are, can be reconstructed a picture of the local government of England as it was at the beginning of the third year of Edward I : a picture which, like that reflected in the Domesday Book of two hundred years before, makes clearer to us both the earlier and the later condition of the country-side.

The Hundred Rolls of 1274–5 are the starting-point of this

book. In interpreting them we shall learn to understand not only the England of Edward I, but the whole system of local government of the early Middle Ages in England; and from Edward's policy in this one matter we may learn to understand what he himself stands for in the history of England—an English Justinian, looking, like his Byzantine prototype, both ways, to the past and to the future.

Disciple : "I don't exactly know what a 'century' or a 'hundred' is.
Master : "Wait a bit . . . The village people know it best."

—DIALOGUE OF THE EXCHEQUER

THE HUNDRED
AND THE HUNDRED ROLLS

PART I

LOCAL GOVERNMENT, 1066–1272

CHAPTER I

THE KING AND THE SHERIFF, 1066–1272

WHAT was the system of local government into the working of which Edward's commissioners were inquiring? It was not the.product of yesterday; it was in its outstanding features far older than the authority of the Plantagenet dynasty itself. But, like everything else in England, it had felt the powerful influence of the great ancestors of Edward. Anglo-Saxon in origin, it had been moulded, modified, exploited by the Norman new-comers, and transformed from a token of local independence to an embodiment of the principle of central control. In this process of transformation the all-important agent was the sheriff; to understand the local government of the twelfth and thirteenth centuries we must begin with him.

When William I made himself master of England he found in every shire an official whose position was somewhat ambiguous. He was called the reeve of the shire; and reeves were stewards, administering the property of a master. The shire-reeve seemed to have two masters. On the one hand, he was looking out for the king's interests in the shire, collecting the revenues arising from the royal estates, the tolls, the judicial payments, and the other dues to which the king was by ancient custom entitled. On the other hand, he was bound to pay over some of the moneys he collected to the ealdorman, or earl, as he was coming to be

called, and he was doing much of the work that the earl had
done himself in the days when he had been ealdorman of one
shire instead of many.   Where once the ealdormen had led the
forces of the shire to war, now the sheriff led them : the sheriff
of Berkshire had fallen at Hastings.   Where once the earl had
presided at the shire-moot, now the sheriff sat there, to see that
justice was done and the king's rights respected.   To the Norman
new-comers, the appropriate name for him seemed to be *vice
comes*—the earl's deputy.   As between the king and the earl
the sheriff was, in fact, securing a position of independence which
might well develop into irresponsibility.   The amount he would
be expected to pay in at the king's treasury might be fixed by
custom, as Domesday indicates, in many shires, but the machinery
for checking his conduct was rudimentary if not entirely lacking.
He had a pretty free hand and was acquiring a territorial position :
but for the Norman Conquest it seems quite conceivable that he
would, like the French *vicomte*, have lost his official character
altogether and become a hereditary magnate.

William I ousted the Saxon sheriffs as soon as he could safely
do so.   The Norman successor to the displaced Englishman,
generally a landowner in the county he governed, was of necessity
entrusted with wide discretionary powers.   The Normans for
years after the Conquest were still in the position of an armed
garrison in the midst of a politically hostile country-side : their
lives had to be guarded by the special *murdrum* fine, not exacted
if the murdered man could be shown to be English.   William's
sheriffs had something of the viceroy about them ; they held
office for long periods, and used their power tyrannically, secure in
the confidence that few would dare to interfere with them.   Picot,
sheriff of Cambridgeshire from 1071 to 1095, was one of the most
notorious.   He bullied the townsmen of Cambridge and the
villagers of Freckenham alike, and did not shrink from invading
the rights of the monks of Ely and insulting by his scornful
ignorance the dear and honoured name of St. Etheldreda, their
foundress.   But even Picot, though there might be no one in
Cambridgeshire able to stand up to him, had to bow to the king's
justice.   After he had secured certain lands for himself by

browbeating a sworn jury in the shire-moot, a former inhabitant of the village who knew the rights of the case reported the injustice at head-quarters, and the jury was summoned up to London where, in the king's court, they told the truth and the sheriff had to surrender the ill-gotten lands.

Behind the sheriff was the king, and if the injured persons were important enough, the king's justice could be brought to bear on the sheriff. But so long as such control only operated occasionally, the sheriff was still a very great man, and in many shires he succeeded in making his position so secure that he was able to hand it on to his son. Some more constant check on him was needed if he were not to become an independent hereditary official. The check was supplied by Henry I. The machinery of the central treasury was overhauled, and a new system of accounting introduced, by which the sheriff found himself sharply brought up if he tried to defraud the central government of any of the revenues which had passed through his hands. Every year the sheriffs had to come up to Westminster to render an account of their stewardship before the great officers of the king's court sitting in the Exchequer, as the central treasury was now called, from the new system of reckoning recently introduced from France. A London chronicler describes the gloomy coun-tenances of the sheriffs ' shaking with terror ' as they assembled to render their account in 1121 ; only one among them, Gilbert, the honest sheriff of Surrey, he says, came forward boldly and gaily when called upon, and took his seat before the Exchequer officials without anxiety. Henry I went further than this ; not content with interviewing the sheriffs at Westminster, the Exchequer officials went on tour round the shires, holding local inquiries into the financial administration of the sheriffs. The county had not now to wait for some extraordinary emergency or outrageous scandal to see the king's justices in their midst. Systematic visitation and inspection had begun, and inquiry into the sheriff's honesty in fiscal matters was bound to lead to investi-gation of all those activities of his which might bring in revenue to the king—his conduct of cases in the shire court, for instance, with their potential profits of justice, or his treatment of the widows or minors of royal vassals, valuable sources of royal income, or his punishment of criminals, whose goods were forfeit to the crown. Forty-four thieves were hanged at Huncote in Leicestershire in 1124 by one such set of visitors. It is even possible that Henry took the further step of setting up a royal justice in each shire alongside the sheriff, to take over some of the judicial business and to keep an eye on him—the forerunner of the later coroner. The references to these local justices are, however, so few and far between that we cannot be sure of their significance.

The death of the Lion of Justice in 1135 meant a severe set-back for law and order. It is too much to say that the whole system of administration broke down ; we know that hundred courts and shire courts still met and that business was still carried on at the Exchequer. But there was great local disorder, and the systematic visitations of the shires must have ceased. The note struck again and again in the official pronouncements of Henry II is : ' Let us return to the good ways of my grand-father '. Stephen's reign was not only an usurpation, but an evil interlude ; an interruption of the process of securing the king's hold over the administration, the finance, and the jurisdiction of the realm. England made a fresh start in 1154, and once the unlicensed castles were down and the king's servants set to the task of making the king's justice available for all land-holders, the need to control the sheriffs effectively led to a revival of the inspection of sheriffs from head-quarters. The first general instructions to itinerant justices were issued at Clarendon early in 1166,[1] and laid down among other important provisions that the sheriffs should bring those formally indicted by the hundred juries before the nearest justices. Four years later came a much more drastic invasion of the sheriffs' sphere of action. Between April and June 1170 a searching examination was made by special com-missioners into the conduct of all the sheriffs in the kingdom.[2] All the barons, knights, and freemen of the shire were required to give evidence on oath as to whether the sheriffs and their underlings had extorted money unjustly from individuals or

[1] Stubbs, *Charters*, pp. 170-3.   [2] Ibid., pp. 175 ff.

communities, with or without the judgement of a court, whether they had retained for themselves dues which they ought to have paid over to the Exchequer, whether they had countenanced false accusations, whether they had taken bribes to let off guilty persons, or bribed men not to complain to the king's commissioners of their conduct. As a result of this general inquest, all the sheriffs in England were removed from office, and heavy fines were inflicted on many of them. Some of them who, like the newly appointed, were officials of the king's court, were restored to office later, but the principle had been established that the office of sheriff was held during the king's pleasure, and subject to the good conduct of the holder. From this time on if the country-side had cause to complain of a sheriff they were justified in assuming that he had the king's government behind him, for the length of the king's arm had been proved. The oppression and extortions of which the chroniclers so frequently tell us might fairly be laid to the charge of the central government, which had shown that it had the power, if it had the will, to punish the unjust and extortionate sheriff.

The point of view of the king and the country-side was bound to differ in this matter. The sheriff was there to look out for the king's interests ; if he used his vantage-ground to fill his own pockets or pay off his own scores it did not necessarily hurt the king's interests. Only if he diverted to himself moneys that should have gone to the Exchequer would conviction certainly entail punishment, and even then a share of the spoils might placate the central government. Something of this partnership in extortion may be fairly charged against the sheriffs of Richard I and John ; on the one hand, we still find men who are prepared to buy the office of sheriff for a large sum, which proves that it could be made to pay ; whilst, on the other hand, the extant Exchequer records go to support the charges of the barons in 1215 that the government was behind the sheriff in his levy of heavier sums from the shires.[1] To the farm of the shire had been added an ' increment ' under Richard ; and ' profits ' were further

---

[1] Stubbs, *Charters*, p. 287 (Articles of the Barons, c. 14), p. 296 (Magna Carta, c. 25).

added under John, increasing the sums exacted by some £2,500 in the period 1189–1216.[1] The complaints put on record by Magna Carta are a testimony to the efficiency of John's sheriffs as fiscal agents : that which made the country loathe them commended them to a vigilant and progressive Exchequer.

It was not only in fiscal matters that the activity of the sheriffs was increased by Henry II's policy. When the king made royal justice more readily accessible to all his subjects by devising attractive writs ; when he offered to all landholders, whosesoever tenants they were, the ' royal benefit ' of a jury for securing quiet possession of their land, he was preparing new work for the sheriffs on a large scale. Every jury for the assizes of Mort d'Ancestor, Novel Disseisin and Darrein Presentment had to be empanelled by the sheriff or his subordinates, and the sheriff had to return the verdict and the names of the jurors to the right quarter. Proceedings of this sort were not new under Henry II, but what was new was the enormous volume of litigation which, attracted by these new facilities, flowed into the royal courts and entailed more and more work (with, no doubt, accompanying perquisites) on the sheriff and his staff. The more royal justice gained on seignorial justice the more there was for the royal official to do in the way of executing writs and empanelling juries, and the more openings for oppression and favouritism in the selection of jurors and the holding of inquests at inconvenient times or in out-of-the-way places. Like many employers of casual labour to-day, the sheriffs preferred to have a safe margin to draw upon ; if they needed a jury of twelve they would summon eighteen or twenty-four men, and fine them ruthlessly for not coming, even though they had their full number of twelve.

It is not too much to say that every extension of royal control of government meant more work for the sheriff. As he grew less independent, he grew more laborious, his staff increased steadily, and with it increased the burden on the country-side. The complaint of a Lancashire hundred in 1334 gives a vivid picture of the growth of a local bureaucracy. Under Henry III, Alan of Singleton was hereditary bailiff of Amounderness, and he

[1] M. H. Mills, *Trans. R. Hist. Soc. for 1925*, pp. 157 ff.

did all the work himself, at his own expense, and so did his son after him, but his grandson found the work grown so much that he appointed a whole-time subordinate to do the work for him, and the process went on till in 1334, Alan's great-great-great-grandson had let the office to a man who employed five others to help him in doing the work of the hundred. In spite of their complaints, the men of Amounderness admitted that at least four were necessary.[1] The increase of population and the increase of business together had multiplied the hundred bailiff's work four-fold in a hundred years, and a large proportion of that work was carrying out the orders received by the sheriff in respect of the residents in that hundred.

Along with this development of machinery in the shires went changes at head-quarters. The fifty-six years of Henry III's reign saw a great advance of the science of government, not only on the judicial side of the king's court, by great practitioners like Pateshull and Raleigh, Bracton's masters, but also on the fiscal side, in the Exchequer. The mere bulk of the new revenue brought in by the extension of royal justice necessitated new methods. As early as John's reign there are signs that good heads are at work tackling these new problems : labour-saving methods, a business-like filing of records are evident. Under Henry III there is a thoroughgoing overhauling of the whole department. Ironically enough, the guiding spirit appears to be one of those very foreigners of whose influence the barons were so furiously and justifiably jealous. Peter de Rivaux, nephew of the unpopular Bishop of Winchester, who has been regarded as a shameless pluralist for having held the sheriffdoms of twenty-one counties in one year, should, it seems, more justly be regarded as an exceptionally efficient civil servant : a reformer who made sure that his new methods should be set going in all the shires of England by taking them into his own hands for a space and putting in under-sheriffs, who would take their orders from him.[2] As a consequence of the reforms effected through him in the years 1232–42, the sheriff of the thirteenth century becomes more than

[1] Coram Rege Roll 297 (Trinity Term), mm. 21, 27.
[2] M. H. Mills, *Trans. R. Hist. Soc. for 1927*, pp. 111–33.

ever before the tool of the central government.   His independence
is now curtailed not only by justices in eyre, but by coroners
whose records are a check on his activities in the criminal sphere,
and by escheators and other agents who take most of the feudal
and royal demesne business off his hands.   His routine work,
however, has increased as his independence has diminished ; he
comes in official contact with more individuals, he has a larger
staff to manage.   His fiscal liabilities have increased also ; owing
to recent 'reforms at the Exchequer he has to levy many sums,
for the purchase of writs, for instance, which would once have
been paid in to the Exchequer by the debtors in person.   Under
Henry III it becomes quite common for the sheriff to find himself
in the Fleet Prison, for failing to satisfy the king, and sheriffs'
heirs are still paying off debts incurred by their fathers when in
office, fifteen years after the sheriff's death.   Under Richard and
John men had paid large sums to be made sheriff ; they are now
ready to buy from the king exemption for life from the office.
Such posts are no longer held by great barons.   The type of man
whom the Conqueror had appointed is replaced by a royal clerk
or a country gentleman, not a tenant-in-chief, but a sub-vassal.
Royal clerks are, perhaps, the more efficient, but on the whole
both king and country-side prefer the squire type, ' a substantial
person, holding land in the county ', as the Provisions of Oxford
say, who will be in touch with local feeling and work well with
the other knights of the shire and who has lands which will serve
as security for his power to make good a deficit in his account at
the Exchequer.

By 1274, then, the sheriff, although, as Maitland says, ' the
governor of the shire, the captain of its forces, the president of
its court, a distinctively royal officer appointed by the King,
dismissible at a moment's notice and strictly accountable at the
Exchequer ', is also very often a country squire, expected to do
right to his fellow-knights of the shire and to live up to a standard
of general decency and good conduct of which the king is not the
sole judge.   To understand more fully the conditions under
which he works, we must now set him against his local background
—the community of the shire.

CHAPTER II

THE HUNDRED AND THE SHIRE, 1066–1272

WILLIAM THE CONQUEROR took over the government of a country whose larger local divisions were in the main those that we know to-day. Of the present forty counties of England thirty-three had practically the same boundaries that they have to-day. Rutland was not yet a county, its area being divided between Northants and Nottinghamshire. Yorkshire and Cheshire between them included the territory which now goes to make Lancashire, Westmorland, and Cumberland ; and Durham, not yet a county, was a great liberty within Northumberland. Monmouthshire was a part of Gloucestershire.

William found these shires or counties subdivided into districts called hundreds, in most parts, but in Lincolnshire, Yorkshire, Nottinghamshire, Derbyshire, and Leicestershire, wapentakes ; in Cornwall, and possibly in Northumberland and Durham also, shires. By the thirteenth century the divisions in the four northernmost counties were called wards, as they are to-day, but it is not clear when the name was introduced. The origin of all these lesser districts is highly controversial and cannot be discussed here ; but of their history since 1086 we can speak more confidently, though their boundaries have been far more drastically modified in the course of centuries than have those of the shires. In some counties, such as Shropshire, Herefordshire, Derbyshire, and Dorset, the system seems to have been completely reorganized between the reign of William I and Henry II, probably under Henry I ; in others, such as Gloucestershire, Berkshire, and Somerset, the eyre rolls show that a process of amalgamation and readjustment has taken place, by which two or three smaller districts have been thrown together to make a better unit for administration ; in others, such as Sussex, one large district has been broken up into two or three smaller ones ; whilst in others such as Cambridgeshire, Norfolk, Lincolnshire, and Essex, the hundred or wapentake boundaries have hardly changed at all between the eleventh and the twentieth century. Though for most purposes the rural district and the poor law union have rendered the hundred obsolete, in Essex at least the tradition was sufficiently alive for Voluntary Aid Detachments in the war of 1914–18 to call themselves by the name of the hundred.

Both in the hundred and the shire courts were held at stated intervals. Before 1066 judicial activities, both secular and spiritual, had been concentrated in these local assemblies, at which the local custom was declared and enforced, titles to property were established, and violence condemned, if not punished. Justice was administered and law declared by those who attended the court : a procedure which sounds democratic, but was probably in practice far from equalitarian. Not only did well-established tradition recognize one law for the rich and another for the poor, as far as proof and penalties went, but, according to all surviving accounts of shire-moots, the assemblies were swayed by the exhortations or threats of one or two influen-tial men, thegns, or even ealdormen. A fair number of lesser freemen, and after 1066 some unfree men, were bound to be present, but the witness or the judgement of the shire was declared by the mouth of a few men. As a writer of Henry I's reign says, ' The opinion of the better men prevails '. A select aristocracy of the chief landholders of the shire must have run the local government in most of the counties of England, with the possible exception of those of the Danelaw. Here there was so much more social liberty and equality that a larger measure of political democracy also may well have obtained in the counties of the wapentakes than in those of the hundreds.

The shire-moot probably met in the open air, at any rate for the two ' great counties ' of Easter and Michaelmas, which are all that the Anglo-Saxon laws specify. The monthly meetings of Norman days, however, would have been at least as necessary before 1066 when no higher courts were easily available ; at these there was probably a smaller attendance and business of a more

personal nature.   Besides these, on occasion an extraordinary
session might be convened by royal command, like that great
Kentish shire-moot held on Penenden Heath in 1071, at which
Lanfranc made good the claims of his church of Canterbury to
the lands and liberties it had enjoyed before the Norman Conquest.   In the specially privileged county of Chester the county
court retained down to 1272 some of that local autonomy which
had characterized the Saxon and Norman shire-moot.   Special
local variations of land law are still preserved there, as in the
older boroughs, and the justice who presides, though armed with
fuller powers than the normal sheriff, defers to those of the county
who know the local usage.   In a case of the year 1260, for instance,
the defendant asserts that he is not bound to answer.   The county
gives judgement that the case ought to proceed.   The defendant
protests that this is an unjust ruling and withdraws from the
county court.   He is thrice summoned—in court, at the door of
the castle hall where the county was being held, and at the castle
gate.   Knights of the county are sent to confer with him, but to
no effect.   ' Then the Justice requested of the whole county that
they should instruct him and show to him what proceedings
should be taken in this matter according to the form of law and
the established customs of the county.   And the county said
that the Justice ought by law now to take the inquest on his own
authority.' [1]   By declaring custom and determining procedure in
doubtful cases the county court was in effect making law, though
law of only local application ; in the Middle Ages no clear dividing
line could be drawn between jurisdiction and legislation.   The
shire-moots of the tenth and eleventh centuries are sometimes
referred to as the *witan* of such or such a shire ; they were indeed
as organs of self-government of far more practical importance
than the central witan, that indeterminate collection of nobles
and clergy whose powers varied inversely with those of the
Anglo-Saxon kings.

It was as the repository of tradition that the Conqueror called
on the shire-moot for co-operation.   For a king who had from

---

[1] Stewart Brown, *Chester County Court Rolls*, p. 30 ; *Eng. Hist. Rev.*, XLII,
p. 119.

the first steadily maintained that he was the lawful heir of the Confessor, and who stood for the principles of justice in accordance with the laws of God and of man, the shire-moot was bound to be the tribunal for settling controversies as to the claims of Norman bishops or earls who had been granted all the lands and the rights of English predecessors.   Not only the Archbishop of Canterbury but many other great men between 1066 and 1087 made good their claims in a county court by the witness of the good men, or, more particularly, the old men, of the shire, a specially appointed royal delegate presiding to see that justice was done and to record the judgement.   By 1086 the shires must have been used to the sight of the king's justice sitting in their court, and to the new procedure of the sworn inquest as a means of getting definite answers to definite questions.   Whether the Domesday inquest was held in shire-moots or hundred-moots, it was new to the English rather by its magnificent comprehensiveness than by its utilization of the local machinery.

William's successors continued to use the shire-moot for their own purposes.   Wherever local knowledge was required by the king, whether for establishing a title to land, or for establishing the nature of a service, or for inquiring into the conduct of some magnate or official, the obvious method to pursue was to order the sheriff to get the information at a shire-moot, and very often a royal delegate came down to preside at the court.   Henry I found it necessary to forbid sheriffs to summon extraordinary shire-moots or hundred-moots without royal warrant ; the practice of holding courts in inconvenient places, at abnormal times, and without due notice, and fining those who failed to appear was probably a frequent means of increasing the profits of office.   Under Henry I, as visits of royal justices became more regular, the transformation of shire-moot into king's court must have become a stereotyped process.   Even under Stephen both the regular and the extraordinary sessions continued.   At a special joint assembly of the counties of Norfolk and Suffolk before a royal steward in 1148, or thereabouts, all the familiar features reappear ; the speeches of the magnates, the witness of the old men, the judgement of the court.   Moreover, the old knight whose testimony settles the matter observes incidentally that for fifty years he has been attending shire courts and hundred courts, since before the days of good King Henry, when peace and justice flourished in the land.[1]

But Henry II did more than return to his grandfather's traditions : he took the decisive step which drew the shire court into the main stream of constitutional development.   It was not merely to use its old procedure on the king's behalf ; it was to be taught a new procedure : the suitors of the court were to become not only judges but jurors.   The king's justices, sitting in the shire court, were to call upon the knights of the shire and the men of the hundred to give answer, in sworn dozens, to questions put to them—not only to specific questions as to royal dues, but to sweeping questions such as : ' Is there anybody in your hundred whom you suspect to be a thief or a receiver of thieves ? '   Gradually there opened up by means of these juries of presentment a way for the complaints and wishes of the country-side to reach the king.   The demand for information was in effect transformable into an invitation to complain ; and complaints came to the king's court of a fullness that would have been embarrassing if they had been seriously taken as a programme for action.   The contact was established, not merely a personal but an official contact, between the shire court and the king's court.   Especially valuable, as we see in the light of later developments, was the arrangement for transferring a case from the shire court to the king's court.   If a man had been accused by a presenting jury in the shire court, or if a dispute between two men had been carried to a certain point in the shire court, and was then called before the king, a body of trustworthy knights— four or more—was sent to the king's court to ' bear the record of the shire ', that is, to report precisely what had taken place in the shire court so that the king's justices had the information before them in dealing with the matter.   These knights spoke for the whole county : they *were* the county in fact—plenipotentiary delegates at the king's court, to see the county's conduct of the case upheld or condemned ; to maintain if need be the dignity of

[1] *Eng. Hist. Rev.*, XXXIX, pp. 568–71.

the county, by taking further steps, such as selecting a champion to uphold its honour. Thus we read in the rolls of the king's courts how the county of Sussex waged a duel with a knight who accused it of wrongful judgement. What with knights bearing the record of the shire, and with juries for the grand assize and the possessory assizes, travelling to the king's court, the men of the shires and hundreds were being drawn more and more into the system of royal justice without, however, losing contact with their base—the old customary courts.

It is, indeed, thanks to this contact that we know so much more of what was happening in the county courts of the thirteenth century than we do at any earlier date. The records carried by the knights were entered upon the roll of the king's court ; and though many of those rolls are lost, from the reign of Richard I onwards a growing proportion survives, and from these we may draw a series of pictures of the county court in action between the death of Henry II and the accession of Edward I.

Except in some of the northern counties, it met every four weeks, sometimes out of doors, but often in the castle hall or some official 'hall of pleas'. The litigation there might involve a judicial combat, as in Wiltshire in 1199, when a victorious champion complained that after he had felled his adversary, a certain Robert Block came up and seized the fallen man's weapon and struck him on the head with it. This was denied utterly by the knights whom the under-sheriff had assigned to keep the field of battle, and the sheriff was ordered to bring a full record of the county to Westminster to settle the matter.[1]

Not only the duel but all the procedure of jurisdiction was controlled by the knights of the shire as well as the sheriff. The whole court was penalized for a technical error, and without the suitors' assistance no judicial business could be done. This is forcibly brought out by a record quoted by Bracton, and after him by Maitland. In 1226 the sheriff of Lincolnshire complained that some of the knights of the shire had been hindering him from holding the courts of the county, the ridings, and the wapentakes. On the shire day at Lincoln he had held pleas from

---

[1] *Curia Regis Rolls*, I, 100.

PLATE II

HEAD AND FOOT OF HUNDRED ROLL, SHOWING 'RAGS'

PLATE II

HEAD AND FOOT OF HUNDRED ROLL, SHOWING 'RAGS'

early morn until evening, and there still remained over many cases ; so he told the plaintiffs and the suitors to come back early next morning.   Next morning, when the sheriff took his seat and the plaintiffs produced their pleas, most of the knights and the stewards who were doing suit to the shire in place of their lords stayed outside the hall of pleas.   The sheriff called to them to come in and give their judgement on the cases before the court, upon which those who were inside went out, and they all went away, declaring that they were not bound to hold the shire-moot for more than one day.   So the sheriff told the litigants that they must come to the wapentake court, and they all departed. Later the sheriff came to Ancaster, the centre of the ten wapen-takes that make up the riding of Lincolnshire, known to-day as the parts of Kesteven, and prepared to hold the adjourned pleas there.   This time a formal protest was made ; the spokesman of the knights declared that the county court was the only place where he and his like were called upon to make judgements.   ' I should like to hear who will give judgement in the wapentake court ! ' said he.   The sheriff said that he was none the less bound to do justice to the poor, and again called on the knights to give judgement.   The knights went out to talk it over, and agreed that the demand was contrary to their chartered liberties ; and they came back and told the sheriff that they neither would nor ought to give judgements, and said other more shameful things to him, asking him by what warrant he was making this use of the wapentake court.   Then one of the stewards present spoke up, saying ,' It is rather for you knights to say by what warrant you are hindering the sheriff, who has the king's authority behind him ! ' and by way of setting a good example he gave his judgement on the first case before the court.   The knights promptly rounded on this servile soul.   ' Make what judgements you please ; we shall see what your lord, John Marshal, will say when we tell him how you have been behaving in the shire court ! '   So the sheriff, in spite of the royal authority behind him, had to give up the attempt to hear the pleas ; and what is more, when he complained to the king, the knights won their case at Westminster.   The king had confirmed the liberties and ancient customs of Lincolnshire, the sheriff had infringed them twice over : by attempting to hold the shire court two days running, and by holding the wapentake court contrary to the .terms of Magna Carta.[1]

This case gives an excellent idea of the school in which the knights of the shire of 1258–9 had received their political training. The king was far off ; the earls and barons were usually absentees, represented in the county by their stewards ; it was the knights who ran the local government, both as holders in turn of the post of sheriff, as coroners, and as suitors and controllers of the county court, where their duties were steadily increasing as the century advanced. Here they were required to discuss taxation, to hear the king's letters and ordinances, to elect the county coroners, to serve on special juries and inquests, and to appoint plenipotentiaries to speak for the whole county in the king's court, both on fiscal and on political matters. If the lord of a manor found it troublesome to spend a day or more every month in a cross-country journey to attend the shire court, once there he would find it, we may imagine, as the later J.P. found quarter sessions, a centre of local gossip and government news, and a field for the exercise of any self-importance or any natural administrative or political ability that he possessed. Alongside the sheriff and his clerk, concerned with the batch of writs to be dealt with, of legal business to be got through, of criminal inquiries to be made, of debts to be collected, if possible before the court broke up, and of royal proclamations to be published, we can see the body of knights, jealous for the custom of the county and their own rights as suitors, not above bribing the sheriff to favour their individual causes, but ready in a moment to sink their differences in defence of the vested interests of their body, and to draft common petitions or representations to the king if any magnate or official had attacked those interests. Thus we find the gentlemen of Devon drawing up the list of charges still preserved at Oxford against their sheriff, Roger of Pridias, in 1272, accusing him of oppression of both rich and poor and of invasion of the liberties of the shire, winding up with the complaint that

[1] *Bracton's Notebook*, case 1730.

he is not a native of the county and a demand for his dismissal.[1] The shire court, in becoming an agent of the central government, had not ceased to be the articulate embodiment of local *esprit de corps*.

The hundred, too, was playing its part in the business of self-administration, as G. B. Adams has called it.   As district and business are on a smaller scale, the process is obscurer and records are very scanty.   But we know enough to be sure that it was functioning steadily under Henry I, and there seems no solid evidence to support the theory that he ' revived ' an enfeebled institution.   The sheriff, he said, was not to hold the hundred court otherwise than old custom sanctioned, but the king would have it summoned at his will for his own royal needs.[2]   It is mainly in connexion with those royal needs that we hear of the hundred court in the twelfth century, especially when information is required about the tenure of land ; many such instances are recorded under Henry I and Stephen.   Sometimes also the king commands the sheriff to see that right is done to some one in the hundred court, ' lest further complaints trouble us '.   Joint meetings of several hundreds are also mentioned, held to secure sufficient witness to some settlement.   Also, at least from the time of Henry I, inquiries were made twice a year at the hundred court as to the enforcement of the frankpledge system, which compelled all men not otherwise guaranteed to be grouped in tithings, or artificial families of ten, jointly responsible for each other's good conduct.   Unless other arrangements had been expressly sanctioned, it was the sheriff's business to ' view ' the frankpledge tithings at the great court or tourn held by him twice a year in each hundred of his county in turn, and from the time of Henry II at least he was at the same time holding inquiries into crimes and nuisances parallel to those held by the king's justices in their eyres from county to county.   He dealt with the lesser offences himself and passed on more serious offences to the justices. A much larger attendance was exacted at the tourn, and it was an event of some importance both to the villagers and to the government, for it produced a good deal of revenue.   But the outstanding

[1] Dodsworth MSS. (Bodl.), vol. 76, p. 33.
[2] Stubbs, *Charters*, p. 122.   See below, p. 168

significance of the tourn is that it links up the hundred to the royal system of police and criminal law, just as the local inquests in land cases linked it to the new royal justice in civil matters. The men of the hundred were doing the king's business as well as their own in their hundred courts, and getting well practised in the new inquest procedure on the juries of the tourn as well as on those of the eyre, where the twelve sworn freemen spoke for their hundred before the king's justices just as the knights of the shire were learning to speak for their county in the king's court.

By 1275 the hundred court was no longer settling important land disputes, as it did under Henry I, but it had a good variety of smaller civil pleas to settle, the perquisites from which brought in a comfortable little revenue for the lord of the hundred, whether it were the king or a subject ; its proceedings were being formally enrolled, and manuals existed to guide the clerk ; it did important business for the crown and was the place for the collection of customary royal dues, and as a whole it was an indispensable piece of the national machinery of government. It may be doubted whether the suitors were as independent in spirit as the knights of the shire, but as far as the forms of procedure went they were the judges and responsible for the judgements of the court.

Apart from the hundred court itself, the hundred was being utilized by the government for judicial, military, and fiscal purposes. The collective liability of the hundred for the murder fine if an unknown person were found dead is as old as the Conquest ; its importance to the revenue is attested by frequent entries in the Pipe Rolls. The hundred jury at the eyre also had a responsibility which entailed serious financial risks. The military and police system was organized by hundreds ; by John's reign, if not earlier, each hundred had an official, to be known later as the high constable, who was responsible for the keeping of the peace, the maintenance of watches, and, possibly, for the mustering of armed men of the hundred. Whether these duties were new under Henry III, or far older, as has been suggested, the constable is an embodiment of local responsibility.

Nor did the township itself escape its share of public duties, though the community of the village was largely made up of men whose personal status put them outside the purview of royal law. The coroner, who had to keep the records of death and wounding, of wreck and of treasure trove, called upon the four neighbouring vills for his inquest ; the two village constables who kept the king's peace and saw to the village arms were chosen by the township ; the township as a whole was held responsible for the escape of a fugitive whom the constable had arrested or who had taken sanctuary in their village church ; and if a villager suspected of a crime were missing and proved not to be a member of a frankpledge tithing, the village as a whole was amerced. Landlords might parcel out the village into manors and holdings ; in the king's eyes it was still an undivided whole : a community which was expected to play its part in the national system of government.

CHAPTER III

GOVERNMENTAL IDEALS, 1066–1272

THE special contribution of the Norman and Angevin kings to the art and science of government may thus be described as the adaptation of the ancient customary institutions of a decentralized system to the uses of their highly centralized administration. Without extinguishing local self-expression in the shire court they made the knights of the shire and the men of the hundred do the work of the central government, creating new traditions which were in their turn to become sacred with well-established use and wont. Not with any conscious aim of statesmanship, but to serve their own purposes, the kings preserved the vitality of these local courts, and so left the country-side an articulate voice, which was, in course of time, to be heard in the colloquies and parliaments of his own central council. Only because the king had again and again demanded from the men of the shire their record, their verdict, their view, their extent, their presentment were the men of the shire in a position to take the initiative and as a body to claim, to petition, and to assent.

When William I promised to his new subjects that they should have the laws of Edward the Confessor and that every man should be his father's heir, in spite of all the drastic exceptions he might make he was, in fact, recognizing limitations to his monarchical absolutism. When he and his successors accepted the principle that the public peace was the king's peace, they were accepting an obligation to the community as well as consulting their own interests. When Henry II, following in his grandfather's footsteps, issued his writs of right, saying to a lord, ' Do right to your vassal, for if you will not, I will ', he was accepting responsibility for justice to all men ; regarding justice, that is, not as a matter to be regulated by personal relations, but as a public, and therefore a royal, concern.   What was implicit in these undertakings was made explicit in Magna Carta.   The king is bound by the law—some of it ancient and customary, some of it made by himself or his ancestors—but whether new or old, he is not the sole judge of what that law is.   The counsel of the realm has a right also to say what is or is not established law and custom.   From 1215 onward some way must be found to reconcile Angevin efficiency with the customary rights of the people of England.

In the long reign of Henry III we see this conception beginning to take practical effect in the working institutions of the country. ' The struggle for the charters ', as the great Stubbs calls it, was in the air ; but its manifestations were far more various than we might guess from his narrative of royal incapacity and baronial criticism.   Fascinated by the development of parliamentary institutions, Stubbs undervalued the judicial and administrative developments of that long and fruitful reign, and did less than justice to a great army of able and energetic workers.   It is not only to the barons, asserting loudly, ' *Nolumus leges Anglie mutare* ', that the laws of England owe their preservation.   The civil servant, once figuring in our history text-books as a ' royal favourite ', later regarded as a mere bureaucrat, deserves more credit than he has yet had for building up and maintaining our precious traditions of law and order.   He was not merely a royal servant : he was a craftsman with a craftsman's pride.   In the apologia of Richard Fitz Neal, treasurer to Henry II and his son, we first hear the voice of the professionally self-conscious public servant : ' There is nothing unseemly to ecclesiastics in the service of kings, for the defence of their rights.   It is fitting to serve kings, not only by maintaining the dignities which adorn the glory of royal power, but also by securing those supplies of temporal necessaries which come to them by reason of their estate. . . . Nor is it beneath the dignity of so great and able a prince as yourself, King Henry, to take thought for these things, amongst greater matters ; for the laws of the Exchequer are not haphazard, but framed by the judgement of great men.'

Seventy years later another public servant set down in

writing the result of his life-work in the service of the State. Henry of Bracton had served for many years as justice in the king's court ; he had sat under and had treasured up the judgements of men like William of Raleigh and Stephen Segrave as they sat at Westminster or went on eyre round the shires, and it was from this practical experience that he deduced the principles applied by him in his treatise on the laws of England.   That treatise, with all its defects, is an embodiment of a new spirit, all the more valuable for its kinship with the past ; the spirit of the common law—national, conservative, independent, if deferential in face of royal authority.   In Bracton, and in his masters and followers, we trace not only the pride of the good workman, but also what is not yet traceable in Richard Fitz Neal—the *esprit de corps* of the professional which enables thirteenth-century judges, royal servants as they are, to protest if need be against the king's overriding of the king's own law.   ' It would not befit the honour of our lord the King or of ourselves,' write the justices in eyre at York in 1219 to Henry III's council, who have been ordering them to wrest the course of justice in the interest of the Earl of Albemarle, ' that we who ought to be judges should have become contemptible in the sight of those to whom we have been sent. . . . We assert most boldly that we have done nothing contrary to the approved custom of the realm.' [1]   Henry II's policy of efficiency had indeed come home to roost when the king's own servants told the king that he was bound by precedent, and when the shire court, ordered to co-operate in safeguarding the royal interest, shouted out its approval of the justices who refused to obey the royal letters.   ' The judgement of the lord King's court and the custom of the realm ' were a strong bulwark against the arbitrary rule of kings and their confidential counsellors.   These justices of 1219 strike the note which sounds again more strongly and clearly in 1259, when judges worked side by side with the baronial party in implementing the rough sketch of reform drafted at Oxford, and in 1264, when the poet of the ' Song of Lewes ' declared, ' Every king is ruled by the laws which he enacts ', and ' We give the first place

---

[1] Hennings, *England under Henry III*, p. 182–3.

to the community ; we say also that the law rules over the King's dignity '.

It was both the king's law and the custom of the realm, ' known better to the nation than to any foreigner ', which Bracton and his fellows administered, upheld, and interpreted. By the end of Henry III's reign the legal profession was well on its way to be a bulwark of English liberty.

The effects of this attitude in the sphere of local government begin to be traceable soon after 1215. One of its most striking manifestations is the change in the instructions given to the justices in eyre. The articles administered by them to the hundred juries are increasing in number and widening in scope. The men of the hundred are being asked for information which really concerns the country-side more than the king. The sheriff, it becomes clear, is regarded as owing a duty to others besides the king ; the king's subjects are invited to report his misdoings even when the king himself has not suffered. For instance, the justices in eyre are instructed to inquire whether he has been keeping the rules laid down in the 1217 Magna Carta about the holding of shire courts and hundred courts, and if he has been obeying the ordinance of 1220 which forbade the compulsary carousals known as scotales. The new articles added for the eyres held in 1254 inquire into all sorts of oppressions and injustices suffered by jurors, litigants, prisoners, and the ordinary people of the shire, few of which would mean pecuniary loss to the king, though they would certainly involve a violation or, in the phraseology of the articles themselves, a suffocation of justice. There is other evidence that new standards of public decency are being applied ; we hear of special government inquiries into the conduct of individual sheriffs in Suffolk, Yorkshire, Cheshire, Nottinghamshire, Derbyshire. The king's government is coming half-way to meet the demand of these localities for good adminis- tration ; and though it is doubtful whether the punishment was as thoroughgoing as the inquiries, the knight of the shire—no great magnate, but the average country gentleman—is establishing his right to demand fair treatment at the hands of the king's sheriff.

There were, in fact, good practical reasons for the central recognition of such a claim. Henry II's policy of setting the shires to do all kinds of governmental work, from reporting on judicial proceedings to the central courts, denouncing criminals, to assessing and collecting royal revenue, made it more and more important that the men who were doing these jobs should be on friendly terms with the central government. Without a good understanding, self-administration would readily become a local conspiracy to defeat the royal ends. The desire to placate local opinion may well have lain behind John's summons in 1213 to the four discreet knights of each shire to come and speak with the king about the affairs of the realm. Fourteen years later John's son is summoning them to discuss the interpretation of the clauses of Magna Carta, and in 1254 he asks them to bring the opinion of their county courts as to the granting of an aid. Such indications prepare us for the situation of 1258–65, when the demand of the greater barons to have a check on the central government is matched by the demand of the knights of the shire to have a check on the local government, and the greater barons, no less than the king, find themselves compelled to make a bid for the support of the shires by meeting the complaints of the 'bachelery'.

Thus the baronial administration is reinforced by the appointment in each shire of four knights to keep an eye on the sheriff and to admonish him, and these knights are commissioned not only to report on the sheriff's conduct to the baronial government but also to bring up any complaints in person to the autumn parliament at Westminster in 1258.[1] The new sheriffs for 1258–9 are elected by them, and take a new oath before the Council to do right to all, not to oppress the poor, and to restrain their subordinates from extortion. The royal justiciar appointed at Oxford, on his great tour of the shires in 1258 and 1259, devotes special attention to the misconduct of local government officials, and the provisions of October 1259 [2] tackle some of the outstanding local grievances thus revealed—matters scarcely worth the attention of magnates like Richard of Clare for their

[1] Jacob, *Baronial Revolt and Reform*, pp. 22–3.   [2] Stubbs, *Charters*, pp. 390–4.

own sake. But the knights of the shire count now ; they are
worth propitiating ; and so we find Henry himself trying in 1261
to appeal to them behind the backs of the great men. Clare and
de Montfort have summoned representatives of the shire to St.
Albans ; the king bids them to Windsor instead to hear his side
of the case : ' To have conference with us, that they may see
and understand that we are proposing nothing but what is for
the honour and the common welfare of our realm.' [1] Henry and
Simon were, indeed, bidding against each other for the backing of
the county gentry, and in the end, it would seem, Henry won.
This may explain why the enactments which met the demands of
the bachelery were not repealed. Whilst the emergency Councils
set up at the Oxford parliament ceased to function in the stress
of civil war, and the baronial ideals of ministerial responsibility in
the central administration seemed frustrated, in local government
the standards of 1259 survived the overthrow of Simon de Montfort. The Statutes of Marlborough in 1267 re-enacted, clause by
clause, the Provisions of 1259 ; those measures which had been
worked out, if their latest historian is right, by the joint efforts of
the baronial leaders and of trained lawyers like Roger of Thur-
kelby.[2] In the eyres of 1268–72 the articles of 1254 were again
administered ; the restored government of Henry III accepted
the standards of the ' bachelery ' for shrieval conduct. When
Edward returned in 1274 it was to an England familiar with the
idea that sheriffs, though royal agents, could be brought to book
like other men at the duly presented request of the country-side.
The influence of the squirearchy and of the county court, even at
Westminster, was an accomplished fact, and there was no putting
back the clock. Here at least the dream of the poet of 1264
seemed to be coming true : ' Therefore let the community of the
realm advise, and let it be known what the generality thinks, to
whom its own laws are best known.'

---

[1] Stubbs, *Charters*, p. 395.
[2] E. F. Jacob, in *Cam. Medieval Hist.*, VI, p. 282.

PART II

THE INQUESTS OF 1274-5

CHAPTER IV

GOVERNMENTAL INQUESTS, 1086-1316

IT is generally accepted nowadays that we owe to the Continent that institution which the eighteenth-century philosophers found so peculiarly and admirably British — the Jury. Brunner established and Maitland taught us that it was 'not English but Frankish, not popular but royal'. If we wish to become fully aware of its royal antecedents we only need to consider the enormous family of inquests of which our petty criminal jury merely is one member. From the early days of the Conquest, William I was making use of this procedure to get the information he required ; ordering his justices or sheriffs to take a group of men, put them on their oath to speak the truth, and then propound to them questions on any subject on which the king required light. Few of such questions and answers were of sufficient permanent importance to be worth preserving ; thus, for most of us, the Domesday inquest stands out in magnificent isolation, and we are unaware of the long series of inquests, both special and general, which are of the same type.

In 1086 the king required facts as to the tenure of land and the incidence of taxation. The questions were framed so as to cover all possible sources of revenue and all degrees of personal liability for payment. Land and money will be found to be the subject-matter of most of the government inquiries undertaken in the centuries following the Domesday inquest, but with the widening of the scope of royal activity, the sources of revenue become more various. When the king begins to tax movable goods he will inquire into the possession of chattels ; when he

27

secures the profits of justice he will inquire into the commission of crimes ; and when he undertakes to provide justice for all— at a price—he will inquire into all sorts of subjects which concern the interests of his subjects rather than of the Exchequer.

It is to this variegated group of inquests that the inquiry of 1274-5 belongs—the parent of the Hundred Rolls. What is unusual about it is not so much that it took place as that its records were preserved. We know of other inquiries, some of which must have been at least as important, of which no records, or only a few stray fragments, remain. Of the inquiry ordered by the parliament of Oxford in 1258 one solitary roll remains of all those once carefully preserved in the Exchequer. The inquiry of 1279, again, had its returns survived in full, would have been a second and a more detailed Domesday Book, giving an account of all England village by village and tenant by tenant as it was in the seventh year of Edward I. But there are returns only for five counties, and even for those five counties there are large gaps.[1] Again the inquiry of 1284-5, known from one of the chief commissioners as Kirkby's Quest, which should give exact and detailed information as to the relations of the local government officials throughout the country with the Exchequer, is only preserved in full for about fifty of the 688 hundreds of England. Though our returns of 1274-5 are incomplete, they cover a great part of the country and are copious enough to fill some 850 closely printed folio pages of the Record Commissioners' edition, printed with the contractions and abbreviations of the clerks who first recorded the jurors' verdicts, and since 1818, when the second volume was published, more stray rolls have turned up, some of which still remain unprinted.

The inquest of 1274-5, then, is one of a long series, other examples of which will show the use made by the Norman and Angevin kings of this adaptable machinery. There was constant occasion to ascertain facts bearing on the king's feudal rights. How many knights is such-and-such a tenant-in-chief bound to supply in return for his fief ? By what service does such a one

---

[1] These returns follow those of 1274-5 in the printed volume, and are also popularly called Hundred Rolls.

hold his land of the king ?   What widows or heirs under age are there in your parts of whom the king should have the rights of marriage and wardship ?   General inquests of this kind recurred frequently in the twelfth and early thirteenth centuries.   There are also the special and local inquests held when a tenant-in-chief dies, when the king asks, ' How much land did he hold of us, and how much of others, and by what service ?   What was the land worth ?   Who is his heir and how old is he ? '   Or again, an inquest into the condition of a royal manor will seek to ascertain its extent, the stock, the tenants, and their services.   Other inquests are of a fiscal nature, to establish a basis for taxation. How many ploughs are there in your village ?   How much movable property does each man possess ?   There are inquests arising out of special circumstances, like the inquests concerning the lands of those Normans who elected to side with the King of France when John lost Normandy in 1204, or concerning the lands of those rebels who fought against Henry III in the barons' wars.   And then there are the inquiries into the conduct of government officials, of which the most famous examples are the inquests of sheriffs in 1170 and the inquests of 1258.   And in 1255 there is the inquiry into the usurpation of royal rights and liberties of subjects, the fragmentary returns of which are printed in the same volumes with the returns of 1274–5 and 1279, and are, like them, known as Hundred Rolls.   Latest of the great surveys is the inquiry of 1316, held probably for military reasons, into the names and lords of all the hundreds or vills of England, the returns to which, called the Nomina Villarum, form an indispensable geographical guide to the student of local government in the thirteenth century.[1]

But of all the royal inquests which took up the time of the country-side and of the royal commissioners the most dreaded was the general eyre itself.   The justices in eyre, travelling round the country at frequent intervals, visiting each county every year or every other year under Henry II, every two or three years under Richard and John, every four or five years under Henry III

---

[1] These returns are printed, county by county, in the six volumes of *Feudal Aids* (H.M. Stationery Office).

until, about 1258, he was made to promise ' not oftener than once in seven years ', and at longer and longer intervals under Edward I, brought with them a set of questions which grew in length and scope till they included most of the matters covered by these special inquests.   They asked questions not only as to crimes committed, but as to feudal tenures, as to the fiscal rights of the Crown, as to the conduct of royal officials, and as to the usurpation of liberties.   By 1272, when all eyres were for the time being prohibited by command of the new king's deputies, the articles of the eyre numbered 69 ; and the fee that a hundred jury would have to pay the clerk for writing out a fair copy of them would be no trifling addition to their other financial liabilities. For the jurors who faced the justices in eyre were often expected to pay a sum down in advance, on account, as it were, for the penalties they might normally expect to incur for speaking foolishly—for making a false presentment, that is, for making a statement which did not accord with the coroner's or sheriff's rolls or with the statement of a later jury, for contempt or for one of a dozen other technical breaches of procedure—and having made this compounding payment, as like as not they would have to pay again when the actual mistake was made.   The experience of serving on a jury might be educational, but it was not a popular one, any more than is the filling up of an income-tax return or the giving of evidence in court at the present day.   It is not likely that a hundred jury, presenting to the justice a sworn statement as to the misconduct of their coroners or sheriffs, would have been consoled for their loss of time and money by knowing that they were the forerunners of the county members of the House of Commons, presenting the national grievances in the Grand Inquest of the nation.   But the fact remains that this favourite procedure of our French kings did in effect provide a valuable training for the English country-side which kept it articulate and conscious, socially and politically, so that no revolution was needed to fit it into the framework of parliamentary government.

The inquest, it may be said, was more of a success politically than judicially.   As a means of detecting and punishing crime the jury of accusation soon proved its inadequacy. Matthew Paris relates how the *patria* of Hampshire conspired to protect the highway robbers who had plundered some Brabant merchants travelling to Winchester. In vain did the sheriffs empanel juries and the justices hold inquiries. When the suspects put themselves upon their county they were acquitted. ' What wonder ? ' says Matthew Paris. ' The whole country-side was after the same mould, and theft was universal.' The men of the jury were themselves accomplices and accessories. Only by imprisoning and threatening to hang two juries did Henry III succeed in getting a presentment out of the free men of Hampshire. This was in 1248, and things became no better as time went on. Edward I added to the articles of the eyre a special question as to conspirators who pledge themselves by oaths to support each other's causes, both in lawsuits and on juries and assizes ; and in the Statute of Winchester he practically admitted the failure of the jury of accusation by providing that the whole hundred must make amends if a robbery takes place within it and the robbers escape free—a rule that was still in force in the seventeenth century. Long before the statute of 1487 had declared that ' little or nothing could be found by way of inquiry ', contemporaries were fully aware of the defects of the criminal jury, both of trial and of accusation. But no better way was devised, and the procedure was used, not only before justices in eyre, but later, when they ceased to function, before the justices of assize and before the new justices of the peace. For better, for worse, the kings of England were committed to the inquest system.

We may suspect that such business-like kings knew their own business. For the obtaining of information substantially the same system is used to-day. The shelves of our public libraries are loaded with the sworn evidence given before hundreds of government commissions of the nineteenth and twentieth centuries, appointed, like the justices and inquisitors of William I, Henry II, Henry III, and Edward I, to collect information for the use of the government, whether as to the conditions of factory labour, the incidence of disease, the working of the university system, the administration of the poor law, or the desirability of the extension of a borough's boundaries. We are used to these commissions and to the blue books that embody their results of their labours ; we are aware of the relation between such inquiries and the statute book. We do not always realize that in the dark and romantic ages of the Crusades and the Gothic cathedrals statistics were being similarly collected, and, if not printed, filed or enrolled for reference with a thoroughness and neatness that would put casual eighteenth-century methods to shame. Later custodians of these archives have allowed the rats and mould of the Tower and the Westminster chapter-house to destroy more than we can calmly bear to think of ; but enough remains for administrators to admire and historians to use with gratitude to the Norman genius. The value of such records is that they were framed to be used by contemporaries, not to appeal to posterity ; that they do not pick and choose, but cover the whole ground (where they are complete) ; that they report everyday rather than the out-of-the-way occurrences. This last statement is only partly true. In records of this kind the working of the ordinary machinery is shown ; on the other hand, those who are asked, as inquests often are, to record misdoing, are selecting their facts as much as the reports of the police courts to-day select from the everyday affairs of men those events which bring them into conflict with the law. Thus, in the reports on officials we hear, as a rule, only of the evil-doers ; it is rarely indeed that a jury presents, as one Yorkshire wapentake does in 1285 : ' We know nothing but good of the bailiff.' But, on the other hand, the complaints often stand unanswered, unchecked by any counter-statement or cross-examination. As a rule we have no means of knowing when a jury's *veredictum* was indeed a true saying and when it was malicious or exaggerated. An inquest as to royal rights and feudal tenures can be often checked by an earlier or later statement ; unless proceedings are taken against an accused sheriff or bailiff the case may, for us, go against him by default. In some few instances, the charges made by one jury are corroborated by another, but this is only if the abuse is notorious and flagrant. On the whole, we are forced to rely on our own judgement, and run the same risks of being misled by prejudice that we run in reading a report in the daily press nowadays.

With all reservations duly made, however, the value to the modern reader of the great mass of statistics accumulated for us in the past is immense : overwhelming, indeed, in face of its bulk. What the Hundred Rolls of 1274–5 offer us is a bird's-eye view of local government all over England at the beginning of the reign of Edward I, seen from two angles : from the king's side and from the side of the governed. The only point of view unrepresented is that of the officials themselves. The king asks ; the country-side answers ; the sheriff and his bailiffs are speechless.

CHAPTER V

THE POLICY OF EDWARD I

THE king who, on 11th October 1274, issued his letters patent ordering this inquiry, is one of the most interesting figures in English history. The first king with an English name since the Norman Conquest, he has been credited with the virtues the English prize most highly—courage and truthfulness ; with the creation of the peculiarly English institution of a representative legislature, and, as a result, with democratic principles. Such an estimate can, however, never have convinced Scotsmen, to whom Edward must always have seemed both tyrant and trickster, and any close scrutiny of his career convinces us that even if he desired it, which seems doubtful, he had no very good right to take ' Keep Faith ' for his motto. In the eyes of the author of the ' Song of Lewes ' he deserved the title of ' Yea and Nay ' fully as much as his great-uncle the Lion Heart. ' A lion by his pride and his ferocity, he is a pard by his inconstancy and changeability, varying his word and his promise and excusing himself by fine words. When he is in a difficulty he promises whatever you want, but as soon as he is out of it he forgets his promise. O Edward, if you desire to be a king, respect the laws ! Shun and detest treachery, and follow after truth. Little have you gained by your guile at Northampton ; treachery warms no man.' He had played fast and loose with them, allying himself now with Simon de Montfort, now with the bachelery of England, now with his other uncle, Richard of Cornwall, now with the Clares, now with his father. He had defied the law and he had sworn to uphold it. He seemed before all else a fighter, plunging into an orgy of tournaments the moment the long-drawn struggle of the civil wars had been brought to an end, and carrying on the Crusade single-handed when his French allies dropped out. His activities as heir to the throne scarcely prepare us for his career as ruler of England. The stamp he has left on English institutions is the stamp of the lawyer and the codifier. He is not the great creative genius ; his gift, it would seem, is for systematization. Like the methodically planned *villesneuves* he founded in England and France, his statutes straighten out the crooked and define the vague ; and his administration aims above all at order, method, and efficiency. Liberty of a popular kind is by no means his ideal ; he is an autocrat in grain ; but he has outgrown the capricious tyranny of his young days, and his absolutism is of a decent and orderly type which will descend as ruthlessly upon a royal servant who neglects his duty as upon a rebel against royal authority.

Edward I, then, is in the true Angevin tradition. Devout, like his father, physically brave, and to the last audacious in war like his great-uncle, he has the business ability, the capacity for hard work and the love of efficiency which had characterized the first two Henrys. His determination to maintain and strengthen the royal authority expresses itself in Gascony and in Wales no less than in England ; in the setting in order of the machinery of administration of court and household ; in the drafting of statute after statute for regulating the government of the country and defining the law of the land. His attitude to the law is his most significant characteristic ; it expresses, we feel, a fundamental and passionate conviction. The royal power is the divinely appointed means for securing the well-being of the realm ; law is also an embodiment of the divine order of things ; therefore the law must be on the king's side. Thus Edward will wrest the law to suit his own purpose ; he will not defy it but coerce it. He is enough the child of the thirteenth century to respect the law ; he is perhaps the first King of England to display the characteristically English trait of wanting not only to have his own way but to have the law on his side. This self-deception or hypocrisy, as it appears to more logical minds across the Channel, has moulded the institutions and traditions of England too long and too powerfully for the student of history merely to smile at it. The fact that Edward I, like Henry VIII, preferred to get his way with the assistance of laws and judges, was in the future to prevent the deadlocks which in other countries made development catastrophic.

Edward I, then, accepts Magna Carta ; he accepts the Statute of Marlborough and the Mise of Kenilworth which register the achievements of the baronial opposition to his father. He accepts the standards of decency and order in the government, both local and central, which have been established in the sixty years since Runnymede. But he is far from admitting the claim of any section of his subjects to participate in the control of policy, and if he calls for their co-operation, it is not because they have a right to give or withhold their help, but because they, as his subjects, have the duty of rendering him service if he demands it.

What was Edward's object in ordering the inquest of 11th October 1274 ? We shall see, when we come to examine the articles of inquiry more closely, that they fall under two headings. On the one hand the king is inquiring concerning royal rights and liberties upon which his subjects have encroached ; on the other hand he is asking for information as to the behaviour of his servants—sheriffs, coroners, escheators, bailiffs, and subordinates. The period nominally covered by the inquiry is the last seven years, beginning, that is, with the close of the civil wars in 1267 ; in fact the replies often go back far earlier than this. How far had the king's subjects taken advantage of the years of warfare to appropriate to themselves royal rights ? How far had government officials taken advantage of the changes of power and the successive experiments in administration to oppress the people and secure profit for themselves, violating the letter and the spirit of the settlement of 1267–8 ? Inarticulate discontent and general charges were of no use ; definite facts were needed upon which the king could act. Edward's action is easily intelligible and thoroughly characteristic. On the other hand, the investigation is no more original in its scope than in its method. Inquiry into the appropriation of royal privileges by subjects had been made more than once in the reign of Henry III. As early as 1238 the royal justices in eyre in Devon had been asking by what warrant the lords of private hundreds held their franchises, and in 1255 an inquest very similar in wording to that of 1274 had been made throughout the country. The clergy had complained bitterly of the royal questioning of their liberties and the strict interpretation that had been put upon their ancient charters. Edward I was asking for more comprehensive, more detailed, and more exact information as to the exercise of liberties than had been given ever before ; but the general line of the inquiry was quite in accordance with tradition. And the same was true of the inquiries as to officials. The articles of the eyre had dealt with the same type of offences, and the inquest of 1258, as far as sheriffs and bailiffs were concerned, had covered much the same ground as that of 1274, particularizing less closely. At one point it looked as if the inquest of 1274 was not going so far as previous inquests. On 28th January 1274, six months before his return, a commission had been issued for an inquiry of much narrower scope, only dealing with encroachments on royal privileges, and apparently limited to eleven counties. A somewhat similar investigation was at that moment taking place under Edward's own eye in his Gascon dominions ; an inquiry into the rights and duties of his French vassals, planned originally in 1259.[1] This inquest of fiefs in Gascony was nearly over by the time the English inquests into rights and liberties began, for the few returns to these which are left are dated March to July, 1274.[2]. The commission of October 11th was, then, a second thought, greatly extending the scope of the inquiry, and increasing the number of articles from two to thirty-nine. The commissions had to begin over again in those counties where they had already taken evidence.[3] It is impossible to say whether this change of plan is due to Edward himself or to his servants and counsellors. But to it we owe that mass of information as to local government which gives the Hundred Rolls their distinctive character and which left its stamp upon the first and second Statutes of Westminster. To contemporaries the inquiry into official misconduct was the main object of the inquest. ' The Lord King sent inquisitors everywhere to inquire how the sheriffs and other

---

[1] See C. Bémont, *Recueil des actes relatifs à l'administration des rois d'angleterre en Guyenne*, pp. xlv–li.

[2] *R.H.*, II, 118–24, 220, 223–4.

[3] At the same time, new sheriffs were appointed throughout the kingdom.

bailiffs had conducted themselves,' says the chronicler of Dunstable Abbey. On the other hand, later historians have laid stress almost exclusively on the inquiry into franchises, and have regarded the Hundred Rolls simply as the preliminary to the Quo Warranto Trials. Both aspects must be borne in mind ; in both the policy of Edward I is exemplified. The king's rights and dignities come first, but the subjects' due rights shall also be maintained. Only there must be no uncertainty as to those rights : all shall be regularly recorded in business-like fashion, by the witness of the country-side, and henceforth the unnoticed accretion of custom, the quiet assumption of privilege, shall be precluded. All shall be definite and clear-cut ; and if any real uncertainties remain as to the boundaries between the rights of king, of official, and of subject, the king's justices shall clear up the doubt, whether by judgement or by statute, on the King's Bench or in his Parliament. That was the intention of the English Justinian.

CHAPTER VI

THE PROCEDURE OF 1274–5

W HETHER the decision to issue the new commissions came from Edward himself or from another we can be pretty sure that the details of the scheme were discussed, and the choice of commissioners made in a council that sat, probably at the Tower, at the beginning of October 1274. On or about October 11th the clerks of the Chancery would receive the list of names to which commissions and copies of the articles were to be sent, and would sit down to make out the king's letters patent —one at least for each pair of commissioners, and possibly one for the sheriff of each county to whom the commissioners were coming. Both commission and articles were entered on the Patent Roll, but the list of commissioners is lacking and the list of articles is almost certainly curtailed, whether by carelessness or by later mutilation of the roll is uncertain. Other evidence makes it probable that the articles numbered thirty-nine,[1] ending with the question about the export of wool, and that the country was divided into ten or eleven circuits,[2] each visited by two commissioners. The commission ran as follows : ' The King to his beloved and faithful A. and B., greeting. Know that we have assigned you to inquire by the oaths of good and lawful men of the counties of D., C., and F. by whom the truth may be fully ascertained concerning certain rights, liberties, and other matters affecting us and our estate and the estate of the community of the said counties, and moreover concerning the deeds and the behaviour of all sheriffs and bailiffs in the said counties, as is more fully contained in the articles on the subject which we have sent to you. We command you therefore to hold these inquests, according to the contents of the said articles, at fixed days and places which you shall appoint for the purpose. And

[1] See Appendix I. [2] See Appendix II.

these inquests, distinctly and openly made, you shall send to us without delay under your seal and under the seals of those by whom inquest was made. We have also commanded our sheriffs of the said counties to bring before you, at the fixed days and places which you shall signify to them, such and so many good and lawful men of their bailiwick that by them the truth of the above-mentioned matters may be well ascertained.'

The men to whom this charge was given were typical of a great class of civil servants. A few of them had served or were to serve as justices of the forest, in Ireland or on the general eyre. Some eight of them had served or were to serve as sheriffs, and one of them was actually sheriff of Warwickshire and Leicestershire at the moment when he was holding these inquiries in Shropshire, Staffordshire, and Leicestershire. Most of them served at one time or another on occasional commissions similar to this one ; many acted as escheators, stewards, constables of castles, bailiffs of manors. Less than half of them were landholders, some by descent, others in right of their wives, suggesting forcibly that a royal clerk had been rewarded for his long service by the hand of an heiress, thus becoming the founder of a county family. As a whole, the commissioners of 1274 are to be described rather as professionals than as amateurs ; as men fully committed to the royal interests and experienced in departmental work.

The earliest dated inquest was held on 18th November at Aylesbury ; the latest, as far as we know, at Malmesbury on 21st March 1275. Thus the work of collecting the information extended over five months. The clerks who wrote out the jurors' replies were more exact in their formulae in some counties than in others ; we have far more precise details in Lincolnshire or Wiltshire, for instance, than in Gloucestershire. But the procedure must have been much as follows. On the day signified by them to the sheriff the commissioners arrived, and found the juries awaiting them. Possibly the jurors had already learned from the sheriff what questions they were to answer ; the articles certainly demanded long and careful consideration. In one case at least they felt that they had been rushed. A Norfolk jury says that many trespasses were committed by the sheriffs and other officials of which they have not at present obtained the exact details, and there is no time to get them or to examine the charges properly.[1] But the commissioners were not able to grant an extension. Each jury was summoned and sworn to reply without fear or favour, the articles were read to them, and a time given for them to draft their verdict and dictate it to a clerk. Then followed the stage of which a Berkshire chronicler has left a vivid little picture in his description of an inquest held at Abingdon Abbey by command of Henry II : ' The villagers filled the corners of the courtyard and the cross ways of the town discussing and conferring together as to what answers they should give. Then when the questions were put to them, they made the following statement, which was set down by their clerk.' When the verdict was written down, the clerk read it over to the jury, who could then supplement or correct it, as a Dorset jury did. ' Insert above the line, " on the death of Ralph Gorges ",' is the note at the foot of this roll, and the correction has been inserted.[2] Then the jurors affixed their seals to the verdict, and it was ready to be handed to the justices.

Each hundred had its own jury, normally of twelve, but for special local reasons there might be six, eighteen, or twenty-four members. There were also jurors for some larger vills and manors, and for boroughs : in Shropshire, for instance, there were separate returns for ten manors, three boroughs, and two liberties as well as the seven hundreds of the county. In the larger boroughs there were more than one set of jurors ; in Lincoln, for instance, the great men, the secondary men, and the lesser men were each represented separately. In London each ward had its own jury. There were also larger groups represented ; in Norfolk there were six different groups of hundreds, for each of which a jury of knights gave a collective verdict ; in Suffolk there was one collective verdict for the eight and a half hundreds of St. Edmund's liberty ; in Herts there was a knights' verdict for the whole shire. In Essex, on the other hand, there are preserved the returns of separate vills, presented probably by the reeve and four men who spoke

[1] R.H., I, 483. [2] Ibid., I, 98.

for their village in the sheriff's tourn.   Here we are told expressly that villeins took part in the inquest ; probably they reported to the knights or other free jurors who incorporated the information in their returns, and the survival of these Essex presentments of vills may be in the nature of a lucky accident.   There must have been local variations of procedure, but one way and another the net was thrown wide, and though there is, of course, overlapping and duplication, the value of the different and converging testimony is clear.   The class feeling in Northampton comes out clearly in the complaints of the lesser men of the borough against their wealthier neighbours, and the cumulative effect of the same report coming from vill after vill of an Essex hundred is considerable.

Even these various types of presentment do not exhaust the material collected on the inquest of 1274–5.   The commissioners had apparently been instructed, like the justices of 1259,[1] to receive petitions or complaints from individuals, and here and there we find appended to the verdict of a jury a *querela* from some injured person.   One such plaint from Devonshire may be quoted.   In 1272 Richard Bysothewimpel of Clifton hundred sued a neighbour, he says, for a debt of eight pounds in the county court.   The debtor acknowledged his liability in the presence of the sheriff, who undertook to collect the debt, and told Richard to come and claim his bond at Exeter Castle on Lady Day.   When Richard turned up he was seized by two of the sheriff's men, who took him to the prison in the Windsor Tower, telling him a prisoner in the castle had brought a charge against him.   They bound him hand and foot so tightly that his blood ran, and he was thus induced to pay down forty shillings, to be allowed bail for his appearance before the justices of jail delivery when they should come.   A neighbour found bail and he was set free, but in January 1275 the sheriff was still holding the bond and the debt was still unpaid.[2]   Other such individual complaints come from Essex and Cambridgeshire ; they give a wealth of detail which the statement of a third party naturally omits.   But they go forward, it seems, with the endorsement of the jury, who accept the

---

[1] Jacob, *Baronial Reform and Rebellion*, pp. 69–70.   [2] *R.H.*, I, 68.

statement handed in to them, ' finding a true bill ', to use the phraseology of the general eyre, enrol it with their own verdict, and present it to the commissioners. In Dengie hundred, Essex, five vills independently present, very briefly, the offence detailed in a long *querela* from a lady of Asheldham.[1]

Every chance, one would say, had been given for abuses to reach the royal ear, yet there was still obstruction. Though new sheriffs had been put in in most counties, who might be expected to have no personal interest in the reports, the whole county staff had not been changed. As the jurors sat round, considering the questions that had been read out to them, receiving the complaints and reports of vills or of individuals for incorporation in their verdict, and discussing the form of the return to be dictated to the waiting clerk, a stray hundred bailiff or sub-bailiff might well find an opportunity of threatening them with heavy penalties if they told too true a tale. One plucky jury in Lincolnshire persisted in face of such threats : ' We who have sworn to the above written inquests show to the lord king that both his bailiffs and other men's bailiffs in this wapentake of Kirton are threatening to oppress us, by reason of this verdict, with greater extortion than ever before.' [2] In Winstree hundred, Essex, the commissioners note, ' We were not able to fulfil our office here, because neither the villeins nor the free men of the hundred would appear before us, being prevented by the present bailiff and by his predecessors.' [3] The most flagrant case is that of Gilbert of Clifton, bailiff of the wapentake of Staincliff in Yorkshire and later sheriff of Lancashire. This man went so far as to threaten the commissioners themselves. ' He used most shameful words against William de Chatterton, justice assigned to take these inquests, because he had told the jurors of the country-side fearlessly to tell the whole truth about the bailiffs of the earl of Lincoln (the lord of Staincliff wapentake). Gilbert said that if he had been present when this announcement was made he would have pulled the justice down by his legs, and that before half a year was up the justice would be wishing that he had lost all his lands rather than be a commissioner. And when Reginald

---

[1] *R.H.*, I, 136–7.   [2] Ibid., I, 308.   [3] Ibid., I, 137.

Blanchard of Waddington appeared before the twelve jurors of
the wapentakes to reveal the wrongs done to him by Gilbert and
the other bailiffs of the earl, Gilbert seized Reginald's beasts and
refused to restore them at the command of the commissioners,
saying that if they entered his lord's liberty he would seize their
persons and all their goods unless they came in his master's
name.' [1]

It is possible that such obstruction led to a supplementary
inquiry in Essex, but if so it must have taken place very soon
after the first one.[2]   In general, the commissioners could feel
that, whether well or ill done, their task was over when they had
received from the juries the written verdicts with their appended
seals.   In a few counties we can actually trace their movements
from day to day.   William de Brayboef and William Gerberd
have been spending February taking the Hampshire inquests ;
at the beginning of March they reach Wilton, in the south of
Wiltshire, where they sit from Wednesday, March 6th, to Tuesday,
March 12th, receiving the verdicts of some nine hundreds and
two towns.   On Tuesday, March 12th, St. Gregory's Day, they
take the three and a half miles' journey into Salisbury, and at
once set to work, hearing the returns of six hundreds that same
day, and receiving some seventeen more verdicts before moving
on on Friday, travelling northwards.   On Saturday, March 16th,
they pause at Great Bedwin to receive the return of the specially
privileged hundred of Kinwardstone, now held by the King's
aunt, Simon de Montfort's widow, as part of the dower inherited
from her first Marshal husband.   From Great Bedwin it is seven
or eight miles on to Marlborough, where they are receiving returns
on Monday and Tuesday from seven hundreds and the borough
of Marlborough.   Thence over the downs by Wootton Basset they
reach Malmesbury, where the last seven or eight inquests are held
on Wednesday and Thursday, winding up, as far as we know, with
the verdict of the borough of Chippenham on Thursday, March
21st.   By this time their clerks must have been well loaded up
with those rolls—between forty and fifty for Wiltshire, forty to
fifty for Hampshire, twenty-three at least for Oxfordshire, and

---

[1] *R.H.*, I, III.   [2] Ibid., I, 137, 148.

thirty-four at least for Berkshire—of which to-day only thirty-nine are left ; then clean and new, with their rolls of seals dangling from them, now grimy with the dust of centuries, and often with only slits to show where the parchment tags for the seals went.[1]

Those bundles of rolls made a great impression on the minds of the countrymen. In later years, when they spoke of the searching inquisition that they or their neighbours had undergone, in the winter after the king came back from the Holy Land, they called it the Ragman Quest, because of those rolled-up verdicts with their dangling seals. The multiplicity of the seals was the outward and visible sign of the collective responsibility of hundred or borough ; a royal charter or a private deed was the act of one man, and bore one seal, a contract might bear two, but the verdict had a seal for every juror. ' Every little freeman has his own seal nowadays,' said one of Henry III's judges superciliously, and where to-day a signature authenticates, in the days when writing was a specialized profession, the seal was indispensable, and when joint responsibility was involved a veritable fringe of tagged seals would adorn a document. In the Record Office in London to-day may be seen that most famous letter drawn up in the Parliament of Lincoln in 1301 to be sent to Pope Boniface VIII which bears the seals of eighty-seven different lords, and the document by which the Scots recognized the overlordship of Edward I in 1291 was similarly adorned. ' They called it the Ragman,' the chronicler says, using the ordinary English name for a charter with the jagged or ragged effect produced by all these dangling strips of parchment on which the seals were fixed. There was a more frivolous kind of Ragman known to the thirteenth century. Medieval ladies, both in France and England, loved to play a kind of fortune-telling game derived possibly from practices of divination older than Christianity and forbidden by the Councils of the Church. A number of different fortunes or characters in verse were written out on a roll, and opposite each verse was a string or strip of parchment, with a weight or seal on the end of it. The roll was rolled up so that only the strips showed ; you pulled one and so ' drew a fortune '.

[1] See Plate II.

Drawith a strynge, and that shal streight yow lede
Unto the verry path of your governaunce,

says the fifteenth-century poem called ' Ragemane Roelle '.
One set of verses of Edward I's reign headed ' Ragemon le bon ',
has fifty such characters.[1] It is a far cry from the good Master
Ragman who tells your fortune to the justices whom Coke has
confused with the Justices of Trailbaston ; the only connexion
is in the many sealed returns. Jurors had often had to seal
inquests before, but never before, one must suppose, had the
villagers seen so magnificent an accumulation of ' ragmans ' as
when they watched the clerks and the jurors adding roll after roll
to the commissioners' store. In a very short time the nickname
was sticking ; within five years the clerks of the justices in eyre
were referring in their entries to the Ragman jurors and the clerks
of the Chancery were issuing orders for the custody of the Ragman
Rolls of this year. From 1278 to the end of the eighteenth
century the rolls now called the Hundred Rolls were known to
archivists and antiquarians as the Ragman Rolls, and one of the
ordinances based on the results of this inquest was generally
known as the Statute of Ragman.

[1] Wright, *Anecdota Literaria*, pp. 76–83.

CHAPTER VII

THE RECORDS OF THE INQUEST

IT is time to look more closely at the records themselves. The *Rotuli Hundredorum*, as printed by the Record Commission in 1812–18, fill two folio volumes of 543 and 877 pages respectively, not counting the indices. These two volumes, unlike the two volumes of Domesday Book, are not printed directly from one great record. They are a collection, that has been sorted and rearranged for purposes of publication, and a cursory inspection of the printed page may easily mislead.

In the first place, it is necessary to remember that the records of at least six separate inquisitions are printed in these two volumes. Taking, for instance, the opening pages of volume one, we shall find returns to the inquest of 1255 on pages 20–34, records of the inquest of 1274–5 on pages 1–4, 9–19, and 35–48, and returns of the inquest of 1285, called Kirkby's Quest, on pages 4–8 and 84–5. If we turn to volume two we find on pages 174–8 a return to an inquest dating from about 1251, and all the returns after page 321 belong to the inquest of 1279, the writ for which is printed in the Introduction. The printed headings and marginal notes must therefore be carefully consulted before we can assume that we are reading replies to the questions of October 1274.

When, however, all the returns to other inquests have been weeded out we have still one more distinction to draw, and that a most important one. If the Devonshire records in the first volume are examined, for instance, it will be found that those on pages 63–88 are headed ' Inquisitions ' and those on pages 89–96 are described as ' Extracts of Inquisitions '. Looking closer, we see that the Inquisitions are printed from forty-three different rolls, whilst the Extracts are all printed from one roll, called ' Extract Roll, No. 2 ', beginning on the twenty-ninth skin. The

Inquisitions are said to belong to the third, the Extracts to the fourth year of Edward I.[1] If we take the records of one hundred, say Haytor, and compare the account on pages 71–3 with that on page 89 we see that the Extracts are in summaries or abridgements of the contents of the Inquisitions. That is, the Inquisitions are the original verdicts handed over by the jurors on the spot, and the Extracts are a compilation made from them at a later date by government clerks, just as Domesday Book was compiled at head-quarters from the original returns to the inquest of 1086, none of which are extant, though a few copies made locally in Cambridgeshire and elsewhere have been preserved. For 1274–5 we are both more or less lucky ; in some cases there is a wealth of detail which we should have lost if no original returns had been kept ; but elsewhere there are yawning gaps which do not exist in Domesday Book. For Berkshire, Somerset, Cornwall, York, Northumberland, Bedfordshire, Huntingdonshire, Leicestershire, Warwickshire, and Worcestershire no original returns have survived, and we are entirely dependent on the Extracts. On the other hand, for Wiltshire, Salop, Hampshire, Kent, and Hereford, only original returns are left ; and for Cheshire, Surrey, Middlesex, Cumberland, Westmorland, and Lancashire there is nothing at all. In a good many counties so few original returns survive that we have in fact to depend on the Extracts.

It is important, therefore, to know what the Extract Rolls are like. As is to be expected, they differ from the original returns which vary widely in form from county to county, in being neat official records of standardized make-up. There are five of them, Number 1 covering Dorset, Herts, Essex, Suffolk, Norfolk, and Northumberland ; Number 2 the counties of Oxford, Berkshire, Devon, Cornwall, Lincoln, Buckingham, Cambridge, Huntingdon, and Bedford ; Number 3 the counties of Stafford, Somerset, Northampton, Rutland, York, Derby, Nottingham, Gloucester, Warwick, Leicester, and Worcester ; Number 4, which is not printed, the same counties as Number 1, and a separate unnumbered roll covering Sussex.[2] If Number 1 and Number 4 are

---

[1] The third year began on 20th November 1274.
[2] Printed *R.H.*, II, 201–19.

compared with the original returns it is seen that the clerk classified his material in making the abridgement, picking out the evidence about erring officials to make up Roll 4, which is labelled ' De Ministris ', and putting the rest of the material in Roll 1, so that the two summaries are complementary. Thus, where the original returns are lacking, both the unprinted and the printed ' Extracts ' are needed to give a fair idea of their contents. Again, the printed volumes break up the Extract Rolls, rearranging the material along with the original returns for each county alphabetically, and they do not even represent all material now available, for a number of returns have been discovered since 1818,[1] so that no one who is studying the history of one special hundred can be certain from the printed volumes that no return for it is extant. All these gaps and defects, however, though distressing to the topographer, are not so important if we are studying local government as a system ; it will take us all our time to exhaust the information we already have.

At what date were the Extract Rolls drawn up ? The date given in the printed volumes is the third and fourth year of Edward I, that is, 1275–6, but the inscription, if we inspect the manuscript, is obviously not contemporary ; it might even be Elizabethan. The roll itself gives a clue, however ; at the end of the Yorkshire entries on Roll 3 there is a note in the same handwriting, to the effect that three of the verdicts are missing now, though they were all delivered to William of Saham and his fellows.[2] The Yorkshire inquests had been handed over to William of Saham and his companion justices on 18th April 1279, for them to keep by them for purposes of reference during their eyre in Yorkshire.[3] The eyre was over by the end of 1280, so that the clerks at Westminster might have had back the rolls at any time after that date ; but they cannot have set to work on their abridgement before then, and the four Extract Rolls look as if they had been turned out at the same time. It seems, then, that the date of compilation may be between 1280 and 1290. The object, presumably, was to put the required information in a neat and handy form for purposes of reference ; the Extracts

[1] See Appendix III.   [2] *R.H.*, I, 135.   [3] *Close Roll Cal.*, p. 558.

are far more compact and easy to consult than the many-sized separate verdicts, with their rags and tags. The scribe made some errors in his copying of names of places and people unknown to him, but on the whole they may be trusted to give the main gist of the returns they summarize. If the original verdict for a hundred is available we shall use it ; but if not we can turn to the Extracts with confidence.

There are a few more points of interest to note in our records. It has been said that they vary from county to county in form, and as we have lost the detailed orders given to each pair of commissioners we cannot tell who was responsible for these variations. We saw that there were different kinds of juries ; when we compare Extracts and Original Verdicts we find that the compilers only used the returns of the hundreds and boroughs and left on one side both the presentments of the vills in Essex and the presentments of the Knights in Norfolk and Suffolk. As a great many of the hundred verdicts are missing, this means that in these counties the Extracts and the Original Returns are largely independent. Usually there was a separate parchment for each hundred ; in Kent several hundred verdicts are entered on one roll, probably because the Kentish hundreds were so tiny that in the ordinary way they were lumped together for many purposes. It seems possible that all the commissioners did not insist on the jurors' sealing their verdicts, but where the bottom of the roll has been cut off we cannot be certain what happened.

Another local variation more easily noticed in the printed volume is that some counties were asked more questions than others. In Yorkshire there are replies to five articles which do not appear in any other county, the first dealing with Church courts and the others with tolls, weights and measures, and farms of boroughs. Six questions are found only in Lincolnshire ; they deal with official misconduct and with resistance to royal agents. On the Gloucestershire circuit questions about clippers and forgers of coin elicit some curious information ; in five out of the eleven circuits there is an article about the collection of the Twentieth granted to Henry III in 1269.[1]

[1] See Appendix I, pp. 248-57.

Lastly, we come to the notes made on the original returns, given at the bottom of the page in the printed volume—such notes as, ' He cannot deny this ' ; ' He has died ' ; ' He has the king's charter, so nothing further '. Such notes are especially frequent on the Gloucestershire and Lincolnshire rolls.[1] Who made these notes ? There is practically no doubt they were made, from 1278 onwards, by the clerks of the justices in eyre who were ordered to follow up the inquest. The rolls of the Chancery contain notes to the effect that the Ragman rolls of this or that county are to be handed over to the justices going there to hold their eyre, as the Yorkshire rolls were given to William of Saham. As they sat in state, holding their great court of justice and inquiry for the shire, the rolls were turned up ; the names of the jurors of 1274 compared with the names of those now before the judge ; their statements compared with those of the earlier jury ; and then the clerk notes on the eyre roll, ' Formerly the Ragman jurors presented that . . .' with the resulting proceedings ; and on the Ragman Roll itself—our Hundred Roll of to-day—some brief comment. By 1287 when the justices held their eyre in Gloucester so many years had passed that often both accuser and accused were dead, and *obiit* is a frequent entry.

These notes are a standing reminder of the wear and tear to which the original returns were subjected. Carried up and down the counties as they were being collected, deposited in the keeping of the chief justice, inspected possibly by the lawyers who drafted Edward's great reforming statutes, handed over to the justices in eyre, rolled and unrolled, searched and annotated, by pleaders, clerks and justices during the eyres, it is hardly wonderful that when the Ragman Rolls came back to head-quarters the compilers of the Extracts found the number short. It is rather remarkable that any of the verdicts that survived the eyres of Edward's reign and the rats of the Tower and the Westminster chapter-house should still retain the jurors' original seals dangling on their ' rags '.

---

[1] *R.H.*, I, 166 ff, 241 ff. See also Plate VIII

PART III

LOCAL GOVERNMENT IN THE LIGHT OF THE HUNDRED ROLLS OF 1274–6

CHAPTER VIII

THE TWO ASPECTS OF LOCAL GOVERNMENT

SUCH is the historical setting of the Hundred Rolls. With this knowledge of the tradition behind them, of the courts and the men that produced them, we are now in a position to use their contents as the raw material from which to reconstruct the local governmental system of the thirteenth century. Every hundred is part of a shire ; what we have to do is to make ourselves at home in the administrative life of an English county of the thirteenth century. We must put ourselves in the place of the royal commissioners, and discover what they are taking for granted as they put these questions, many of them technical in form and elaborate in detail, to the jurors.

The commission assumes, to begin with, that the shire is a unit, if not a unity. It mentions ' the estate of the community of the shire '. That community is constructively present before the commissioners in the persons of the different juries—the representatives of the vills, the good men of the hundreds and boroughs, and the knights of the shire. Again, the field of the inquiry is the whole shire. No one is to be allowed to escape these questions on the ground of special privilege, as may happen on some judicial visitations. On the basis of these questions we can, as it were, make a political map of the typical county : it will not be simple, but all the ground will be covered.

In the second place, the commissioners have a twofold interest in this unit. They are to inquire into encroachments on the king's rights and liberties, and they are to inquire into the misconduct of sheriffs and other officials. The two classes of facts they are pursuing concern the king's property and the king's servants. Taking this standpoint, it at once becomes clear to us that two systems are at work in the shire—the tenurial and the administrative—and that these two systems overlap. The king is both landlord and ruler, and his rights and obligations can be regarded in either light. By 1275 he has differentiated his officials to some extent ; the escheators look after his feudal, the sheriffs his sovereign, rights and revenues. The first questions [1] concern his rights as a landlord, his demesne manors, his escheats, his dues as feudal overlord. Then come the questions as to the rights of his tenants which accrue to them by their tenure of land from him ; and here the overlapping begins. For many of the king's tenants are claiming as landholders rights which the king enjoys as ruler, not as landlord. The liberty or franchise is at once a feudal and a governmental unit, and as a governmental unit it comes within the sheriff's sphere of action. The escheator or steward or marshal can deal with the purely feudal rights of the crown, but when the tenant is exercising regalian rights— performing, that is, any of the functions which the crown has undertaken to discharge—then the sheriff comes into play.

When we pass from reliefs, wardships, ancient demesnes, and tenants-in-chief to hundreds and vills, tourns and views of frank-pledge, we are in the sheriff's province. He is the centre of control. He is responsible to the Exchequer for the revenues of the shire ; he is responsible to the king's justices for putting in motion the machinery of royal justice in the shire, and for carrying out its judgements. With his colleagues the coroners and a large staff of subordinates he administers the shire ; with the co-operation of the knights and freemen he holds the monthly shire court.

Within this comprehensive whole are the smaller units : the hundreds and the liberties. For each hundred a hundred bailiff is responsible, ultimately, to the king. If the hundred is in the king's hands, he takes his orders from the sheriff ; if it is in a subject's hand the bailiff may be responsible both to the sheriff and to the lord of the hundred ; but whatever the privileges of

[1] See Appendix I for the actual articles of the Inquest.

that lord, the hundred bailiff is the king's bailiff.   This is not only the king's view of the situation ; it is shared by the lords of the private hundreds themselves, even though this theoretical subordination may break down in practice, as we saw in the case of the bailiff of Staincliff wapentake.   A study of the everyday working of the governmental machinery, however, leaves the impression that such breakdowns were the exception rather than the rule.   The extent to which subjects shared with the king the burden of government is hardly appreciated by those to whom feudal privilege implies encroachment on royal power.

Some rough idea of the place of the liberties and hundreds in the shire system may be formed by taking two counties as examples—Suffolk and Wiltshire.   Suffolk,[1] which contains twenty-four hundreds, falls then as now into three main sections. The western third of the county forms one of the largest franchises in England, the eight and a half hundreds of St. Edmund, where the Abbot of Bury exercises rights equivalent to those of a sheriff. In the south-east of the county are the five and a half hundreds of St. Etheldreda, grouped round Woodbridge, where the Prior of Ely enjoys similar privileges.   But though there is a separate shire-moot for St. Edmund's liberty, and though the abbot's officials account directly to the Exchequer, some men of the liberty also owe suit to the shire-moot at Ipswich or Beccles, and all writs executed by the abbot's seneschal have passed through the hands of the sheriff of Suffolk.   The rest of Suffolk outside the franchises of the two abbeys is the ' foreign county ', or ' the geldable ' ; in these ten hundreds the customary revenue is still payable to the king, and the hundred bailiffs take their orders direct from the sheriffs.   But the hundreds have various lords.   Hoxne is in 1275, as it was in 1086, the Bishop's Hundred, held by the Bishop of Norwich, who also holds a quarter of Wangford hundred.   Lothingland is held by Devorguilla of Balliol ; Samford is held, during the king's good pleasure, by Ralph of Ufford ; Mutford is held by Edmund de Hemgrave. The remaining five and three-quarter hundreds are royal.   In the private hundreds of the geldable the profits of government are

[1] See map facing p. 208.

shared between the king and the lord of the hundred. But there
are other liberties besides the private hundreds ; there are manors
whose lords exercise petty governmental functions like holding
the assize of bread and ale or the view of frankpledge ; there
are others whose lords exercise a jurisdiction equivalent to that of
the hundred court ; there are large complexes of feudal jurisdiction extending over many hundreds, and these are found both
within and without the other franchises. In Suffolk the Earl of
Gloucester's honour of Clare has its head within the liberty of
St. Edmund, and its limbs in half a dozen hundreds ; and the
royal hundred of Hartismere contains the head of Edmund of
Cornwall's honour of Eye. It is a network of rights, bewildering to twentieth-century eyes, but no more impracticable in the
working than is our modern system of local government, whose
division of function between county, district, and parish councils
would be unintelligible to the thirteenth-century Suffolk squire.
To complete our survey of the shire we must remember the
ɔboroughs of Orford, Ipswich, and Dunwich, which exercise most
of the functions of local government and, like the liberties of St.
Edmund and St. Etheldreda, execute the king's writs by their
own officials, having the right to exclude the sheriff and his
bailiffs.

Wiltshire contains thirty ɔne hundreds, of which twelve are
in the king's hands and twenty-seven in those of subjects.
Ecclesiastical lords are the most numerous. Knowell and Down-
ton are held by the Bishop of Winchester ; Elstub, in four
scattered fragments, is held by the Prior of Winchester ; Damerham, in eight widely separated fragments, is held by the Abbot of
Glastonbury ; Cheggelewe and Sterkely by the Abbot of Malmesbury ; Bradford by the Abbess of Shaftesbury ; Whorwelsdon by
the Abbess of Romsey ; Chalk by the Abbess of Wilton ;· and
Melksham by the Prioress of Amesbury, whilst the Bishop of
Salisbury holds Canning, Bishops Rouburgh, Ramsbury, and
Underditch, in which last his borough of New Sarum stands.
There are no large compact liberties like those of St. Edmund's
and of Ely, though the Winchester hundreds form part of a great
administrative system organized as scientifically as that of St.

Edmund, with its centre in another county, Hampshire; and the Winchester and Glastonbury hundreds share the governmental privileges granted by royal charter to their abbots for all their hundreds. The other ecclesiastical liberties are less highly privileged; while the Abbess of Wilton and the Prioress of Amesbury execute the king's writs by their own bailiffs, the Abbesses of Romsey and Shaftesbury and the Abbot of Malmesbury admit the sheriff's bailiffs, and he holds the tourn twice a year in their hundred courts. The same is true of the lady of Heytesbury hundred, Parnel Dunstanville, of Joan Mauduit in Warminster hundred and of Reginald de Pavely in Westbury hundred. Geoffrey Wascelin, lord of Chippenham hundred, admits the sheriff twice a year to hold the tourn, but excludes the bailiffs and serves the king's writs by his own bailiff; and the Earl of Cornwall in Mere hundred, Maud Longsword's husband in Alderbury and Amesbury, the Cantelupes in Calne, the Countess of Albemarle in Highworth and Cricklade, and Eleanor de Montfort in Kinwardstone can exclude both the sheriff and his bailiffs. The remaining twelve hundreds are royal; they are administered in groups of three by four of the sheriff's hundred bailiffs. The boroughs of Wilton, Chippenham, Devizes, Marlborough, and Old and New Sarum also have the return of writs and can exclude the sheriff's bailiffs, but there are no other lords who can do so, except the Abbot of Glastonbury, in one stray manor of his that lies in the royal hundred of Thornhill.

Two counties whose previous histories differ widely have been taken as examples. In a county like Buckinghamshire, where all hundreds are royal but there are many liberties; in Lincolnshire with its many sokes but only two private hundreds; in Cornwall, where the whole county had been granted by Henry III to his brother as a hereditary domain, and was held by the king's cousin Edmund in 1274, the same standard pattern can be traced under the local variations.

In the following analysis of this standard pattern the articles of 1274 will serve as a starting-point for a survey of the thirteenth-century shire from its two aspects, the administrative and the tenurial. We have seen that the two cannot in fact be separated, but it will be simplest to begin with the shrieval system of government, first examining the sheriff's position, functions, and colleagues throughout the shire and then proceeding to his subordinates in the hundred, with their more localized work.   In postponing specifical feudal concerns until this administrative survey has been completed we are reversing the more courtly order of the inquest, which puts the king's rights first and his servants' second.

CHAPTER IX

THE ADMINISTRATIVE ASPECT OF THE SHIRE

I. The Sheriff and his Task

' Even as the children of the night—the owl, the nighthawk, and the vulture—love darkness rather than light, so from the King's Court are sent sheriffs, under-sheriffs and beadles . . . men who at the outset of their office swear before the highest judge to serve honestly and faithfully God and their master, but being perverted by bribes, tear the fleeces from the lambs and leave the wolves unharmed.'
                                                WALTER MAP, about 1181

' As sheriffs let loyal folk, good men, and landholders be appointed, so that in each shire an under-vassal of that same shire be sheriff.'
                                                PROVISIONS OF OXFORD, 1258

' In this year (1258) died William Heron, sheriff of Northumberland, the hammer of the poor, passing, as we believe, from the thirst of avarice in this temporal world to the thirst of Tantalus in the nether regions.'—MATTHEW PARIS

OF the forty articles of the inquest of 1274, seventeen refer expressly to the sheriff. Articles 15–34 form in effect a section with the heading ' Concerning Sheriffs ', ending, ' All these inquiries shall be made about sheriffs, coroners, their clerks and bailiffs and about all lords and bailiffs of liberties '. We must then begin with the sheriff, the very pulse of the machine.

The first question that arises is, How does the sheriff come to be where he is ? The articles do not touch on this, for in 1274 the appointment of all sheriffs lay entirely with the king, except in the palatinates of Chester and Durham and in the counties of Rutland, Westmorland, Worcester, Cornwall, and Lancaster, where the office was hereditary. This meant in practice that the sheriffs by birth, like the Beauchamps of Worcestershire, put in an acting sheriff, who did the work in the ordinary way, but was appointed and removed by his lord and not by the Exchequer, though no doubt pressure could be brought to bear on the king's behalf if it was desired to remove him.   In the rest of England appointments were made in the Exchequer ; that is, in practice, by the treasurer, and the term of the appointment was the king's good pleasure : ' The King has committed to A. the county of B. to keep as long as the King shall please so that he answer at the Exchequer for the outgoings thereof.'   Sometimes, as in Somerset in 1211 or in Devon in 1230, the men of the county are able by a money payment to avert the appointment of a stranger, but this is an act of grace on the king's part.   The newly appointed sheriff took an oath before the treasurer and barons in the Exchequer, and in the ordinary way he would appear before them to answer for any alleged misconduct.   The baronial opposition of 1258, however, were not satisfied with this responsibility.   They felt that the sheriffs, many of them royal clerks or poor men entirely dependent upon the king, had not enough responsibility towards the shire they administered, and they demanded at Oxford that the men who were appointed should be men of substance, holding land in the county where they held office. The appointments made in the following autumn were in accordance with this demand ; the four knights appointed in each shire to keep an eye on the local government and receive complaints against ex-sheriffs and other officials, when they brought their reports to the October parliament at Westminster were invited to nominate the sheriff for next year.   In most cases they chose one of themselves.   The new sheriffs, thus chosen from the knights of the shire, by knights of the shire, took a new form of oath, ' in the form provided by the King's council ', promising to avoid those precise abuses of which the barons had complained, and which the royal proclamation of 20th October [1] had condemned, encouraging men to report any such misconduct to the king.   The new sheriffs carried back with them to their shires a royal charter written in English to be read aloud in the shire-moot, the first public proclamation that has been preserved

[1] Hennings, *England under Henry III*, p. 202.

in that language.[1] The citizens of Oxford keep their copy to this day among their archives. The language used is yet one more proof that the country-side was beginning to count politically. The churchmen could readily follow a Latin charter, and the magnates used French for their business correspondence ; the use of English meant that it was thought necessary that the knights and freemen of the shire should understand what new reforms were intended, and that the king was definitely pledged to them.

As regards the appointment of sheriffs, the king was committed to three undertakings : the sheriff was to be elected by the men of the shire, he was to be a landholder in the shire where he held office, and he was to hold office for one year only. The first rule was very soon abandoned. A year and a half later Henry took the law into his own hands, removed the elected sheriffs, and appointed his own all over England. This led to great local disorder. The counties often refused to recognize the king's men and the baronial council backed up their resistance by appointing ' Keepers of the Peace ' alongside the king's sheriffs, so that in each county there were two rival authorities between which men could choose. In some counties this dyarchy lasted until after Evesham. The royal nominees complained bitterly that they were not allowed to hold shire-moots or tourns or collect the king's revenues, and in some counties they declared that elected subordinates refused to obey them. The election of sheriffs came thus to be associated with resistance to royal authority, and there was no question of continuing the practice after the barons had laid down their arms in 1267. On the other hand, coroners were continually being elected in the shire courts, by royal command, so that the system could not be considered impracticable, and it was again tried at the close of Edward's reign. In 1300, by the *Articuli super Cartas*, every county except those with hereditary sheriffs was given the right to elect its sheriff. The sheriff-elect was to be presented at the Michaelmas Exchequer by a trustworthy delegate from the shire, bearing the letters patent of the county sealed by the six most worthy knights ; if no such nominee appeared, the treasurer and barons

---

[1] Stubbs, *Charters*, pp. 387–9.

would provide a sheriff themselves. This is, in fact, what generally happened; the advantages of election did not apparently outweigh the trouble. Whereas the rolls of the Exchequer are crowded with the names of mayors, thus elected and presented by their fellow-burgesses, hardly any entries of elected sheriffs are found. One practical difficulty lay in the joint sheriffdoms; Oxfordshire and Berkshire always shared one sheriff, as did Cambridgeshire and Huntingdonshire, Surrey and Sussex, and several other groups; it was not probably the easiest thing in the world to contrive that two county courts should freely elect the same man. However that may be, little use was made of the permission granted in 1300, and it was withdrawn in 1311. Edward III tried the experiment once more in 1339 during his quarrel with the great departments, rather, it would seem, as a hit at the Exchequer than as a bid for popularity. By the Walton ordinances of 1338 the sheriffs were to be elected in the county courts; but only eight shires obeyed the ordinances, and those under protest. In 1340 five shires which had held elections obtained exemption from electing, and a number of suitors to the county court of Cambridgeshire definitely refused to take part in the election.[1] After 1340 the old system was resumed. The knights of the shire, it seems, preferred that the Exchequer should select their sheriff.

On the other hand, the second rule—that he should be a landholder of the shire—seems to have been pretty generally observed. Most sheriffs between 1258 and 1307 were landholders, and a fair proportion of them held land in the county they administered. Both Henry III and his son, however, used to transfer men from one county to another, employing them in counties where they held no land. Thus William de Boyville who held land in Cumberland and York, was sheriff in turn of Northamptonshire, Rutland, Cumberland, Bedfordshire with Buckinghamshire, and Warwick with Leicestershire. John de la Ley, who had an estate in Shropshire, was sheriff in succession of Essex with Hertfordshire, Somerset with Dorset, and Hampshire. Thomas of Belhus, who held land in Norfolk, was sheriff

[1] B. H. Putnam, *Trans. R. Hist. Soc. for 1929*, p. 36.

of Cambridgeshire with Huntingdonshire. William de Lisle, lord of several Northamptonshire manors, was made sheriff of Berkshire with Oxfordshire in 1270, after serving twice as sheriff of Northamptonshire, but thereby hangs a tale. In 1256 he was removed from office and a special commission, including both Simon de Montfort and Richard of Clare, was appointed to investigate his conduct. He had, it was alleged, impounded a fine herd of oxen and thrown the cowherd into prison, where torture was applied until the peasant said that the oxen had been stolen by his master and himself. William de Lisle then released the man and imprisoned his master, a well-known knight of the shire who had on previous occasions taken an independent line against him in the county court. When the case came up for trial before the justices of jail delivery the cowherd, though in fear of his life, declared his master's innocence and denounced the sheriff. William was found guilty by the special commission and condemned to death and forfeiture, if we may trust Matthew Paris. His wife, who with her children was sharing his quarters in the Fleet Prison, managed to get at her friend the young Queen of Scotland, Margaret, who was then on a visit to her father, Henry III, and through her intercession William's penalty was commuted for a fine. The county, it would seem, was too hot to hold him, and not long after he effected an exchange of manors with an Oxfordshire gentleman and moved to that county, where, fourteen years later, he was made sheriff, and where he died in 1277.

A case like this, though the ending is somewhat ironical, helps to explain the barons' desire that sheriffs should be local landholders. If they had a stake in the county they would be less likely to offend their neighbours or betray the interests of their class. But the Exchequer also found it a sound plan to employ men who had lands that could be seized if their accounts were in arrears, as often happened : men whose sons inherited solid assets from their father to balance his liabilities. Sheriffs' heirs were constantly appearing at the Exchequer to pay off their fathers' official debts, incurred ten, twenty, or even thirty years earlier. The heirs of one of William de Lisle's contemporaries, sheriff in

Sussex 1255–7, only cleared off his debt in 1333. In 1276 Henry la Zuche, brother and heir of William la Zuche who had been sheriff of Sussex in 1261–3, was trying to put off the responsibility for his brother's debts on to William's son-in-law, but in vain : with the late sheriff's goods and chattels, his debts had gone to his brother, and Henry was sent to the Fleet Prison till he should make satisfaction for the £63 13s. 4d. owing to the king from William's term of office fifteen years before. As the wishes of county and Exchequer agreed on this point, it is not surprising that the ' substantial man ' demanded in 1258 is the dominant type of sheriff, and that the royal clerk or professional civil servant is the exception rather than the rule.

The third demand—that the sheriff should hold office for a year and no more—was not accepted as a standard by Edward I. Of the twenty sheriffs removed in October 1274 thirteen had held office for two years and more, and of the twenty who replaced them, fourteen were to hold office for three years or more, and one for as many as seven years. For three-quarters of his reign Edward was keeping his sheriffs in office for two or three years on the average. In individual cases they might hold office for as long as ten years together. After 1300 the average tenure of office became shorter, but in no year of his reign were new sheriffs appointed for every county, and in two years no new sheriffs at all were appointed. The reasons for preferring a longer term of office were such as modern administrators will readily appreciate : a sheriff's work was highly technical, and the sheriff must have been a far more useful and efficient servant of the Exchequer in his second and third years of office. In 1325 the official view is clearly stated : just as the Exchequer prefers to have men ' with a good estate of land within the counties where they hold office ', so it holds that ' sheriffs ought not to be changed so often as they have been, for by the more often changing of sheriffs it frequently happens that the king is ill served and his mandates not executed and the people vexed '.[1] But here the popular view diverged. In the parliament of 1340 it was alleged that sheriffs were emboldened to oppress the people grievously and to serve

[1] *Red Book of the Exchequer* (R. S.), p. 961.

both king and people ill by the fact that they held their offices for a term of years, and a statute was passed providing that no sheriff should remain in office for more than a year, the appointment to be made in the Exchequer every year on the morrow of All Souls (November 3rd). The statute was not observed. Fourteen years later it was again provided in parliament that sheriffs should be removed every year, but it was not until 1370 that a year became the normal duration of a shrievalty, ex-sheriffs only serving again after an interval. By 1370 the political importance of the sheriff had received its final blow from the development of the powers of the justices of the peace, and his routine work, with its technical complexities, was coming more and more to be discharged by the under-sheriff. It is possible also that the expenses of the office were contributing to make the sheriff himself refuse to hold office for more than a year.

However selected, whether by the treasurer or by the shire, the actual appointment was made by letters patent under the great seal, and the whole county was commanded to acknowledge and respect his authority. Commands were also issued to his predecessor to hand over to him all documents and moneys in his keeping, and also, more often than not, the castle in the county town which serve as official head-quarters. One such transaction of the year 1278 is recorded in an indenture between an outgoing and an incoming sheriff of Herefordshire,[1] and it is worth quoting at some length by way of introduction to our survey of a sheriff's responsibilities and activities :

'Be it remembered that on the Wednesday next before the feast of All Saints in the sixth year of King Edward's reign, Giles of Berkeley handed over to Sir Roger of Burghull the county of Hereford and the castle with its appurtenances.

'Also the statutes under the seal of the Lord King, and the letters patent as to the keeping of the new statutes.[2] Also five writs to be returned on the morrow of Martinmas [specifying the names of the litigants], six writs to be returned on the

[1] *P.R.O.* Sheriffs' Accounts, 18/2.
[2] Probably the Statutes of Gloucester, of August 1278, and the explanations added later by the justices. See *Stat. Realm*, I. 50. Possibly also the statutes of 1275.

octave of Martinmas, four writs to be returned on the quinzaine of Martinmas, one writ of Novel Disseisin and some writs of Mort Dancester.

' Also two prisoners ; Osbert of Lugwardine who is appealed of homicide and has been arrested under the King's writ, and Lucy Baldwin who was convicted in the hundred court of Irchenfield of complicity in the death of Roger Oleyn and Wervella his wife.

' Also the distresses taken for the summons of the Exchequer, namely three beasts of Walter of Bastwick, taken for an amercement . . . and for having a writ ; four beasts of Adam of Wygmore . . . for a Jew's debt ; five pieces of Bruel, one of Brimenmow, and one of Russel ; and one horse of Richard Manwood's, taken for tallage.

' Also the rolls of the county and of the hundred of Irchenfield, with the writs touching them.'

To understand the sheriff's duties in connexion with castle, writs, prisoners, distresses, and rolls we shall have to survey the whole field of his administration, and travel with him and his subordinates through the length and breadth of the shire.

Of the accompaniments of office the castle comes first. In most of the counties of England, at any rate at the beginning of Edward's reign, it formed the outward embodiment of the sheriff's functions, and its upkeep was one of his responsibilities ; sometimes a special board of knights was appointed to survey it at the time of transfer. The castle might on occasion become a military centre of importance ; a number of gentlemen up and down the shire might be called on to garrison it if required ; but it was in steady and constant use for more peaceful purposes. It contained the office where the sheriff's official records were stored, the writs and rolls needed at the shire court, the writs and vouchers and tallies that he had to produce at the Exchequer, the judicial writs that he had to return to the justices at Westminster and elsewhere. It is the treasury or local exchequer where money is paid in to his receiver, and here are kept the local rating lists which outsiders come up to the castle to consult. It serves as a county prison, where the sheriff keeps the prisoners arrested by himself or by others, either in the deep dungeon reserved for worst offenders, or in the cells or cages of wood which stand in the castle yard and are so often broken by the more hardy prisoners, to the sheriff's discredit and financial loss. Here also is the castle pound, where beasts taken as distresses are kept until redeemed by their owners or sold.[1] In the castle hall or the castle yard, in many counties, sits the monthly county court ; and here at longer intervals sit the king's justices. Here, on occasion, the sheriff may have to entertain other official guests, as when an Oxfordshire lady, left widowed and with child, was ordered to repair to Oxford Castle for her confinement, placing herself in the sheriff's keeping.[2] The castle focuses in itself all those various activities by which the king's work in the shire goes on, whether Roger or Giles be sheriff.

II. THE SHERIFF'S EXECUTIVE FUNCTIONS

(a) The Arrest and Custody of Criminals

' *What sheriffs and bailiffs have taken gifts to conceal felonies done in their bailiwicks, or have been negligent in attaching felons of this sort, out of favour to some one ? What sheriffs have permitted imprisoned felons to escape from prisons free and unpunished, or have extorted money from prisoners for granting bail which they have a right to have freely ? What sheriffs have induced approvers in their custody to appeal innocent and law-abiding persons, as a means of extorting money, or hindered them from appealing the guilty ? '*

cc. 15, 27, 26.

That work can be classified roughly under the headings of executive, fiscal, and judicial work. If we take the castle as our starting-point we may regard it first in the light of prison, and consider the police functions of the sheriff.

The sheriff's duty is to guard his prisoners safely ; how have they come into his keeping ? They may have come in various ways ; in a sense it was anybody's business to arrest a criminal.

[1] e.g. Exeter Castle, *R.H.*, I, 87.   [2] *Bracton's Notebook*, Case 137.

Any one who considered that the king's peace was being broken
could raise the hue and cry, and then every one within earshot
was bound to help. At his tourn the sheriff had to inquire if
this had been duly done. Again, the frankpledge groups were
penalized if any member of a tithing escaped scot-free after
committing a crime. The village as a community was penalized
if it failed to help the coroner in his work of inquiry, and the
hundred was fined if a murder was not brought home to some
person. If a criminal were caught redhanded or seriously
suspected, the village as a whole was liable for his custody until
they had handed him over to safe keeping. Henry of Normanton,
sheriff of Yorkshire, fined one village eight pounds and another
twenty-four marks for allowing prisoners to escape—in one case
quite unjustly, as the jurors show.[1] The amateur jailers sometimes inflicted great cruelty on the captives in their eagerness to
be on the safe side. Alan Blunt, arrested on Friday 19th June
1254 by the bailiffs of Lincoln, on suspicion of theft, was put in
the charge of Alan Williamson, who placed him in the stocks in a
room opening off his yard, put an iron collar, heavy and close-
fitting, round his neck, shut the door, and went away. On
Saturday the prisoner was found dead, and the inquest found that
this was not the fault of Williamson, but due to the stiffness and
roughness of the collar and the discomfort of the prison, so that
his jailer was guiltless of his death. Naturally the great desire
of the township was to get the prisoner safely off their hands ;
not till they had handed him over to the sheriff could they feel
safe. The sheriff, on the other hand, was not always eager to
receive them. The jail might be full up ; if he took in the
prisoner he might be able to get no payment from him ; he might
take up the room of more profitable inmates, and at any time he
might break jail and render the sheriff liable to a fine for escape.
The barons complained in 1258 that after their bailiffs had made
an arrest the sheriff would often refuse to accept the prisoner
when brought to him. The villages made the same complaint.
The township of Fulbourn in 1259 brought to Cambridge Castle
a woman suspected of the murder of her husband, handing her

[1] *R.H.,* I, 110.

over to the sheriff in full county court for custody, but the sheriff, one of the new baronial appointments, refused to accept her. As the village would not take her back she was allowed to escape, and it is not clear whether the sheriff or the township was held liable for the fine incurred. The woman, however, came of her own free will before the justices in eyre who were investigating this piece of slackness, and put herself on a jury who acquitted her. Another case of a prisoner's escaping by falling between the two stools of sheriff and vill came up in the Cornish eyre of 1302. The sheriff's officials attached a man and gave him into the keeping of his tithing until the sheriff's tourn. At the tourn he was not indicted, as the jury thought it superfluous to indict a man whom the sheriff had already arrested, so though the man escaped he could not be hanged for his escape when recaptured.[1] An escaped prisoner was guilty of a capital offence, and could be beheaded at sight if captured before he reached sanctuary. Even at Cambridge and Northampton, where there were churches very near the castle, the castle officials sometimes caught the fugitives in time and so saved the sheriff the fine for escape by taking off their heads.

Though prisoners might be handed over to the sheriff by seignorial bailiffs or by village constables, normally speaking he had himself been responsible for their arrest. Whether a man were indicted by a jury, presented by a bailiff, or appealed by a private person, it was the sheriff's part to order his arrest, or attachment, to use the medieval phrase. Here at once begins the evasion of duty. The Hundred Rolls give numberless instances of the taking of gifts to conceal felonies. Walter of Stirchesley, sheriff of Wilts 1272–4, took twenty shillings from a man suspected of larceny, not to have him attached.[2] Three men indicted of felony at the sheriff's tourn are still wandering about Yorkshire, through the failure of the under-sheriff to attach them.[3] Another Yorkshire official drew a steady payment of eight shillings a year for allowing Dandy of Skyren to lurk at liberty in his bailiwick.[4] The negligence is often that of

[1] *Year Books*, 30 Ed. I, p. 502.
[2] *R.H.*, II, 275.
[3] Ibid., I, 109.
[4] Ibid., I, 114.

a lower official ; a bailiff of Broxtow wapentake, Notts, received commands from the sheriff to attach a man for felony, and gave him warning so that he escaped.[1]   In one Essex hundred the jurors complain that men are indicted over and over again at the sheriff's tourn, and yet they are neither attached nor imprisoned, and they suspect that the bailiffs take bribes to leave them in peace.[2]   Worst of all is the charge that the ex-bailiff of a Lincolnshire wapentake, indicted of robbery before the justices in eyre in 1271, has not yet been attached ; this looks very much like official collusion.[3]

A formal accusation in one of the local courts was the normal preliminary to an arrest.   In his tourn, held in the different hundreds of his shire twice a year, the sheriff required the hundred juries to accuse suspects, and on their presentments made arrests if the accused could be found.   Presentments were also made in the shire court, probably by the hundred bailiffs on behalf of their hundreds.   Besides these collective accusations, individuals could bring charges, and very often did, by the procedure known as appeal.   Both in the hundred and in the county court a man could appeal another of theft or murder and a woman could appeal a man of the murder of her husband.   Wherever the appeal was made it was the duty of the executive official to arrest the accused and hand him over for safe keeping to the nearest custodian of a safe jail.   Such individual charges were very often made by persons who were already in jail.   It was exceedingly common for a prisoner, arrested on the indictment or presentment of a juror to turn king's evidence and denounce his alleged accomplices.   Such persons were called approvers, and sometimes earned their freedom by acting as champions in the duel by which the appealed persons sought to vindicate their innocence.   There is preserved in the Public Record Office a drawing, from a roll of Henry III's reign, of an approver, Walter Bloweberme, fighting a judicial combat with the accomplice, Hamo Lestare, whom he had denounced and whom he was to defeat ; for in the background is drawn the gallows upon which Hamo was hanged after his failure in the duel.   Matthew Paris,

---

[1] *R.H.*, II, 315.   [2] Ibid., I, 146–7.   [3] Ibid., I, 372.

in his story of the Brabant merchants, mentions an approver who fought six duels and rid the king of as many thieves.   In 1274 the jurors of Pickering wapentake tell of an approver in York castle who appealed thirteen honest men, from whom the sheriff extorted forty shillings, while the jailer made even more by threatening the country people with similar appeals from another man in the prison.[1]   The sheriff had these suspects completely at his mercy ; in every castle, it seems, there was an especially deep and dreadful prison into which men were cast, and if this was not sufficient sharper means of coercion were used.   William de Lisle was by no means the only sheriff who tortured his prisoners, and a suspected thief had much to gain and little to lose by turning approver and appearing in open court to appeal those persons against whom the sheriff might have a grudge, or whom he knew to be wealthy.   The Nottinghamshire jurors mention an approver who was rewarded by a gift of oxen for appealing a perfectly honest and respectable parson.[2]   In Lincolnshire the under-sheriff arrested Peter de Hycham, declaring that he had been appealed by an approver, and so extorted twelve marks from him ; but when accuser and accused were brought face to face, the approver declared that he had never seen Peter before.[3] Those law-abiding and innocent persons who were not able to pay such sums had to face a long imprisonment, for though the sheriff was bound to arrest felons he had no power to try them, and unless bail was allowed, they had to await the coming of the king's justices in jail.   Joan of Hereford, suspected of stealing a lady's surcoat, was kept in Guildford Jail ' among the thieves ' for forty-seven weeks by the sheriff of Surrey until the justices of jail delivery came round, when a jury found her innocent of both theft and of complicity with thieves.[4]   To escape such a fate the well-to-do could be induced to pay large sums, and the Hundred Rolls are full of examples of such extortion.   Robert del Estre, sheriff of Cambridgeshire, got an approver to appeal a Grant-chester man of homicide, though he had already been acquitted of the charge before the justices of jail delivery, and demanded

---

[1] Ibid., I, 115.   [2] Ibid., II, 316.
[3] Ibid., I, 313.   [4] Ass. R. 541 A, m. 15d.

four shillings for his release.[1]   We have seen how the Devonshire
sheriff, Roger de Pridias, extorted four marks from a man thus
falsely accused, by casting him into a pit for four-and-twenty
hours.[2]   The Lincolnshire rolls tell of a man thus appealed who
was tortured to death by the sheriff's underlings for refusing to
make the payment demanded.[3]   Most outrageous of all perhaps
is the case of Hugh the Butcher of Northumberland.   This man
paid five pounds to the sheriff who declared that a felon recently
hanged had appealed him ; he was then appealed a second time
by another approver, produced by the next sheriff, and this time
had to pay ten pounds to be allowed bail ; he was then appealed,
as was asserted, by a third approver, and paid eight marks to be
at peace till the coming of the justices, and when the justices came
this approver said that he had never appealed Hugh ; and
finally the county coroner warned him that unless two marks were
paid to prevent it, he would be appealed a fourth time.[4]

Accusation could thus be obtained by irregular means, but
even so the jurors report many instances of persons arrested
without any formal accusation, whether by appeal or by indictment.   Two Wiltshire men, attached by the sheriff on suspicion
of homicide, had to pay 6s. 8d. to be freed, though they had
never been indicted.[5]   Richard of Southchurch, sheriff of Essex,
by his official authority caused Master Auvre le Ku to be arrested,
alleging that he had broken the king's peace, ' who had never in
all his life trespassed against the king's peace as much as the said
Richard did in one day '.[6]   When the same Richard attached a
well-to-do gentleman and took twenty marks from him the jurors
declare, ' We know not why he attached him unless it was because
he wanted his money.' [7]

Less frequent is the complaint that the sheriff has suppressed
an appeal.   There is one pretty bad story from Yorkshire of this
sort.   A countryman appealed Gilbert du Bois of the death of his
son, in full county court, and the keeper of York Jail, at Gilbert's
instigation, imprisoned the appellant on the pretext that he was a
thief, tied him up to a post in the prison, and kept him naked and

---

[1] Camb. Hundred Roll (unprinted) 3, m. 2.   [2] *R.H.*, I, 67.
[3] Ibid., I, 274.   [4] Ibid., II, 20–21.   [5] Ibid., II, 275.
[6] Ibid., I, 149.   [7] Ibid., I, 148.

starving until he paid down forty shillings to the sheriff and ten shillings to the jailer.[1]

Finally, the sheriffs are accused of making money by refusing to give bail freely. In view of the scanty accommodation for prisoners there was a very elaborate system of giving security, and if a man could find pledges who would undertake to produce him for trial when called upon the sheriff was bound to release him if the offence was not too grave. The hundred jurors report cases of extortion of money for bail, or replevin, to which the accused had a right, and, on the other hand, of concession of bail to men charged with ' irreplevisable ' offences. William of Stowe, sheriff of Cambridgeshire, allowed bail to a man who was appealed by his mistress of the murder of her husband. He fined the pledges mercilessly, it is true, when they failed to produce the murderer in court, but he had no more right to fine them than he had to accept their security in the first place. In the end he himself had to pay a hundred shillings for his breach of the law. On the other hand, a later Cambridgeshire sheriff, William de Roothing, took twenty shillings from a man indicted of theft when he had a right to free replevin. According to the jurors of Bingham wapentake all the sheriffs of Nottinghamshire since Evesham had taken money from men who should have had their replevin freely.[2] Seven sheriffs are named, but the present sheriff, who had been appointed three months before the inquest, on 14th October 1274, does it more freely and openly than any that came before him. If a prisoner is poor he remains in prison as a matter of course until the justices of jail delivery arrive.[3]

It should be observed that exactly the same offences are charged against the bailiffs of those lords of liberties who had the sheriff's power of arrest and custody. Into the liberty of the Peak, Edward's own estate, whose head bailiff is Sir Roger Lestrange, one of the commissioners for the Shropshire circuit in 1274, no sheriff ever comes, the jurors say ; but the underlings of Sir Roger play just the same game as the sheriffs do elsewhere. They come and attach offenders, and let them go free for a bribe. When the wounded man dies they attach the father and brother

[1] Ibid., I, III.   [2] Ibid., II, 320.   [3] Ibid., II, 316.

of the actual homicide and exact ten more marks ' for the use of their lord, Sir Roger ', allowing the man who struck the blow to escape.   Another manslayer is allowed to go scot-free because he is the bailiff's brother.[1]

The same kind of reports come from the Bishop of Ely's Norfolk hundred of Mitford ; a woman indicted for her husband's death is allowed to go free and unpunished after paying ten marks to the bailiffs, whilst another indicted of theft buys her replevin with 6s. 8d.   The Bishop of Ely's jail in Ely is still standing, like the prior's jail in Melton, Suffolk.   But there were many liberties whose lords, though it was their duty to arrest, had no jail, and had to hand over their prisoners to the sheriff for safe custody, just as they might on occasion borrow the king's gallows when they had the right to hang thieves.   It was, however, steadily maintained that all such felons were the king's ; he might grant out to a subject the right to try, to imprison, or to hang them, or even to take their goods for a year and a day ; but those who exercised such functions were responsible to the king for the enforcement of his peace and the execution of his justice ; the king's coroner kept a record, which had to be produced for the king's justices, whose clerks noted on the rolls all the profits of criminal proceedings, even though they went into the pockets of some baron or bishop and never reached the king himself.

(b) The Execution of Writs

' Have sheriffs or bailiffs of liberties failed to summon men according to the form of the king's writ, or otherwise executed the lord king's commands fraudently or inadequately ? '—c. 25.

The castle served the sheriff not only as a prison but as an office.   Amongst the official records and other documents kept there there must, at any given moment, have been a large number of writs.   Not long ago there was discovered a roll coming from the office of a sheriff of Bedfordshire early in the reign of Edward III on which was entered the writs received by the sheriff during seventeen months ; they numbered two thousand.[2]   Sixty years

---

[1] *R.H.*, II, 288.   [2] E.H.R., XLIII, 24.

earlier the work may not have been quite as heavy, but it will be remembered that in 1278 the outgoing sheriff of Herefordshire had some eighteen or twenty writs to hand over to his successor, most of them returnable within a month. Some of these referred specifically to lawsuits, and may simply have commanded the presence of litigants in the king's courts. But a large proportion of the writs received by the sheriff were commands involving not merely the responsibility of serving them but the labour of executing them. When private persons hand writs to the sheriff in the county court or elsewhere, or when the king's messenger brings him a bundle of writs from head-quarters, he will have to sort them out. He will put on one side those concerning persons or places within the liberties whose lords have the return of writs. These, or rather copies of these with a covering letter, he will hand over to his bailiff errant, or some other subordinate, to take to the responsible official of the liberty, whether he be the seneschal of Glastonbury Abbey or the bailiff of the Peak, or Gilbert of Clare's bailiff of the hundred of Tewkesbury, and the duty of executing the writ is passed on to them, with orders, however, to report to the sheriff when action has been taken, so that he can make a due return to the Exchequer or the King's Bench or wherever the writ came from. A roll from St. Edmund's liberty, preserved at Oxford, has copies of writs thus passed on to the seneschal of St. Edmunds by the sheriff of Suffolk, with the seneschal's notes, whilst in the archives of the Exchequer, in London, are many writs which have been executed by bailiffs of liberties, returned with the sheriffs' endorsements to head-quarters.

There will remain for the sheriff himself to execute a great variety of writs. They can be broadly classified under the headings of royal or private concerns. A great many will be concerned with litigation, the direct consequence of Henry II's policy of putting the machinery of royal justice at the disposal of his subjects who wished to vindicate their claims to land. The execution of these writs only concerns the king indirectly as affecting his honour and to some extent his revenues ; it is the subject who will suffer from delay. Into the other class fall the writs commanding the collection of sums owed to the Exchequer, the summoning of troops, the provision of supplies, the holding of inquests or surveys of royal lands or castles and the like.   The jurors of 1274 are not invited to discriminate, however ; any royal command, whatever its contents, should be promptly obeyed.

Perhaps the commonest type of writ is that which commands the sheriff to compel the attendance of persons in court.   This is a long-drawn-out business.   ' The law must be slow in order to be fair,' as Maitland says, and it is in the sheriff's hands ' to turn the screw that brings pressure to bear upon the defendant '. The first command may be to summon the party or parties ; the next to attach ; the next to distrain ; the last to seize the body of the reluctant litigant.   Our sheriff, as each fresh batch of writs reaches him, will be sending out the messengers bearing summonses, or orders, to his hundred bailiffs to attach persons by pledges or seize their cattle or other movable property, or even, it may be, to take their lands into the king's hands by way of compelling their attendance at the king's court.

The summons may be simply to appear in court, but here at once is an opening for oppression.   The sheriff of Lincolnshire, it is alleged, summoned twenty-seven men of Lincoln to be in the king's court in London on Midsummer Day, whereby they had to miss Boston Fair and lost at least twenty pounds ; and the writ was a forgery, devised by the sheriff at the instigation of the other party.[1]   Far more common than the charge of forgery, however, is the complaint of delay in execution or the suppression of a writ altogether.   The jurors of one Yorkshire wapentake assert that ' almost all the sheriffs and their bailiffs, as well as the bailiffs of liberties which have the return of writs, do not make due execution of the commands of the lord king according to the form of his writ—for example, Henry of Normanton, under-sheriff of Yorkshire, his clerk John de Foxoles, and the sub-bailiffs of the Bishop of Durham in Howdenshire '.[2]   In Essex also ' all the bailiffs have not executed the Lord king's writs as they ought to have done '.[3]   One sheriff who had a writ to execute against a

[1] R.H., I, 113.   [2] Ibid., I, 130.   [3] Ibid., I, 148.

rector charged with violence delayed proceedings by alleging that
the other party had been unable to find pledges that he would
prosecute, when his hundred bailiff had already reported the
names of the pledges to him.[1]   In another case not the return but
the writ was falsified ; both the date for appearance and the
amount of land involved was altered ; and Julian de Pochow
lost fifteen pounds, presumably because the case went against
her by default.[2]   Henry of Normanton had neglected for four
years to execute a writ which Isabel Darel brought against
William de Bussy concerning a debt which he owed her, whereby
Isabel lost sixty marks ; like many another woman she had failed
to master the art of judicious bribery.[3]   When a woman of
Saundby handed the king's writ to the bailiff of a Notts wapentake
for him to execute, he flung it at her feet saying, ' Go and ask for
another writ ! '[4]   This slackness in the county staff had long
been a scandal ; thirty years before a formal complaint had been
lodged against the sheriff of Worcester for doing nothing in a
certain matter though three successive writs had been delivered
to him.[5]   Thirteen years later another sheriff of Yorkshire was
accused by one man of ignoring the king's writ for eleven successive
county courts, which in Yorkshire means a year and a quarter,
and by another man of refusing to execute four writs in succession,
and then exacting forty shillings before he would execute a fifth.[6]
Sometimes the sheriff simply suppressed the writ and declared
that he had never received it.   It was to prevent such abuses
that new rules were laid down in 1285.   ' Forasmuch as justices
. . . are often impeded in the due execution of their office,
because sheriffs do not return writs . . . or make false returns to
them . . . Our Lord the King hath provided that they which
fear the malice of sheriffs shall deliver their writs, whether original
or judicial, in full county court or in the rere-county, and shall
receive a *billet* from the sheriff . . . or under-sheriff '.[7]   The
receipt was to be dated and sealed either by the sheriff or by some
of the knights of the shire there present.   Copies of such dated

[1] Ibid., I, 112.   [2] Ibid., I, 128.   [3] Ibid., I, 123.   [4] Ibid., II, 303.
[5] *Royal Letters*, II, 48–9.   [6] Ass. R., 541 A, m. 39d, m. 52.
[7] *Stat. of Realm*, I, 90.

receipts are preserved in the records of religious houses, among other legal documents.[1]   In order to prevent the sheriffs putting the blame unfairly on the bailiffs of liberties, the justices were to be supplied with lists of those liberties who had return of writs. Yet even after the statutes of 1285 the trials of 1289–91 show that sheriffs still did grievous wrong to litigants by slowness or refusal to execute writs, and pretended that the fault lay with bailiffs whose lords had not the return of writs.

(c) Empanelling of Juries

' What sheriffs and bailiffs have taken bribes for removing men from juries, or have amerced men summoned to inquests for default when there were enough without them ? '—cc. 16, 17.

Besides the summons to appear in court there was the summons to serve on a jury.   A very large proportion of the writs which the sheriff has to execute command him to get together a body of jurors.   It might be a jury to inquire whether the building of a wall or the digging of a conduit would be to the hurt of the king or the country-side : a jury to make a valuation or ' extent ' of royal property, or a recognition of customs and services ; a jury to give a verdict in a case of Novel Disseisin ; or an inquest into the age of an heir of a tenant-in-chief.   In selecting the man to serve, the sheriff and his underlings had almost unlimited opportunities both of harassing the ordinary freeman and of influencing verdicts.   In 1274 information is demanded as to sheriffs who have unfairly penalized men for failure to attend for jury service or have taken bribes for altering the composition of juries.

The returns suggest that such alterations were made generally at the juror's own request.   The average freeman was no more anxious to serve on a jury in the thirteenth century than he is to-day ; the Rolls of Chancery are sown thick with grants of exemption to individuals from serving on assizes and recognitions for the rest of their life.   The barons in 1258 complained that

[1] e.g. of Beaulieu Abbey ; B. M. Cott. M. S. Nero, A. XII, fo. 75d ; of Thorney Abbey ; C.U.L., Add. MS. 3021, fo. 278.

such exemptions were really making it difficult for legal business to be done,[1] and the sheriff must have made large sums of money very easily by granting exemptions on his own authority. In Suffolk one shilling seems to have been the usual fee or bribe ; instances abound both in the royal hundreds and those of the Abbot of St. Edmunds. The same story comes from all over England. 'All the sheriffs and bailiffs have done this and still do it,' say the jurors of Ryedale wapentake in Yorkshire.[2] The four knights who drew up a return for nine Norfolk hundreds give a list of twenty-eight persons who had made payments ranging from sixpence to seven shillings, not to mention gifts of oats and barley, to be let off jury-service.[3] There is also an abundance of evidence of fining persons for non-attendance at inquests, even though they were not needed to make up the number of jurors. Two men in Wangford hundred, Suffolk, had to pay 6s. 8d. on this pretext, though they had not really been summoned at all.[4] The actual work of summoning was performed by subordinates, and when the hundred bailiff or sheriff's clerk pocketed the money the villagers were hardly in a position to know how the spoils were shared. But the sheriff was ultimately the responsible agent, and the sheriff, it must in fairness be remembered, might be penalized if he failed to produce a full panel. The sheriff of Northumberland was fined ten pounds in 1270 because only seven jurors turned up at Westminster to make a recognition in a plea of land, and the case in consequence had to be adjourned.

The Hundred Rolls do not afford many instances of the packing of juries. In an assize of Mort d'Ancestor between two ladies of Lincolnshire, twelve men were removed from the jury in return for a payment of eighteenpence, and owing to the consequent delay the plaintiff had to get a fresh writ.[5] On the other hand, there are cases of intimidation. The under-sheriff of Yorkshire imprisoned twelve jurors of an assize of Novel Disseisin 'amongst the thieves' till they gave him twelve shillings to be free.[6] Presumably they also gave the verdict he wanted, for one of the litigants procured a writ to have a second jury,

---

[1] *Petition of the Barons*, cl. 28 ; Stubbs, *Charters*, p. 278.   [2] *R.H.*, I, 117.
[3] Ibid., I., 474.   [4] Ibid., II, 180.   [5] Ibid., I, 349.   [6] Ibid., I, 109.

known as a jury of attaint, to overhaul their verdict, and even then the under-sheriff, on some pretext or another, got six and a half marks out of them.   It is the jury of presentment which is fined by a Gloucestershire sheriff for concealing a felony ; this would appear to be an attempt to coerce a jury into accusing some one they would otherwise have let alone.[1]   Sheriffs are also accused of empanelling juries either akin to or hostile to one of the parties to a suit, and the Exchequer often issued specific directions to prevent this when ordering an inquest.

A sidelight is thrown on this question by the naïve narrative of the canon of Barnwell.   In his account of the prior's lawsuits under Henry III and Edward I he boasts of the prior's skill in getting a ' good inquest ' which would speak ' marvellously well '. In one case, in the Cambridge eyre of 1286, the jury found against the prior.   ' On this the prior was exceeding wroth with the twelve jurors, and sent his canons into Cambridge to find lawyers to attaint the twelve of swearing falsely, and the twelve hearing this were gravely alarmed.'   The winner of the lawsuit, however, came to the prior in tears, and a compromise was made out of court.   In every other lawsuit, however, the prior was successful.   By gifts of grazing, bread, ale, and wine to the authorities, prudently bestowed, he escaped amercement in every case but one, and ' even that amercement was never paid nor entered on the estreats of the eyre, for the justices were favourable and the clerks benevolent, and when they left Cambridge they lavished gracious thanks on the prior and the canons, declaring their obligation to them.'

Concerted attempts to defeat the ends of justice must from a very early date have attended the use of the jury system.   We have seen evidence of the intimidation of the jurors of 1274–5, and the justices of the eyres of 1278–9 and subsequently had orders to inquire into conspiracies of this kind.   ' Whereas we have been given to understand,' the king's letters ran, ' that certain malicious persons in many counties of our realm, to serve their own ends, being more prone to evil than to good, have presumed to make certain detestable confederacies and evil plots

[1] *R.H.*, I, 170.

PLATE III

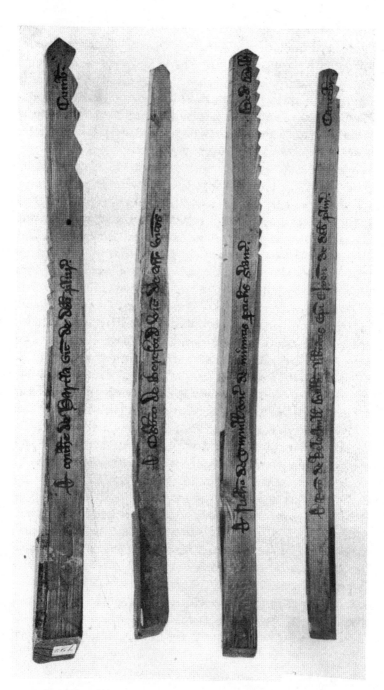

EXCHEQUER TALLIES OF SHERIFFS' PAYMENTS

amongst themselves, taking oaths to each other to uphold the
cause of their friends . . . in pleas . . . coming up in the courts,
by deceitful conduct on assizes, juries and recognitions, . . . and
in like manner, to grieve their enemies, and where possible
disinherit them . . . we command you to inquire diligently in
every county to which you shall come on this eyre concerning . . .
conspirators of this sort.' But, even so, the only machinery for
detection was the inquest itself, and it was setting a thief to catch
a thief. The Statute of Winchester six years later used more
drastic means to deal with at least the presenting jury. Juries
refused to indict malefactors, the statute asserts, choosing rather
that homicide and robbery of strangers should go unpunished
than that their neighbours should suffer. Henceforth the
country-side as a whole is to share the penalty for such offences
if the criminal in person cannot be brought to book ; the whole
hundred in which the robbery was committed shall be answerable
for the damage done.

The sheriff, it is true, had not much to say as to the composition of the eyre juries ; they were selected by the two knights
of each hundred, who had themselves been nominated by the
four chosen knights of the whole shire. All the same, he had a
hold on the hundred bailiff, who certainly co-operated in the
presentments of their hundred juries, and he may have had some
influence on the knights. It is safe to say that his active co-operation would be needed if the justices were to detect and defeat
conspiracies among the jurors.

If in judicial inquests the sheriff's position was strictly
subordinate, and ended with the production of the jury, in fiscal
inquests he might well have more scope. If categorical information was required by the Exchequer as to the condition of the
king's property, or the possessions of a minor tenant-in-chief, or
the assets of a royal debtor, he might himself have to convey
the information to head-quarters. In the central archives are
hundreds of returns to such inquests endorsed with the date and
place of their holding, often in the shire or hundred court, but
often elsewhere. An examination of such returns drives home
alike the indispensability of the sheriff and his opportunities for

coercion of jurors and cooking of verdicts.   There is one instance
of complete suppression : an under-sheriff of Herts who held an
inquest at Hitchin into a trespass against the king's peace refused
to make any return of its verdict to the king's justices.[1].   Henry
of Normanton, that under-sheriff of Yorkshire whose enormities
seem to stagger even the compilers of the extract rolls—' Numberless and marvellous are the misdeeds alleged against him ' [2]—
falsified a return by tearing off the seals of the twelve jurors after
they had affixed them.   This he did because one of the litigants
had promised him one hundred shillings a year until such time as
an ecclesiastical benefice should be available.[3]

(d) Distraining

In executing the king's writs, as in carrying out the less
formal legal processes of the local courts, the sheriff and his staff
found themselves constantly compelled to distrain.   The tenants
of those houses which lay within the precincts of the county castle
must have been well used to the sight of cattle and horses being
driven into the castle ground, and of their owners coming to
reclaim them and to give pledges of their appearance in court or
of their readiness to pay the debt for which they had been distrained.   Such parks or pounds for distresses must have been
scattered up and down the county, as well as in the castle.   In
Somerset the park at the royal manor of Somerton had been used
as a pound for all the distresses taken from those who owed the
king money, from all over the county ; if the beasts had not been
claimed within three days from their taking they had been driven
to Somerton ; but in 1274, according to the hundred jurors, the
lords of the private hundreds in the county were no longer
allowing this.[4]   At Godmanchester, in Hunts, there was a place
called ' Le Pondfolde ' outside the gates of the house of the
Prior of Merton, where all the beasts distrained in Toseland
hundred were kept.[5]   Private parks also were used by the sheriff's
underlings.   In Cornwall Roger de Carmynou had by customary

---

[1] Ass. R., 541A, m. 11d.   [2] R.H., I, 109.   [3] Ibid., I, 125.
[4] Ibid., II, 123.   [5] P.Q.W., 304.

right the parking of all distresses taken in Kerrier hundred, with the right to demand a penny for each animal parked.[1] This would be paid by the owner of the beasts when he came to recover them, which was not always a simple matter. On one occasion a litigant brought the sheriff of Essex a writ for the delivery of two of his beasts. The sheriff gave him a mandate which he carried to the hundred bailiff, and the bailiff took him to the Earl of Hereford's park at Pleshy, where the cattle were grazing, and told him to pick his own out of the herd. He picked two, but found on closer inspection that one was not his own, and drove it back to the park, but he was not allowed to take his own second cow because the park extended over two hundreds, and the hundred bailiff said he had no power to let him take a beast out of the next hundred. So the cow remained in Pleshy park, and continued to run up a bill payable to the sheriff or the hundred bailiff.[2] These pence for distresses were amongst the most valuable perquisites claimed by the sheriff, and this no doubt explains the large number of complaints made in 1274-5 of the abuses connected with distraining. As the actual process was carried out by subordinates, a great many of the charges are brought against bedels and hundred bailiffs ; but there are also complaints of sheriffs selling the beasts (under cost price) and refusing to give them back,[3] and of coercion applied to the owner when he came to the castle to recover his beast, to make a grant of his land to the sheriff's clerk.[4] The sheriff certainly had the duty of selling the distresses taken for money owing to the king, and as certainly abused it. Seignorial officials, like Gilbert of Clare's seneschal, are accused of the same kind of unjust distraint as the sheriffs.[5] The right to inquire into cases of detention of beasts when pledges were duly tendered was a regalian privilege, exercised only by the sheriff and by those lords to whom the king had given the right ; such cases most often arose, however, from unofficial distraint by an individual.

The actual seizure of the beasts, as was only to be expected, produced a great deal of irritation and violence. There are a

[1] *P.Q.W.*, 109.   [2] Ass. R. 541 A, m. 1.   [3] Ass. R., 541 A. m. 52.
[4] *R.H.*, I, 118.   [5] Ibid., II, 156.

good many stories of forcible resistance to the sheriff's officials
when they came to distrain, and of recapture of the beasts
taken.   The vicar of Ditton in Suffolk rescues the beasts which
the king's bailiff has distrained.[1]   In Calceworth wapentake in
Lincolnshire the servants of the owner of the castle attack and
seriously wound the men driving off the distresses, and are fined
ten marks by the sheriff—though three years later the jurors doubt
exceedingly whether any of that money has reached the king.[2]
On one Norfolk manor the courtesy of the sheriff's underling
proves his own undoing ; he comes to distrain upon Nicholas de
Lenham, and invites the servants of Nicholas to select the beasts
he shall take, and thereupon the village reeve and the servants
fall upon him and flog him so that he cannot take any beasts.[3]
In Stanborough hundred in Devon when the bailiff comes to distrain some beasts at Boltbury he is slain by the squire.[4]   After
this the weapon of excommunication used by the dean and chapter
of York in 1260 to prevent the king's bailiffs from using their
powers seems a gentle and peaceful form of resistance.[5]   The
fault, then, is not all on one side ; the jurors who report high-
handed distraining have also to report that the villagers have
' impeded the execution of the Lord king's mandates ' [6] ; but
the score is very much longer against the officials than against
the country-side.   In some cases also the sheriff was definitely
to blame for sending men without evidence of their official position ; a statute of 1285 forbade sheriffs to use strangers unknown
to the country-side to take distresses, as this provoked resistance.[7]
There are a few, but very few, instances of failure to take the
distresses, through slackness or in return for bribes.   The chief
abuses are perhaps best summarized in the statutes of October
1275, based on the evidence of the Hundred Rolls : ' Because the
commonalty of the land have sustained great loss by wrongful
taking of distresses by the sheriffs and other bailiffs, it is provided
that those to whom the beasts belong may feed them themselves,
whilst they are imparked, without giving anything for their keep.
Also that no beasts be sold within a fortnight of their taking.

---

[1] *R.H.*, II, 199.   [2] Ibid., I, 269.   [3] Ass. R. 562.
[4] *R.H.*, I, 79.   [5] Coram Rege R. 167, m. 9d.   [6] c. 12.
[7] Stat. West., II, c. 37 ; *Stat. Realm*, I, 89.

Also that no man be distrained by the beasts that till his land, nor by sheep, either by the king's bailiffs or by any other men, as long as any other distress can be found.' [1]   In this matter, as in several others, the first statutes of Edward's reign completed the work of the Statute of Marlborough ; he was building on the foundations laid by the barons and the ' bachelery '.

(e) Military summons

' *Who have summoned any to be made knights and have allowed them respite for money ?   What magnates have distrained any to take up arms without the king's command ? '—c. 24.*

There was one type of writ which on occasion imposed a heavy responsibility on the sheriff—the writ commanding him to summon the military forces of the shire.   The fyrd, as it had been called before the Norman Conquest, the musters, as the Elizabethans called them, the fencible men of the Napoleonic wars, and the militia of the nineteenth century were only supposed to serve for purposes of home defence.   An emergency like the French invasion of 1217, when the sheriffs were summoned to bring up all fit to bear arms in their shires, would not recur frequently in south-eastern England ; the counties neighbouring the Scotch or Welsh marches were more likely to receive such summons, as Gloucestershire had done in 1231.   But a rebellious subject might have to be coerced, and the sheriffs had been ordered to levy a force with horn and hue from vill to vill of their counties in 1224 to subdue the insurgent William de Bréauté, who had flung a justice-in-eyre into prison and was defying the royal authority in Bedford Castle.   In the baronial wars the control of the armed forces of the shire became of considerable importance, and the extraordinary keepers of the peace appointed in those years kept a check on the sheriff, if they did not supersede him in this department.   In 1263 and 1264 foreign invasion had again been feared, and the sheriffs of Norfolk, Suffolk, and Essex guarded the coasts with all the forces of the shire.   But such military charges were exceptional ; in a general way the

[1] Statutes of the Exchequer, c. xiii ; *Stat. Realm*, I, 197b.

sheriff's duties were auxiliary rather than directive.   He had to keep the strongholds in his charge in good repair ; to procure victuals and munitions for the troops ; to pass on the royal commands to the military tenants, and when appropriate enforce the obligation of knight-service ; to hold periodical inspections of the men of military age and standing ; and, most probably, to keep lists of the freemen liable to bear arms.[1]   A series of regulations issued by the king and his council from 1181 onwards had defined the obligation of freemen and villeins in the way of equipment, the obligation of boroughs and hundreds to appoint constables for their mustering, and the obligation of the sheriff, with special assistants, to inspect the arrays of the hundreds periodically.[2]

The line dividing military and police functions was narrow. The sheriff had to supervise the keeping of watch and ward against breakers of the peace, whether thieves or rebels ; the constable of the hundred was responsible both for the military musters and for the watchmen and local keepers of the peace. The military array of the shire—the *posse comitatus*—was at the sheriff's disposal for the enforcement of his authority if it was resisted.   He could call upon the law-worthy and fyrd-worthy men to support him if the bailiffs of a liberty refused to execute the king's writ and defied him in the person of his sheriff.   The first Statutes of Westminster, issued six months after the returns of 1274–5 had been completed, provided for the case where such bailiffs had taken a distress and kept it within their lord's castle, refusing to hand it over to the sheriff for him to restore to the owner, as the law bade, in return for proper security.   In such a case the sheriff might call out the *posse comitatus*, or as many of them as he need, and beat down the castle.[3]   The second Statutes of Westminster, ten years later, went farther, declaring that henceforth it was to be no good return to a writ for a sheriff to say that he was unable to execute it ; if his underlings reported that they had been resisted he was to put aside all other business and take the forces of the shire to assist him in making execution.[4]

---

[1] *Curia Regis Rolls*, I, 45.
[3] c. 17 ; *Stat. Realm*, I, 31.

[2] See below, pp. 188 ff.
[4] c. 39 ; *Stat. Realm*, I, 90

The need for some such regulation appears in the returns made to the twelfth article of the inquest of 1274, demanding the names of those lords or bailiffs who had resisted the execution of the king's command, whether passively or actively. Not only in rescuing distresses that had been driven off by the sheriff's men, but in open and insulting defiance of royal officials, especially in the remoter districts like Yorkshire, it had been made evident that the sheriff needed effective force in his own shire to back him up. The bailiff of the Earl of Lincoln, who had threatened to arrest the Yorkshire commissioners, needed to be taught his place, and though we have no information as to his punishment, fuller details are preserved in a Lincolnshire case. ' Three years ago,' the jurors report in 1274, ' the men of Sir Norman d'Arcy rescued some beasts from Ralph of Ingham, the king's bailiff, to the Lord king's dishonour.' Their verdict is annotated by the justices of the eyre of 1281, ' *Suspensi sunt*—they have been hanged '.[1] Under the statute of 1285 it was the duty of every resident of the shire, from the archbishop downwards, to back up the sheriff's authority actively.

There is no direct reference to the sheriff's military functions in the Hundred Rolls ; the only article remotely concerned with them is article 24, which inquires whether sheriffs have taken bribes to respite men from assuming knighthood. To this question a few returns are given, of no great interest ; in Manlee wapentake, Lincolnshire, two men are said to have paid half a mark a year for two years to be respited,[2] and the Norfolk knights report eight instances by connivance at evasion.[3] The enforcement of knighthood on young men of sufficient substance by Henry III and his son was, however, rather a financial than a military measure.

III. THE SHERIFF'S FISCAL FUNCTIONS

' *Who have received the king's debts and not acquitted his debtors ? When fines for hiding treasure and the like pertain to the king, who have taken them ? Who have received the king's commands to pay his debts and have accepted from the creditors a part of the sum paid ?*

[1] *R.H.*, I, 342.   [2] Ibid., I, 342.   [3] Ibid., I, 465, 479.

*What sheriffs or keepers of castles have accounted for a greater sum
than they have reasonably spent, and have retained to their own use
material bought or purveyed for such works ? '—cc. 23, 20, 22, 29.*

Of the writs which the king's messengers delivered to the
sheriff, those which involved the heaviest work were the mandates
from the Exchequer twice a year, at Michaelmas and at Easter,
sealed with green wax, commanding him to collect moneys owed
to the king.   The collection of revenue, both customary and
occasional, was from the point of view of the crown the sheriff's
most important function ; it was the Exchequer which took the
most lively and continuous interest in the appointment and in the
behaviour of the sheriffs.   Of those all-important duties and
the abuses arising in their performance the Hundred Rolls give
us abundant evidence.   They throw some light also on his duties
as a spending official, called upon, on occasion, to execute royal
commissions, to supply royal needs, and to pay royal debts.

Where was the fiscal business of the shire transacted ?   Payments were received both at the county court and at the tourn,
whilst the sheriff's subordinates must have collected payments in
all kinds of places up and down the country ; but the regular
and permanent place of receipt and account was the castle,
where the sheriff's receiver was normally to be found, like William
Lovel at the castle of York or Philip de Pres in Shrewsbury
Castle.[1]   The sheriff, like the great lords,[2] talked of his
' exchequer ' in the castle ; his office would almost certainly be
furnished with an abacus or counting board.   Any business man
would need one ; Henry III in his orders for alteration and
improvements in his palace at Woodstock directed what Latin
verses should be inscribed on the chequer board for his chamber.
In this office the sheriff's receiver sat to receive the sums brought
by private persons in debt to the king and by officials.   The
farm due from two lords of private hundreds in Norfolk was
payable at Norwich Castle ; [3] the customary payments due from
the Abbot of Glastonbury in lieu of suit or service in Cornwall
were payable at Launceston Castle ; [4] a Wiltshire tenant-in-chief

[1] *R.H.*, I, 130 ; cf. *R.H.*, II, 92.   [2] e.g. at Eye, *R.H.*, II, 186.
[3] *R.H.*, I, 441, 454.   [4] Bodl. MS., Wood 1, fo. 213d.

paid his rent at Marlborough Castle.[1]   The Essex Hundred Rolls constantly associate payments with Colchester Castle.[2]   But more important for the sheriff and his receiver were the accounts of the hundred bailiffs or other subordinates charged with the collection of local revenue.   Of such interviews, in the nature of things, we only hear when something goes wrong.   The bailiff who came to render his account did not always return as easily. Thomas Silvester, bailiff of Wonford hundred in Devon, came to Exeter Castle one Monday to render his account of all his receipts for his time of office, and on the balance it appeared that he was still owing thirty-six pounds, for which he was arrested, being, by his own account, seized and flogged by six ruffians unknown, then fettered and thrown head first into the lowest dungeon, fifteen feet deep without a ladder, and left there manacled till the Friday, without food and drink, in which period he swooned nine times.[3]

The sheriff or his deputy also received payments at a supplementary session held after the main business of the county court was over.   In a statute of 1285 this session is called the *retro-comitatus*, or rere-county ; it was probably conducted in a less public and formal and more businesslike manner than the full county preceding it.   On one occasion when the sheriff and under-sheriff of Staffordshire were at work receiving the king's dues at the rere-county in the shire-hall of Stafford they heard shouts outside.   The under-sheriff ran out to see who was raising the hue and cry and found Thomas Spicer with his knife drawn attacking two men.   When the under-sheriff interposed Thomas turned against him, for which trespass, says the under-sheriff, ' I led him into the shire-hall before the sheriff, and had him arrested till he brought pledges to make amends for his attack on me.' [4]

A great number of payments, mostly of ancient customary dues, were made twice a year at the sheriff's tourn, and from the stories and songs it seems clear that there was a good deal of door-to-door collection by the bailiffs.

[1] Ass. R., 998, m.34d.   [2] *R.H.*, I, 136, 144, etc.
[3] Ass. R., 541 B., m. 40.   [4] Ass. R., 541 A, m. 20.

What were the moneys which the sheriff had to collect for the king ? In the first place come certain ancient customary payments, which are a charge upon the land—fixed renders or assized rents as they were often called. They have a bewildering variety of names.[1] Some of them undoubtedly go back to the days before the Norman conquest, and very probably represent the commutation of service or tribute in kind. One such payment, possibly originally given in lieu of entertainment, is sheriff's aid, which may once have been a perquisite of the sheriffs, but by 1274 had long been part of the revenue he had to pay in at the Exchequer. It is constantly mentioned in the Hundred Rolls among the obligations of landholders ; it appears that the sheriff generally collected it at his tourn twice a year. In Rothwell hundred, Northants, for instance, held in 1274 by Gilbert of Clare, the sheriff had formerly held two tourns in the year and had there received from sixteen contributories £5 12s. 4d. as payment for sheriff's aid or for view of frank-pledge.[2] All this revenue, the jurors say, has been intercepted for the last twenty years by the Earls of Gloucester. Again, in Sussex, we hear that the hundreds of the rape of Pevensey between them pay £9 17s. 6d. by way of sheriff's aid.[3] In Suffolk this payment is called sheriff's silver and is coupled with the payment of ward silver.[4] In Norfolk it is called sheriff's scot,[5] in Northants sheriff's yield.[6] Sheriff's welcome in Essex may be the same due.[7] In the west country a similar payment collected at the sheriff's tourn is called the horderesgeld or horderesgift. In Nottinghamshire there is an aid called sheriff's palfrey,[8] which again seems to point back to a commuted obligation of entertainment, like the Cheshire *puture*. Men whose lands are liable to these dues were described as being ' geldable at the tourn ', which was certainly the normal place for collecting all such ancient customary dues—the tithing penny or head money, the *certum* or cert-money due at view of frank-pledge, wardpenny,

---

[1] See N. Neilson *Customary Rents* (Vinogradoff, *Oxford Studies*, II).
[2] *R.H.*, II, 13.
[3] Ibid., II, 205.
[4] Ibid., II, 172.
[5] Ibid., I, 457, 483.
[6] *P.Q.W.*, 557.
[7] *R.H.*, I, 445.
[8] *Cal. Ch. R.* I, 143.

the common fine, paid for exemption from attendance at the tourn, and probably hidage. On the other hand, one such payment called wodewelleshot is said by Norfolk jurors to be payable once a year at the shire-moot at Norwich.[1]

A reference in one Exchequer document to the tallies of the tourn shows that the sheriff kept his record of receipts there by the procedure used at head-quarters.[2] Complaints that the sheriff had increased these dues are to be expected. It was a constant practice among government officials in the Middle Ages to offer to commute some service or grant some exemption from a penalty for money down, and then when the payment had hardened into custom to exact the service when required and inflict the penalty when incurred as if no payment had been made. This habit accounts for the fear and suspicion with which ' new customs ' were regarded by the country-side. But in spite of government promises and the resistance of the villagers the Hundred Rolls show a great increase in the customary payments. In Essex we hear of villages which have had to pay seven shillings at the tourn in place of sixpence ; of a hundred being compelled to pay twenty shillings above the *certum* due at the view.[3] The fine ' for fair pleading ' ' *injuria que vocatur beupleder* ',[4] which had been expressly forbidden by the Statute of Marlborough in 1267, has been exacted in hundred after hundred, ' in contempt of the king's mandate '.[5] Of one Master Lawrence, bailiff of the lathe of Shipway in Kent from 1265 to 1275, the jurors say that he took eighteen shillings a year for ten years from one hundred at the two lawdays for this fine, and yet charged them none the less, and by these and other exactions he so flayed the men of the hundred that many of them have left the district.[6] A similar charge is made in the Oxfordshire hundred of Banbury.[7] Before the barons' wars complaints had been made of new exactions in the tourn ; a new payment called lathescot is mentioned in the justiciar's eyre of 1259 as having been introduced by an under-sheriff before 1248,[8] and this complaint is repeated in 1275, as if the abuse continued.[9] In

[1] *R.H.*, I, 483.   [2] Mem. R.K.R. 29, m.4.   [3] *R.H.*, I, 145.
[4] Ibid., I, 38.   [5] Ibid., II, 207.   [6] Ibid., I, 229.   [7] Ibid., II, 32.
[8] Jacob, *Baronial Reform and Rebellion*, p. 351.   [9] *R.H.*, I, 232.

the Sussex hundreds the unjust levying of the common fine is reported.[1]

After the fixed or nominally fixed payments due at the courts came the profits and perquisites of the courts themselves, which could be averaged over a series of years, but were bound to vary in detail. We can still turn up the accounts for some of the county courts of Henry III's reign.[2] In the year 1258–9 the sheriff of Essex collected £5 12s. 7d. from the litigants of his county by way of fines, fees, and amercements. The county court of Kent in its sixteen sessions from June 1264 to August 1265 produced £79 12s. 8½d., and this in spite of the fact that at two sessions Simon de Montfort presided on behalf of the king, who was there present, and pocketed all the takings. The payments include amercements of hundreds for giving wrong or incomplete information by their presenting juries; fines from litigants for permission to come to an agreement out of court; fees for litigants for having the aid of the court—very likely in attaching or distraining an opponent to appear. There is one payment ' for having a good inquest ' which looks like a bribe; if so the bribe is accounted for at the Exchequer. Other payments are for not prosecuting a complaint, for failing to appear, for refusing to produce a litigant after becoming his security, and for refusing to accept the oath-helpers of the opposing litigant. There are besides amercements from those who have lost their cases. Occasionally we find recorded a payment for release from attendance at the county court—the fine *pro secta relaxanda*. One way and another, the pleas and perquisites of the county court made a considerable item in the revenues for which the sheriff accounted to the king, and their collection, whether at the rere-county or from house to house, needed careful recording. In the Hundred Rolls the jurors report both extortionate fines and amercements imposed by the sheriffs in court, and exaction by his underlings of sums in excess of those imposed. Magna Carta had provided that the amounts of amercements should be assessed by a man's neighbours, and it is alleged that this rule has been evaded. As to the collection, the Suffolk sub-bailiffs

[1] *R.H.*, II, 203, 204.   [2] Morris, *Early English County Court*, pp. 197–230.

had the simple device of levying one shilling when a man had been amerced at sixpence and half a crown when the sum was eighteenpence.[1] We shall meet more examples of this abuse when we come to consider the hundred bailiff's work.

An important heading of the sheriff's annual account was the farms of the hundreds. In many private hundreds the lord paid an annual rent or farm, occasionally at the Exchequer direct, but more often to the sheriff at the castle or at the tourn. With royal hundreds there was a fixed farm due from the hundred bailiff in respect of some of the profits of administration, whilst he rendered an account separately of other items. Thus in Greystone hundred, Herefordshire, for instance, the farm of the hundred was four marks, and the sheriff took the pleas and perquisites of the hundred courts, but left to the bailiff, apparently, the common fines and the hundred silver;[2] whilst in Knightlow hundred, Warwickshire, the sheriff retained the profits of the tourn.[3] In Holford and Greston hundred, Gloucestershire, the bailiff's farm of five marks covered the pleas and perquisites, but not the assized rents.[4]

A very general cause of oppression, according to the hundred juries, was for the sheriff to raise the amount at which he farmed the hundred, leaving the bailiff to recoup himself at the expense of the country-side. This might be the result of pressure from the Exchequer, but the hundred jurors of 1274-5 were not in a position to know this; and the form of the question, ' What sheriffs have delivered hundreds to extortionate bailiffs, oppressing the people, in order to raise their farms ? ' suggests that the responsibility lay with the sheriff. The returns show that both sheriffs and lords of liberties are guilty. The complaint is universal. In Suffolk the farms of two royal hundreds have been raised in one case from fifteen pounds to £23 10s. 0d., in another from twenty pounds to thirty-six pounds,[5] whilst the Abbot of Bury St. Edmunds has raised the farms in St. Edmund's eight and a half hundreds by amounts ranging from four pounds to ten pounds a year.[6] In Somerset the sheriff has raised the farm

[1] R.H., II, 145. [2] Cal. Misc. Inq., No. 1271. [3] Ibid., No. 278.
[4] R.H., I, 170. [5] Ibid., II, 191. [6] Ibid., II, 155.

of Williton hundred, with the result that the hundred bailiff has
been grievously oppressing the people to make up the new
amount.[1] In Essex three successive sheriffs have been putting
up the farm of Chelmsford hundred.[2] The jury of Kirton wapentake, Lincolnshire, deliver their souls energetically : ' Kirton
wapentake is let to farm at ten pounds, and it would not be
worth as much if the men of the county were treated justly, but
it has been delivered to extortioners who oppress men beyond
measure.'[3] The Hertford jury is equally forcible : ' All they
know is that W. de Roothing gave ten pounds more than other
bailiffs have usually given, to flay the country-side ; which he
has done.'[4] In five instances the farm had been ten marks up
to 1267, and the sheriff who raised it to ten pounds had been
appointed in 1270. The same complaint is made as to the farms
of the lathes of Kent and the ridings of Yorkshire.

This raising of farms is a standing complaint in the shires.
It had been forbidden by the Statute of Marlborough ; petitions
against it recur in the parliaments of Edward II and Edward III.
There is no doubt that we have in the Hundred Rolls a one-sided
statement. An Exchequer official, describing the situation,
might have said : ' There was a great deal not only of corruption,
but of slackness, in the collection of the county farms in former
years, and I am sorry to say that we were not nearly strict
enough with the sheriffs. Since we have begun to demand exact
accounts in detail and stopped making allowances for alleged
difficulties of collection, the money has come in much more
satisfactorily.' In other words, in many cases it is rather
efficiency than extortion which is the grievance.[5] And there are
other sound reasons for an increase of farms. So long as the
wealth and population of a hundred were on the increase
the amount that could be made out of it, and therefore, from the
point of view of the central government, the amount that should
be made out of it, would rise also. The king's object, in such
cases, would be to check the profits of the sheriff, and secure a
share if the increase of the farms seemed practicable. It would

---

[1] Ass. R., 759, m. 3d.   [2] R.H., I, 153.   [3] Ibid., I, 307.   [4] Ibid., I, 188.
[5] So Miss Mills interprets the Exchequer documents.

not be surprising either if the farms were raised more rapidly than economic development warranted, or if the residents grumbled at any change, however justifiable financially.

No special authority was required by the sheriff to levy the payments mentioned so far. He was also, however, the king's agent for collecting sums imposed by higher authority or incurred outside his jurisdiction : he was the indispensable servant of the Chancery, the Exchequer, and the law courts. Any man who sought the king's justice might thereby become the king's debtor. In spite of the high-sounding phrase of Magna Carta, ' To none will we sell, to none will we delay or deny right or justice ', a royal writ had to be paid for, and most processes in the king's courts were initiated by a writ. Again, any man found guilty of a trespass, or losing a suit in the king's court would be liable to an amercement. The clerks of the justices at Westminster, of the justices in eyre, of the justices of assize, of the justices of oyer and terminer would all constantly be drawing up *estreats*— extracts from the court rolls of the sums which had to be exacted from culprits or litigants. When the general eyre in any county was over it was the duty of the justices (who were often dilatory in performing it) to send in these estreats to the Exchequer. Similar lists were supplied by the justices of the King's Bench and the Common Bench. From these lists the clerks compiled the so-called summons of the green wax, which they forwarded twice a year to the sheriffs and to the seneschals of liberties which had, like St. Edmunds, the right to levy the summons of the Exchequer. The payments due for the services of the Chancery for charters and the like were recorded under the curious heading of ' The summons of the Pipe ', on the same parchment with the green wax entries, and the two lists forwarded to the sheriff for action.[1] These were ' the king's debts ' which the sheriff had to collect, as a rule, through his underlings ; for which the strictest account would be exacted at head-quarters ; which, nevertheless, as the Hundred Rolls amply prove, could also be made the means of private profit to both sheriff and underlings.

[1] This account is based on M. H. Mills, *Surrey Pipe Roll*, p. v.

A common device was to refuse to give a proper receipt for payment, and then exact the king's debt a second time. In Thingoe hundred, Suffolk, some men fined for giving a false verdict have paid ten marks, but received no quittance from the seneschal of St. Edmunds.[1] A Sussex bailiff carries round with him out-of-date summonses of the Exchequer, with the green wax seal still appended, and though the seal is broken, he extorts large sums of money by this means, for which he gives no receipt. Further, he compels a widow to pay two shillings to have respite from paying a debt of 13s. 4d., which she had already paid to another official; he takes from her two cows worth twenty shillings on the same count, and after all this still gives her no quittance.[2] The tally is mentioned as the form of receipt given when the Chelmsford jurors report how the sheriff took twenty pounds from the men of Writtle, but kept the tallies, so that they had no quittance to show.[3] The contemporary poet does not take more than poetic licence when he sings, 'More than ten times over I have to pay my debt.' The Exchequer Statutes of 1275 and 1285 to some extent remedied this abuse. But there were other ways of extortion open. Men bribed the collectors to gain a respite. One royal debtor in Thedwastry hundred, Suffolk, has been paying twenty shillings a year for several years to have a respite : the jurors do not know the amount of the debt.[4] A merchant is distrained for a debt to the king which was really owed by another person ; then, for a bribe of eighteenpence the true debtor is given a respite till the next collecting day and is then persuaded, quite contrary to the facts, that she has been amerced.[5] There are instances of beasts being distrained to secure payment of a debt to the king, and the distress being restored for a bribe, and the debtor respited till the time for squeezing comes round again. By the use of the green wax persons are compelled to contribute when a common amercement is laid upon the hundred though they are not by custom liable.

Occasionally the sheriff was required to take part in the collection of a tax imposed by the king's council. So much of

<hr>

[1] R.H., II, 158
[2] Ibid., II, 218, cf. I, 187.
[3] Ibid., I, 154.
[4] Ibid., II, 158.
[5] Ibid., II, 145.

the royal revenue was customary that a general tax could still be regarded as exceptional and the procedure of collection varied on each fresh occasion. These extraordinary taxes, as levied in the seventy-five years before 1274, have been examined in detail [1]; they include scutages and aids collected from military tenants; tallages collected from the king's non-military tenants-in-chief, in the boroughs and on the king's own estates; gifts or aids from the clergy; and taxes upon movable property in the form of fifteenths, twentieths, fortieths, and the like. In 1274, the last scutage had been levied in 1257 and the last tallage in 1269, whilst the last tax on movables was still in process of collection in 1273. This was the twentieth which had been granted in 1269 for the crusade of 1270, on which both Edward and his brother had gone. As a rule special collectors were appointed for the levy of each tax, and the sheriff was not necessarily one of these. The Hundred Rolls make it clear that whether as official collector or merely as an auxiliary to the collectors the local sheriff had taken an active part in levying the twentieth in at least ten counties, for an article inquiring ' about the collectors of the twentieth penny ' was administered to the jurors on five of the circuits of 1274–5.[2] The question was not directed against the sheriffs as such, and many of the answers concern only the special collectors; for instance in Rutland, where they are accused of receiving forty shillings more than they paid in to the Exchequer,[3] or in Blengate hundred, Kent, where they are said to have taken fifty shillings beyond what was right.[4] But it appears from the jurors' replies to this question that the task of the special collectors was to assess and to render account at head-quarters, whilst the actual levying of the sums they fixed was in the hands of the sheriff and his underlings. An Exchequer tally is still preserved which records the payment of the arrears of the twentieth by Osbert of Bereford, sheriff of Warwickshire and Leicestershire 1273–5, who was also one of the Hundred Roll Commissioners.[5] The collection of the tax dragged out over four years and offered the local officials admirable opportunities to

---

[1] See S. K. Mitchell, *Studies in Taxation under John and Henry III.*
[2] c. 40. [3] *R.H.*, II, 51. [4] Ibid., II, 200. [5] See Plate III

line their own pockets. The sheriff of Rutland's bailiff had collected fourteen shillings under this head ; but they doubt if he paid it over to the collectors.[1]   Another bailiff having collected almost the whole amount due from a village kept a mark for himself when he paid it in, so that the village had to pay that mark a second time.[2]   The tenants of Stoke Goldington in Bucks paid twenty shillings to the sheriff towards the twentieth, and sixty-six shillings to five other junior officials to have a respite from paying the twentieth.[3]   The sheriff of Devon had taken £12 11s. 4d. from the citizens of Exeter for the twentieth and given no receipt.[4]   In Lexden hundred, Essex, the sheriff had been taking sums ranging from forty pence to forty shillings from each village in excess of the amount they had been rated at ; here a number of smaller local collectors are mentioned who handed over the money to the sheriff.[5]   If the jurors spoke truly, the sheriff must have made a profit of some fifty pounds out of the transaction in Essex.   A collector in Lincolnshire kept eighteen shillings for himself because when he went to Lincoln to pay in his collection the sheriff refused to give him a tally of quittance.[6]

The example of the twentieth may fairly be taken as typical. The hundred jurors have nothing to say about the collection of tallages or scutages, but we can be pretty sure that the sheriffs and their staffs got their pickings out of the collection of any tax sanctioned in those special sessions of the king's council which were coming to be called parliaments.

Of the casual dues which the sheriff might have to collect on occasion there are one or two reports.   The feudal incidents and dues were the escheator's concern, but it was the sheriff's business to look out for treasure-trove and wreck and such other royal perquisites as had not been granted to lords of liberties.   In the Hundred Rolls these are generally mentioned only when subjects have usurped them.[7]   A fine of £6 3s. 4d. has been exacted from a dweller in the Derbyshire hundred of the Peak for concealing treasure-trove.[8]   In Lincolnshire three cast-up whales, which

---

[1] *R.H.*, II, 51.   [2] Ibid., II, 54.   [3] Ibid., I, 38.   [4] Ibid., I, 70.
[5] Ibid., I, 139.   [6] Ibid., I, 269.   [7] See c. 20.   [8] Ibid., II, 289.

are ' royal fish ', have been appropriated by the prior of Spalding and by William Longsword,[1] and in Essex the bailiffs of Colchester have done the same.[2] A wrongful seizure of felon's goods, another royal perquisite, is reported in Tendring hundred ; a woman had committed suicide and beasts which belonged to her son had in consequence been taken.[3] In Hartwell, Northants, a chest had been found containing a great sum of gold and silver, formerly the property of a woman convicted of felony. The tithing man of the village had handed it over, as in duty bound, to the hundred bailiff, and he in turn to the sheriff, but the jurors doubted whether it had ever reached the king.[4] In Clackclose hundred, Norfolk, a certain Gilbert of Wells had intervened to prevent the king's bailiffs from taking possession of the lands and chattels of a robber recently hanged.[5]

The returns of 1274-5, then, give an abundance of information as to the sheriff's exercise of his powers and duties as a collector of royal revenues—both customary and judicial, both taxes and perquisites. They illustrate also, though less copiously, his functions as a purchasing and spending agent of the crown. In spite of the fact that the royal estates were no longer in his charge some functions of a steward or reeve were still his. Amongst the royal mandates he received orders to obtain or furnish supplies for domestic, charitable, or military purposes, were not infrequent ; he might be required to furnish the royal table with food, to supply the king's friends with deer to stock their forests, to send corn for the use of the king's troops or timber for the repair of the king's palaces. And in carrying out these commands he could make use of the royal privilege of prise—what the later Middle Ages called purveyance ; he could requisition what the king needed regardless of the owners' wishes, and pay at a later date. For payment he needed royal authority ; he would have to show up the writ authorizing expenditure before he was credited with the sum he had spent— ' allowed ' it, as the phrase went, on his account at the Exchequer.

In the previous reign, Henry III's especial devotion to Edward

---

[1] Ibid., I, 271.   [2] Ibid., I, 139.   [3] Ibid., I, 141.   [4] Ibid., II, 11.
[5] Ibid., I, 460. In this hundred felons' goods belonged to the Abbot of Ramsey, and the ' king's bailiff ' was appointed by him.

the Confessor had made St. Edward's feast on October 13th a
centre of festivity and banqueting which taxed the resources of
all the shires within a reasonable distance of London. In 1252,
for instance, orders were sent to the sheriffs of Buckinghamshire, Kent, Sussex, Essex, Norfolk, Cambridgeshire, Northants,
Berkshire, Wiltshire, and London to send up to Westminster, by
the Wednesday before the feast, a total of 76 boars, 60 swans, 72
peacocks, 1,700 partridges, 500 hares, 600 rabbits, 4,200 fowls,
200 pheasants, 1,600 larks, 700 geese, 60 bitterns, and 16,000
eggs.[1] In 1257 the sheriff of Cambridgeshire was credited with
£15 15s. 10d. at the Exchequer for expenditure on such supplies.[2]
Another occasion for provisioning was war. As the sheriffs had
had to supply munitions for his father's French wars, so Edward's
Scotch campaigns were to keep them busy. In 1300, for instance,
the sheriff of Cambridgeshire was ordered to supply 1,000 quarters
of wheat, 1,000 of oats, and 500 of malt ; the wheat to be ground
into flour, well bolted, placed in new, strong barrels, salted so that
it would keep a year or two at need, and three hazel rods to be
placed at the top of each barrel, and so to be sent by a given day
to Berwick-on-Tweed.[3] The rolls of the justices in eyre give a
good idea of the procedure of requisitioning such supplies. In
1297, when Edward was preparing for a campaign in Flanders,
Cambridgeshire was ordered to supply 1,000 quarters of wheat
and as many of oats, and a royal clerk was sent as a special agent
to assess men's contributions. In the eyre of 1299 a series of
charges are brought against the sheriff : of taking bribes to let
men off the king's requisitioning, of taking ten quarters of wheat
where the king's clerk had fixed the contribution at two, of taking
bribes for exemption and levying the corn notwithstanding, of
compelling men to buy corn to make up their quota, of keeping
the good wheat for himself and sending the inferior grain to the
army. Again and again the sheriff's pleas are dismissed by
the justices ; altogether his amercements on this score come to
fifty marks, and the efficacy of the eyre machinery is thoroughly
vindicated.[4]

[1] *Close Roll Cal.*, p. 259.   [2] Mem. Roll., L.T.R. 32, m. 19.
[3] *Pat. Roll Cal.*, p. 487.   [4] Ass. R. 95, mm. 52, 54.

This side of the sheriff's activity was undoubtedly developed considerably by Edward I : it was, in fact, one of the many devices by which in his later years he anticipated the royal revenue and enhanced the financial difficulties to which his son succeeded.[1]   But the Hundred Rolls show that similar prises had been occasioned by the baron's wars.   Though the *tempus guerre* ended officially with the battle of Evesham, fighting went on up to December 1267, and the king's troops had to be fed.   The sheriff of Suffolk in 1266–7 took large stocks of barley, malt and salt fish from some seventy-eight persons, and eight years later they have not been paid.[2]   Nevertheless, the sheriff's accounts show that he has been credited at the Exchequer with £22 8s. for cartage of wheat, malt, oats, oxen, porkers, salt, herrings, and wine, and his underling has been allowed fifteen pounds for expenses incurred in Norfolk and Suffolk in securing victuals and other necessaries for the king's use.[3]   Similarly the sheriff of Oxfordshire has been allowed thirty-six shillings at the Exchequer for salt fish taken from Henry of London, who, in 1275, has not yet been paid.[4]   This prise is probably part of the requisitions for the use of the army besieging Kenilworth : requisitions so heavy as to exhaust the revenue in ten of the counties of England, whose sheriffs bring ' nothing but writs ' to the Exchequer in 1267.[5]   The jurors of Knightlow hundred, Warwickshire, say that their sheriff took thirty sheep, three calves, and five oxen— one ' to draw the engines ' for the use of the besieging forces—as well as corn.[6]   A less protracted siege left its trace on the returns for Essex.   In April 1267 the baronial forces under Gilbert of Clare entered London, which rose in their support, and the king's army, abandoning the siege of Ely, marched south and lay at Stratford, outside London, for seven weeks.   During this period provisions ran short and the sheriffs of both Kent and Essex scoured the country-side for military stores.   Richard of Southchurch, the sheriff of Essex, according to the villagers of Chafford hundred, took ' for the sustenance of the king's host ' wheat, oats, cheese, bacon, pease, and beef, as well as ropes for making

[1] See M. H. Mills in *E.H.R.*, XXXVIII, 340. [2] *R.H.*, II, 170.
[3] Jacob, *Baronial Reform and Rebellion*, p. 252. [4] *R.H.*, II, 36.
[5] Jacob, p. 253. [6] *R.H.*, II, 225.

cords for the arbalests and catapults ; picks, calthrops and spades
to lay low the walls of London ; tow and eggs for dressings, linen
for bandages, chickens to feed the wounded, and finally cocks,
forty and more of them, which he proposed to use as incendiary
bombs, by tying fire to their feet and sending them flying into
London to burn it down.   This surprising stratagem was attributed to several viking heroes in the stories and sagas of those
days, but the jurors are not concerned about its feasibility or the
cruelty involved to the cocks.   For them the noteworthy fact is
that Richard took all these supplies to his own manor of Southchurch—the modern Southend—in the opposite direction from
London ; that he was allowed two hundred marks at the
Exchequer for all the things he had taken for the king's use ; and
yet, as they declare on oath, he has never paid a penny for them.[1]

Here again we may take leave to doubt their stories.   The
Exchequer officials were too well aware of sheriffs' habits to
credit them, on their own word alone, with sums which they
should have paid ; receipts as well as writs had to be produced
at Westminster, and though forgery was possible, it was not
simple.   It was probably easier to extort by threats a full receipt
for a part payment.   But only a few returns expressly assert that
this has been done in their reply to the question concerning the
payment of the king's debts.   The bailiffs of Lincoln have been
ordered to pay £10 9s. to a merchant of that city for some scarlet
cloth, out of the farm they owe the king annually : they have
refused to make the payment until the creditor agrees to let them
keep £2 9s. for themselves, and yet have claimed allowance for
the whole amount at the Exchequer.[2]   Few such complaints are
alleged against the sheriff beyond those already mentioned.   Nor
are there, it would seem, any complaints against him as the royal
almoner, whose duty it was to supply friars with timber for
building their schools, nuns with tunics, and old men with their
little pensions from the royal bounty.   Here it may be that
religious sanctions operated to keep the sheriffs honest.

One duty of the sheriff's, however, closely allied to his functions
of requisitioning, is referred to in many counties as a source of

[1] *R.H.*, I, 148 ; cf. Jacob, p. 259.   [2] Ibid., I, 313.

peculation. This is the obligation of keeping the king's castle, bridges, and highways in good repair. The jurors are specifically asked if any funds or material destined for castle works have been embezzled by sheriffs or other responsible officials.[1] In the typical county of 1274, as we have seen, the castle is in the sheriff's keeping and is the head-quarters of county government, so that its upkeep will be a matter that concerns him nearly, as well as the king, to whom he is accountable for its condition. But each castle has its own history. Its repairs and building operations can often be traced on the Exchequer records. At Cambridge, for instance, the average expenditure on the castle under Henry III was very low—not much more than a shilling a year, and it was clearly getting into a bad condition. In 1285 things had changed. Sums varying from £116 to £408 a year were being spent by the sheriff on the buildings which were going up, and which included a hall, a chamber, kitchen and bakehouse, certain walls and gates. The wages bills for 1286–95 are extant. Two Cambridge burgesses supervised the work as viewer and ganger under the sheriff, who had to answer at the Exchequer for the cost of labour, building material and carriage of the stone, clunch, timber, and lead from Peterborough, Lynn and elsewhere.[2] At Northampton Castle, on the other hand, the great period of activity was under Henry III. 'Much building has been done there by your faithful sheriff William de Lisle,' the surveyors report to the king in 1253, and the Exchequer records supply the details. Henry III, a discerning connoisseur of art, made frequent use of Northampton Castle as a royal residence, and the rolls show that not only had walls and towers been repaired with hewn stone, but a new chapel had been built for the queen, the king's wardrobe, the great hall and the chaplain's room had been built or rebuilt, and stained glass windows had been provided for both hall and chapel.[3] Even though special clerks of the works were appointed, the responsibility for executing these detailed instructions that came from the king rested with the sheriff. His labours were increased, and so were the openings

[1] c. 29.
[2] W. M. Palmer, *Proceedings of Cambridge Antiquarian Soc.*, XXVI, pp. 66–89.   [3] R. M. Serjeantson, *The Castle of Northampton.*

for fraud. Accounts could be faked and material misappropriated. Thus the Wiltshire jurors report in 1275 that two sheriffs had kept for themselves the money allocated to the purchase of stone and sand for building a wall at Clarendon.[1] One of the viewers of the works at Old Sarum had converted twenty-four feet of lead to his own use and another had appropriated the timber destined for the castle mill.[2] Both in Oxfordshire and Northants the sheriffs had converted timber to their own use.[3] On the other hand, the sheriffs of Shropshire had allowed part of Shrewsbury Castle to fall into decay.[4] Scandalous doings are reported from Rochester. After the fire that occurred there during the war three thousand tiles from the great hall, two gates and a quantity of lead, stone, and timber were carried off by the constable, John Potyn, who built a cellar in the town with the stolen material, employing the king's workmen on the job.[5] Forty pounds' worth of timber, stone, tiles, and ropes had been misappropriated by the sheriff's serjeants in the castle of York.[6] In Rutland the hall where the king's justices held their pleas when they visited the county had been burnt down during the civil war, and the sheriff had levied fifty shillings from Martinsley hundred for rebuilding it, but so far he had kept the money for himself and done nothing with it.[7]

The sheriff also received many commands concerning the king's highway. The king's taste for hawking and hunting might necessitate work on ridges. In 1235 the sheriffs of twenty-two counties had received orders to build or repair the bridges in their shires so that the king might pass freely with his birds over all the rivers. Whether in Windsor or Epping Forest or on the moors of Somerset the countrymen had often the king's sporting tastes to thank for the fact that they went dry-shod.[8] Apart from such special commands, the sheriff was expected to inquire twice a year in his tourn as to the condition of bridges and causeways, whilst the justices in eyre, at longer intervals, held inquiries into his performance of this duty. The eyre juries often report

---

[1] *R.H.*, II, 243. [2] Ibid., II, 269. [3] Ibid., II, 4, 36.
[4] Ibid., II, 107. [5] Ibid., I, 225. [6] Ibid., I, 120.
[7] Ibid., II, 51. [8] See Flower, *Medieval Public Works* (S.S.) II, xxiv.

breakdowns or encroachments.   Here men have been digging for gravel in the king's highway and made a hole which completely obstructs passage ; here a causeway has broken down ; here a ditch is blocked and has flooded the road ; here a wall has been built which narrows the road unduly.   In some cases the sheriff is ordered to distrain the person or persons responsible for the upkeep of bridge or causeway ; in others he himself is charged to repair, remove, fill up, or pull down as circumstances require. To carry out such orders he could requisition the services of the country-side.   Magna Carta had forbidden him to compel men or villages to do such work unless they were bound by ancient custom ; but it would seem that where they were so bound, no royal writ was needed for the enforcement for ' bridgebote ' or for the levying of the due called pontage which replaced it.   The Cambridgeshire Hundred Rolls record a shameful abuse of this right by Robert del Estre, sheriff from 1270 to 1274.   Sixpence a hide was the usual amount levied as pontage from those lands in the county which owed this payment, but according to the jurors Robert took two shillings a hide from the whole county for the repair of the great bridge, promising that he would build a fine bridge of stone and mortar.   But he made instead a cheap bridge of hurdles and timber which had already broken down by 1279, when the commissioners of that year came to Cambridge ; [1] and, not content with the one fraud upon the county, he employed a subordinate in the castle to pull planks out of the bridge by night, thus delaying its completion for three months, during which time the country-folk coming into the town had to pay to be ferried across in the sheriff's boat, by which he made a hundred shillings.[2]

As a whole, however, the hundred jurors have little to say of the sheriffs' activities in road and bridge-making.   In response to Article 13 they report encroachments on the public roads in numerous hundreds, but leave us to suppose that the sheriffs have rather erred through slackness than through oppressiveness in this respect.   This is probably a fair reflection of the comparative importance in normal conditions of the sheriff's different fiscal duties ; his work as an active agent of the Exchequer throws all

[1] *R.H.*, II, 407.   [2] Ibid., I, 50 ; Hundred Rolls (unprinted) Camb., 2, 4.

else into the shade, and the king's debts matter much more than the king's highway. The outlook of the jurors of 1274–5 corresponds pretty closely to that of their contemporary, the anonymous author of the ' Song against Sheriffs '[1].

Who can tell truly
    How cruel sheriffs are ?
Of their hardness to poor people
    No tale can go too far.
If a man cannot pay
    They drag him here and there ,
They put him on assizes,
    The juror's oath to swear.
He dares not breathe a murmur,
    Or he has to pay again,
And the saltness of the sea
    Is less bitter than his pain.

When a sheriff comes
    To abbey or to hall
The best of meat, the best of drink,
    Is brought at his call.
But all this store of dainties
    Does the host no good
Unless a gift of jewels
    Is dessert after food.
His grooms and his beadles
    Must each have his share,
And his lady wife must have a gown
    Of rainbow hues to wear.

Oh, the sheriff's clerks !
    Needy folk at first,
Poor like others, suffering
    From hunger and from thirst ;
But when they get a bailiwick
    How they grow and swell !
Their teeth grow long, their heads grow high,
Houses, lands, and rents they buy,
    And pile up gold as well.
They scorn their poor neighbours,
    They govern by new rules,
That is reckoned wisdom now
    In our modern schools.

[1] Translated from MS. Harl. 913.

IV.   THE SHERIFF'S JUDICIAL FUNCTIONS

(a) The County Court

' Concerning ancient suits withdrawn from the lord king.'—c. 7.

Lastly we have to examine the courts which the sheriff held— the shire court and the tourn.   In spite of the steady shrinkage of judicial business in the local courts resulting on the centralization of justice under Henry II and his successors, there still remained much work for the shire court to do, some of which could be done in no other court in the kingdom.   The rere-county at which, as we have seen, the king's debts were collected, was held the day after the county court ; the sheriff could not get both the judicial and the fiscal business done on one day.

In most shires the county court was held every four weeks, always on the same day of the week.   In Yorkshire, Lincolnshire, Lancashire, Cheshire, and Northumberland it was held every six weeks, but riding courts were held in between in Yorkshire and Lincolnshire.   It was not till the reign of Philip and Mary that the four-weekly interval was adopted for the northern counties also.

As to the place of meeting, by rights it was determined by ancient custom.   In some counties this sanctioned the use of several different places.   In Essex, according to the Hundred Rolls, the county met in a green place in Chelmsford hundred,[1] but other evidence shows that it also met at Writtle and at a place called Langethorn, which may or may not be ' the green place '.   In Herts, Cheshunt and Hertford ; in Berkshire, Grandpont outside Oxford, Newbury, Sutton, Ockbridge, and Remenham were all used at different periods.   In Sussex, Shoreham and Lewes had been the customary centres ; the jurors of 1274 complain that Richard of Cornwall ' attracted ' the county court to Chichester, to the grievous loss of the whole shire.[2] There was naturally competition among the towns for the place of meeting, for the county day must have brought custom to the town, and Guildford claimed and clung to its monopoly after the grant of 1256, which transferred the court to it from Leatherhead.

[1] *R.H.*, I, 142.   [1] Ibid., II, 202, 215.

Not till 1928 did it surrender its judicial priority to Kingston, with the transfer of the assizes to that ancient borough. In like manner Richard of Cornwall granted at some date between 1225 and 1256 that eight county courts a year should meet at Launceston. In the fourteenth century, however, his son had transferred the seat of the court to Lostwithiel, and the burgesses of that town were vehemently protesting against a possible shift to Bodmin, where some courts had been held as early as 1267.

Penenden Heath, north-east of Maidstone, was the meeting-place for the shire court of Kent, as it had been in 1086 and as it was still to be in 1786, but by 1274 open-air assemblies were beginning to be out of date. Upon the heaths and green places halls of pleas were being built, like the county house on the north side of Penenden Heath, where the sheriff held his county court monthly in the eighteenth century. Edmund of Cornwall built a fine hall at Lostwithiel, at great expense, for the holding of the county courts, when they ceased to be held at Launceston.[1] The jurors of Martinsley hundred complain that the sheriff of Rutland had levied fifty shillings from them to rebuild the hall where the county pleas were held, presumably at Oakham, which had been burnt down during the civil wars, but had so far kept the money himself.[2] A Suffolk petition of 1302 indicates that the knights of the shire were less ready to face the English climate than they had once been. The great court of the Abbot of Bury St. Edmunds, a sort of private county court, had formerly been held at Catteshill, some two miles to the east of the town, where the justices in eyre had also held their sessions. It was proposed to transfer the site of the court to Henhow, north-west of the town, where the name Shirehouse Heath is still preserved, and the Friars Minor, whose house at Babwell was hard by, petitioned the king that the new hall might not be too near them: ' If it is placed where some people have provided and ordained, it will be a great trouble and damage to the brothers, for if rain or tempest come, people will have no shelter for themselves or for their horses save in the friars' church, as has happened before when meetings have been held there, so that the

---

[1] *Rot. Parl.*, I, 296.   [2] *R.H.*, II, 51.

brothers cannot say their masses in their church, nor do any other good thing, because of the noise and press of people. Wherefore, sire, take pity on the friars, and do not suffer the orisons and masses which they say for you to be disturbed, but give command by your letters that, if the aforesaid house is to be removed, it may be planted somewhere nearer the town, so that people can more readily have shelter there than with the friars.' [1] The petition suggests what earlier and later descriptions of county courts confirm—that a large number of those who came to the county court remained outside the hall of pleas for a good part of the time, whether on horseback or on foot, gossiping or doing business. The Lincolnshire knights who refused to give judgements two days running stayed outside the door of the shire-house and would not come in. The shire-hall of Norwich was not large enough in 1461 to hold the many people of small substance and no value who wished to take part in the election of the county members, and the sheriff had to adjourn the court to the castle yard. In the thirteenth century people were not as a rule at all eager to attend the shire court if they could avoid it, but the great six monthly ' general counties ' in spring and autumn must have required more space than the ordinary four-weekly courts, and it may well be that proceedings then took place in the open air unless a storm of rain drove the sheriff and the leading knights of the shire to take shelter in the hall of pleas. This would be all the simpler if the county was meeting at the castle. Bracton, writing some twenty years before 1274, treats the castle as the normal place of meeting ; but as the century went on specially erected shire-halls were becoming commoner. The open-air tradition, however, did not die out ; as late as the Commonwealth a Northamptonshire county election was held in the open air on Kettering Heath.

What men attended the county court ? Here the Hundred Rolls have much to say. The jurors were asked what ancient suits had been withdrawn from the king, and their answers show pretty clearly how the duty of attending the shire court was distributed. It was the land which he held that determined a

[1] *Rot. Parl.*, I, 157.

man's duty of attending the county ; the land owed suit to the
shire court, as the phrase went. In Suffolk, for instance, Nicholas
de Wynton held a tenement in Mendlesham which owed two suits
a year to the ' general ' county court, but for the last five years
the suit had not been paid.[1] The monks of St. Remi held one
hide of land at Marston in Cuttlestone hundred, for which they
owed suit to the county court of Stafford every month.[2] A complete list of suits due to the county court of Cambridge about the
years 1230–40 is to be found in the chronicle of Barnwell Abbey,[3]
whose compiler observes that he has thought it well to insert a
list of all the services owing from the different villages of the
county so that men may be saved the trouble of going up to the
castle to consult the sheriff's roll. According to this list, 162
suits were owed to the county court from the 130 villages of
Cambridgeshire. Generally the person who owns the suit is
clearly a gentleman, and occasionally it is said that his suit is
performed for him by another, doubtless his tenant, and twice it
has been commuted for money. In seven villages the suit is
owed by the whole village, and done by one man, who bears the
name, at Wicken, of John le Shiresmen. One result of the suit
being owed from land was that women owed it ; thus Denise de
Munchensy is given leave to appoint an attorney to do suit in
her place to the county of York in 1271, as she is old and feeble.[4]
Again, not only freeholders but villeins could and did render suit,
chiefly to the ' general ' counties, taking turns, probably, to discharge a communal responsibility. It is most unlikely that they
took as active a part in the proceedings, when there, as did the
knights ; they were probably needed rather to present than to
judge. Another result was that the division of the holding
divided the responsibility. The Cambridge list of suits mentions
thirds and two-thirds of suits, as do the Suffolk Hundred Rolls,
very frequently.[5] Again, the performance of suit could be made
the condition of a grant of land ; Richard of Barkway holds his
land in Oakington from Crowland Abbey by the service of attending the Cambridge county court and so acquitting the abbot of

[1] R.H., II, 193. [2] Cal. Misc. Inq., p. 135.
[3] Liber Memorandorum de Bernewelle, pp. 238–63.
[4] Pat. Roll Cal., p. 514. [5] R.H., II, 147, 172, 188, 194.

his obligation. Numbers of such bargains are on record by which a tenant agrees to discharge his lord's obligation or a lord undertakes to find a ' doomsman ' for the shire court.

On the presence of the suitors the work of the county court depended. As we have seen, they could hold up all proceedings if they pleased, though for this collective action was needed. In 1225, when the suitors of Somerset county disapproved of the sheriff's proceedings, and tried to coerce him by their withdrawal the plan miscarried, because two or three remained and the sheriff was able to carry on with their assistance till the close of the day.[1] The importance of the suitors' presence was fully recognized, and withdrawal of suit, when reported by the jurors of the hundred in 1274-5, was closely investigated by the justices who came round later. A Bedfordshire knight who asserted that he had never done suit and therefore ought to be quit was told by the king's counsel that either he or his steward must be present ' lest the pleas of the county court should fail for lack of suitors '. [2] Only the king could grant exemption, and this he sometimes did because the suitor was employed on the royal service, sometimes as the reward of merit, sometimes, one guesses, simply in consideration of money paid. Such exemptions were freely granted by Henry III, though not as freely as the exemptions from jury service, which actually made it difficult to get juries of knights for the Grand Assize. Possibly some of the withdrawals of suit reported by the jurors were thus justified.

It is not often that the personal note is struck in the accounts of proceedings in county courts. Bracton speaks of the men on whose nod the opinion of the others depended ; and Matthew Paris describes, though he does not name, the Northamptonshire gentleman who drew upon himself the wrath of William de Lisle by taking the lead in resisting his unjust judgements and headstrong opinions. Chief Justice Bereford used to tell a tale of a knight of Staffordshire who lost his temper in the county court and declared that he would one day pay out one of his neighbours there, and the other knight on his way home from the county

[1] W. A. Morris, *The Early English County Court*, p. 106.
[2] *Plac. Quo. War.*, p. 4.

court that very day was waylaid and murdered, and all men attributed the murder to him who had uttered the threats and he was found guilty and hanged, though later the crime was brought home to an old servant of the murdered man. There is another story of the whole body of suitors imploring a vassal not to pursue his case against his lord, but as the authority for this is the lord himself, the narrative is suspect. No doubt the thirteenth-century knights of the shire, like the justices of the Elizabethan bench, had their Shallows and their Silences, but no Chaucer or Shakespeare has drawn their portraits.

The business to be tackled by suitors and sheriff might be heavy enough to fill a busy day. In 1224 there were 140 cases left to deal with at the end of the day's work. In 1225 a Cambridgeshire lady spent a good part of the day at the county court making good her claim against the Abbot of Eynsham. When she arrived early in the morning she and her champion and the abbot's attorney were ordered to withdraw until more suitors had turned up. Later, when the county court was assembled in full force, Agnes presented herself with her champion, but the abbot's attorney, though summoned again and again, failed to appear, and she was told again to wait, and at last, when the county court was almost at an end, after the ninth hour, she presented herself a third time and secured a judgement from the county in her favour, since her opponent had failed to appear.[1]

In 1275 the press of litigation may not have been as heavy as fifty years earlier, but there was undoubtedly a great variety of business to be got through. In the first place, the county court was the place where official communications were published; it served the purpose of a 'Royal Gazette'. Not only national announcements, like the English proclamation of 14th October 1258, were made there, but also local ones, like that which the sheriff of Gloucestershire published in his county court in 1283, declaring the causes for the excommunication of the prior and convent of Malvern, and forbidding men to buy from them or sell to them and theirs.[2] The publicity of the shire court was used also for the registration of personal agreements, as in

[1] *Bracton's Notebook*, case 1672.   [2] *Giffard's Register*, pp. 211–12.

PLATE IV

THE COLLECTION OF WROTH SILVER, KNIGHTLOW HUNDRED

pre-Conquest days. Acknowledgements of suit and service were made by the witness of the shire, a deed conferring an advowson on a religious house might be read out or a transfer of land in mortmain by royal licence effected—all in the county court, before the sheriff, by the witness of the knights of the shire. So when a royal grant confirmed a liberty, the sheriff would read the king's letters to the county, displaying the royal seal, and all would know that such liberties must be respected at their risk. Thus, also, even before the law so directed in 1285, men would hand writs to the sheriff in county court, so that they could find witnesses to the fact that he had received them if he failed to execute them.

Another matter that required publicity was the swearing-in of officials. The sheriff's subordinates, chosen by himself, and the bailiffs of liberties, who also acted in collaboration with him, were sworn by the sheriff in the shire-moot, so that all might know them and recognize their authority. A London writer who stated in John's reign that sheriffs were elected in the shire-moot was generalizing from London, then as now unique in its government ; such elections, as we have seen, were exceedingly rare. But keepers of the peace were ordered to be elected there in 1277, escheators were occasionally chosen there, and coroners were regularly chosen there from 1219 onwards. Moreover, the specially appointed knights who bore the record of the shire, whether to the king's courts at Westminster or to the king's council in parliament, were chosen in the county court, as were those who gave their consent to a grant of customs at the parliament of Westminster a month after the Hundred Rolls Inquests ended.

This publicity made the county court the appropriate place for the holding of many inquests. Of the miscellaneous assortment of inquests still preserved in the national archives a good proportion were held in the county court. Such inquests, for example, concerned the liberties of the abbey of Ossulston in Leicestershire ; the names of the criminals who maltreated two bailiffs of the sheriff of Nottinghamshire ; the extent of the lands held of the honour of Peverel ; the circumstances in which a

Kentish boy of twelve caused the death of a girl of eleven ; the amount of profits arising at the sheriff's tourns ; the desirability of enclosing a strip of land between two highways in Hoddesdon ; and the value of a holding whose lord is suspected to be liable for knight service. For holding many of these inquests the coroners rather than the sheriff were primarily responsible ; in the county court they often acted as colleagues and could on occasion act as his substitutes. The inquests held by them into the cause of death sometimes took place in the county court.

Besides occasional special inquests, presentments were regularly made in the county court of matters relating to pleas of the crown. Both townships and bailiffs, for instance, reported or presented deaths by misadventure there, and it was alleged that the sheriff amerced the townships for defects in presentment just as if he had been a justice in eyre.[1] Both coroners and sheriffs had to keep a roll of such presentments against the coming of the royal justices.

Whilst only a royal justice could hear charges presented by a jury, the county court could deal with a criminal case if the old procedure of appeal by the injured party was followed. This process is described by a writer whose account is some thirty years later than the Hundred Rolls : ' A man wounded, or, it may be, badly beaten, comes in a cart to plead in an appeal in the county before the coroners, and his guardian shall make his plaint in this manner : " A appealeth B for that whereas he was in the peace of our lord the king on such a year, day and hour, in such a place upon his own land, the said B there assaulted, and wickedly wounded him in the head with a sword, as may be seen, and this he is ready to prove where and when he ought." The appellee being called in the county court does not come. The coroners are sent to see the wound, and it is $1\frac{1}{2}$ inches long and so deep that his life is despaired of. The sheriff takes security that the case will be pursued, and commands that the appellee be arrested wherever found, save in church or churchyard.'[2] This process ' according to the use of men of old time ' was distinctly old-fashioned by 1307, but it was still available

[1] *R.H.*, II, 29. [2] *Court Baron* (S.S.), pp. 85–6.

down to 1819, and appeals of murder, rape, arson, robbery, and wounding were all heard in the county, which testified, when necessary, with the coroners, that wounds had been shown in the court. The persons appealed might be tried in the county court by the old methods of proof, either ' making their law ' by formal oath, supported by oath-helpers, or waging a duel, but some cases initiated by appeal were transferred to the king's court.

Of all the criminal proceedings in the county court the most impressive was outlawry. The obstinate evader of justice was solemnly summoned to appear, or ' exacted ', as the phrase was, for four successive county courts, and on the fifth he was declared an outlaw. Outlawry could only take place in the county court ; in the eighteenth century John Wilkes's outlawry was found to be invalid because the county courts of Middlesex, at which the process was carried out, had not been held in due form.

Whilst the county court was no court of record in the legal sense, the sheriff kept notes of outlawries and presentments to check the coroners' rolls, which had to be produced to the king's justices ; it will be remembered that the rolls of the county court were among the documents handed over to the new sheriff of Hereford in 1278. The sheriff also kept notes of the civil proceedings in the shire court for his own convenience, as memoranda of the sums he would have to collect by way of fees and fines and account for to the king. The headings under which he noted the ' profits of the county court ' in his accounts give us some idea of the pleas upon which the suitors had to adjudicate. The cases that recur oftenest are pleas of trespass, of contact or convention, and of debt. When Richard Bysothewimpel sued Henry de la Willehurde in the county court of Devon for twelve marks in 1272 the statute had not yet been passed which limited the jurisdiction of the shire court to pleas involving forty shillings and less ; after 1278 such cases were reserved for the king's justices, unless one of the parties got a writ of *justicies* authorizing the sheriff to hear the case, and this meant some falling off in the importance of the civil business. Pleas of *vee de naam*, about the taking and holding of distresses, could be heard in the county court without a writ, though elsewhere a special grant from the king was necessary to give a court this jurisdiction. Pleas of land were also still held there. Some of these had been taken from a seignorial court under the writ of right, which authorized the sheriff to deal with a case if the lord of the litigant had failed to take the matter up. Such incidents sometimes led to a wrangle between the two courts; a lord would maintain that he had never refused to do justice, and that the county had wrongfully invaded his rights, and the dispute would be referred to the king's court for settlement. If a plea of land remained in the county court it would have to be decided by wager of battle, each party finding a champion. The sheriff took charge of the proceedings, appointing certain knights to ' keep the field ' and act as referees in the combat between the two champions, who hacked at each other with their archaic little pickaxes, tipped with horn, until twilight fell or one of the combatants yielded himself as ' craven '. Though the duel was far less fashionable in 1275 than it had been at the beginning of the century, it continued in use for long after. On one occasion the county itself undertook to prove its case by battle. A Sussex gentleman alleged that the county had given a wrong judgement and that its record was incorrect, and the county (represented presumably by four knights) came to the king's court with its champion prepared to wage battle; but on the set day they failed to appear and the duel was not fought. The county was not infallible; there are many instances of the king's justices amercing it for false judgement.

Now and then a case, instead of being taken from a lord's court into the county court, was taken out of the county into a private court. This was ' Claim of court ' and was entirely regular. The Earl of Lancaster had an agreement with one of his tenants that he should perform suit for him at the county court of Westmorland, and if any case came up that concerned the earl's tenants he should claim the earl's court and get the plea transferred to his jurisdiction. In like manner the Abbot of Evesham had an accredited representative who attended the county court of Worcester to look out for his lord's judicial interests.

Besides all the litigation which could take place in the county court without a writ there was a number of pleas which the sheriff could hold by special writs. A villein could be claimed by his lord by writ *de nativo habendo*, and, conversely, villeins could claim by writ of *monstraverunt* to be free of the services exacted by their lord. Also, by writ of *justicies* the king could authorize the sheriff to hold almost any plea in the shire court, overriding the ordinary limitations to his powers, so that he could even, at need, employ a jury to decide a matter in dispute. A Kentish writer about 1295 drew up a list of twenty-two pleas which the sheriff may hear by writ in the county court : disputes as to who should repair a bridge, as to the custody of deeds, as to rendering accounts, as to assigning dower, as to the communal bull or boar, as to watering flocks, as to carrying off hay or corn, as to suit of mill, and the like. The king's writ in effect makes the sheriff a royal justice, not merely the president of the court ; he, not the suitors, will give the judgement. These writs may not arrive very frequently, but they will increase the business of the court, as they will involve more elaborate pleadings than the simpler cases that need no writ.

All the civil litigation brings in revenue. Men have to pay for failure to appear, for failure to pursue a claim, for leave to come to terms out of court, for bringing a false complaint, and so on. They are ' in the king's mercy ' as to the amount to be paid ; but ever since Magna Carta the amercement is not supposed to be fixed by the sheriff, but by the neighbours, who know each man's resources, and ' affeer ', or assess, the amount he is to pay. A fourteenth-century sheriff of Lancashire, instead of calling on good and lawful men, sworn in the county court, to affeer the amercements, took to himself three or four of his bailiffs and fixed the penalties high or low according to his hate or love for the parties, to the great oppression of all the community.[1] The Hundred Rolls, without giving so much detail, allege repeatedly that the sheriff imposes oppressive amercements. He is also charged with defying the Statute of Marlborough by fining men ' for fair pleading ' and by fining juries for mistakes in presentment, probably compelling them to make a fixed payment

[1] P.R.O., K.B., 27/455.

in advance as a kind of insurance against error. In Bonestow hundred, Buckinghamshire, where this ' injury ' is said to have been introduced since 1249, it is described as a fixed charge of nineteen shillings a year on the hundred.[1]

It is not always clear in these complaints where the fines and amercements were exacted. All the sheriff's judicial work was not done in the county court ; he had a freer hand and possibly greater opportunities for oppression in the hundred courts, when he held his tourn there.

(b) The Sheriff's Tourn

' *What sheriffs have made their tourns oftener than twice a year ?* '—c. 19.

Twice a year, by a custom of old standing, possibly older than the Norman Conquest, the sheriff was bound to make a tour of his shire, visiting every hundred whose lord had not the privilege of excluding him, and holding a court which was a small-scale copy of that held by the king's justices when they went on eyre through the counties. The sheriff considered himself, as the barons complained in 1258, justice for the day—*justitiarius quoad diem.* As the justices in eyre expected a county court of extraordinary fullness to appear before them, including every magnate, from the archbishop downwards, who held land in the shire, so the sheriffs had been insisting on the presence of lords and gentlemen who might hold land in half a dozen other hundreds and counties ; and thus at Easter and at Michaelmas these unfortunate landlords were being penalized for not being in half a dozen places at once. Not their presence so much as their amercement for absence was the sheriff's object, and the barons very justly protested at the Oxford Parliament against this insistence upon a physical impossibility. By the provisions sanctioned by the baronial council at Westminster in October 1259 the burden was lightened. Only those actually resident in a hundred were required to attend the sheriff's tourn there, unless their presence were demanded for some special reason.[2] The Hundred Rolls

[1] *R.H.*, I, 37, 38.   [2] Stubbs, *Charters*, pp. 375 (17), 391 (4).

make it clear that not even all the residents were present ; a township was allowed to discharge its communal obligation by sending four men and a reeve, some men were bound to attend in respect of their land, which implies that some were exempt, and in some cases a landlord was allowed to hold a private tourn, or ' leet ', as it was called in Norfolk, which was allowed to serve as the equivalent of the sheriff's tourn for those who attended it. In Norfolk, for instance, in 1275, the Abbot of Langley had withdrawn his tenants from the king's leet in his hundred of Loddon to his own leet in Langley, and Earl Warenne had withdrawn the reeves and four men of eight villages from attendance at the tourn of North Erpingham hundred.[1] Women and regular clergy were also exempted from attendance, except on special grounds, and the rules laid down in Magna Carta were to be enforced—that is, the tourn was to be held at Easter and Michaelmas, at the right and accustomed places, and view of frank-pledge was to be held at the Michaelmas tourn.

Although these provisions were included in the Statutes of Marlborough in 1267, it is evident from the returns of 1274–5 that they were often disobeyed.   Only one instance has been noted of an attempt to enforce the attendance at the tourn of an ' ordained clerk ',[2] but on the question of frequency, the sheriffs of Somerset, Devon, Gloucestershire, Lincolnshire, and Essex are all accused of having held the tourn oftener than they ought.   In two of these instances it is also asserted that the tourn ought to be held only once a year.   Devonshire claims this right by charter ;[3] the Lincolnshire wapentakes merely repeat that the sheriff in fact holds it only once a year until Kirton wapentake protests bitterly against two sessions.[4]   North of the Humber the tourn is a detested innovation.   Northumberland and Lancashire say it was first introduced about 1247 by their respective sheriffs,[5] and Northumberland further quotes the charter of 1267 that abolished it, for which sixty marks had been paid in 1272.[6]   In Yorkshire, it is said, only private tourns exist ; the bailiffs of Tickhill hold theirs three or four times in the year.[7]   In 1285 the jurors of

---

[1] *R.H.*, I, 496, 470.   [2] Ibid., I, 456.   [3] Ibid., I, 81, 82.   [4] Ibid , I, 307.
[5] Ibid., II, 19, *P.Q.W.*, 371.   [6] *Pat. Rot. Cal.*, p. 633.   [7] *R.H.*, I, 113.

Kirkby's Quest say that there is no tourn nor view of frank-pledge, but the only inquests held by the sheriff are those held in the county court by the king's writ.[1] And yet the Hundred Rolls speak of men indicted in the tourn in Yorkshire. Staincliff wapentake is alone in lamenting the lack of a sheriff's tourn, which the jurors apparently felt would be some check on the outrageous conduct of the bailiffs of the Earl of Lincoln—those defiers of the king's commissioners.[2] In Norfolk the jurors of Launditch hundred report that ' a new sheriff's tourn ' has been set up by the seneschal of the Honour of Richmond in addition to that held by the sheriff, so that the tenants of the Honour have to attend four in the year.[3] But there are fewer complaints about the frequency of the tourn than about the transactions conducted there.

The business of the tourn was fourfold : the sheriff and the coroners received presentments of offences which were matters for the crown ; the sheriff dealt summarily with the minor offences presented, whilst the more serious were recorded, and if necessary orders were given for the apprehension and custody of the accused against the coming of the king's justices ; the frank-pledge tithings were surveyed, and a number of customary payments, as we have seen, were taken.

The criminal indictments were the work of a system of double presentment. Each township, whether by their five representatives or by the heads of the frank-pledge tithings, who would normally be villeins, reported to a jury of twelve freemen who formally presented the offences under a number of headings called the articles of the tourn. These articles varied from time to time and from place to place, even more than the articles of the general eyre ; numbers of different versions exist, and the only official set is that included in the constitution drawn up for Wales in 1284, when Edward I was imposing the English system of local government on his Welsh conquests. This version defines the sheriff's duties at the tourn and enumerates twenty-nine articles for inquiry.[4] Some deal with the upkeep of roads and bridges,

---

[1] Surtees Soc., Vol. 47, pp. 68–7.
[3] Ibid., I, 435.

[2] R.H., I, 112.
[4] Stat. Realm, 57.

others with the keeping of watch and ward, the selling of second-
hand clothing, the stealing of corn, doves, sheep, game, the brewing
of ale and the like : by-law business, as one might say.   Others
dealt with more serious crime : treason, homicide, rape, arson.
The expressions used by the jurors of 1274–5 indicate that they
regarded the tourn as the normal place for indictments of theft or
murder.   The complaint is equally common that the sheriff has
imprisoned persons for theft who have not been indicted in the
tourn, and that he has corruptly concealed the felonies of those
who have been so indicted, either he or his bailiffs having been
' negligent ' in performing their duty.[1]   In one case the hundred
clerk had accepted a gift of beasts and of carcases and of other
trifles to suppress the indictment of a woman who was charged
with theft.   Another bailiff is accused of having forced himself
upon a tourn jury as their clerk, and then having inserted amongst
the secret presentments charges of which they knew nothing,[2]
for, as at the general eyre, some indictments had to be kept
private lest the accused should get wind of the charge and escape
before he could be apprehended.   A Sussex jury reports that the
seneschal of Arundel refused to allow the sheriff to hear the secret
presentments without him, because he wanted to have the first
chance of imprisoning any of the men of his jurisdiction at
Arundel, whence they generally escaped with ease after they had
made gifts to the seneschal.[3]

Tampering with indictments in the way the Hundred Rolls
describe led to a stricter system of recording them.   Under the
statutes of 1285 the presenting jurors had to put their seals to
their indictments, and in 1327 the sheriff was ordered to make a
duplicate record by indenture, the jurors retaining one portion
and the sheriff and coroners the other.[4]   Even so it was not easy
to protect the innocent from the malice of the sheriff ; in 1371
we hear of a sheriff of Lancashire who always planted himself
amongst the jurors as their acting clerk and succeeded in procuring
whatever indictment he desired.[5]

Another abuse in the tourn, as in the county court, was the

---

[1] *R.H.*, I, 144, 477 ; II, 441.   [2] Ass. R., 1233, m. 4.   [3] *R.H.*, II, 214.
[4] *Stat. Realm*, I, 81, 257.   [5] K.B. 27/455, Rex, m. 2.

sheriff's habit of fining juries wholesale for irregularities in the form of their presentments. The sheriff of Hereford in his tourn in Wolphy hundred expected a categorical reply in a set form to every one of the *capitula* he delivered to the jurors, and amerced them at his will for any slip in replying.[1] This practice, which is mentioned in the Great Charter of 1217, had hardened into a fixed custom early in the reign of Henry III ; in both private and public courts the fine ' for stumbling ' (*ne occasionetur, beupleider, pro stulta presentatione*, or whatever it was called) was being regularly imposed, sometimes as a kind of compulsory insurance against error before any error had been made. The baronial opposition had condemned it, and the Statutes of Marlborough had forbidden it ; but it still went on, and it figures in the official sheriff's accounts as well as in eyre records. A Sussex official in 1274 made the hundred jury pay two and a half marks ' for fair pleading ' and then asked his subordinate if he had anything more to add, and if he had, the jury had to pay another twenty shillings.[2] In another Sussex hundred, although the composition had been paid, the poor folk had to pay in addition for every slip they made.[3] The Bishop of Norwich took the same fine at his private tourn in Hoxne hundred ; [4] in fact, the habit was universal, and was still in full force when the *Mirror of Justices* was written about 1290.

Besides the presentments in reply to the articles, on occasion special inquests might be held in the tourn. In 1280, for instance, the sheriff and coroners of Worcestershire were ordered to inquire who killed Walter Codard, and their return is still extant, showing that at the sheriff's tourn held at Cokeswell on Saturday 30th August 1280 a jury found that John of the Dean was being distrained by the bailiff, as he alleged, unlawfully, and that when he resisted the bailiff, who was very drunk, struck him with a stick, and Walter Codard, the bailiff's man, ran up with a knife behind John, who, being warned by a woman's cry, turned to defend himself, and struck Codard with an axe, so that he died a fortnight later.[5] As a matter of fact, when the inquest was held,

---

[1] Ass. R. 300 c, m. 22.　　[2] *R.H.*, II, 204.　　[3] Ibid., II, 214.
[4] Ibid., II, 186.　　[5] *Cal. Misc. Inq.*, No. 2240.

a pardon for John had already been issued at Westminster, but probably no one in the tourn was aware of that fact.[1]   Another inquest, enrolled on the records of the King's Bench, is dated from the sheriff's tourn held at Crowden, for Armingford hundred, Cambridgeshire, on Tuesday 2nd December 1320, and shows how twelve jurors, whose names and seals were appended to the return, charged fifteen persons with the robbery of goods worth a hundred pounds.[2]

Over the serious crimes enrolled in the indictments of the tourn the sheriff had no jurisdiction ; the coroners took charge of the records and were there to see that he did not exceed his power. One case recorded on the roll of the Somerset eyre in 1280 illustrates the limits of his jurisdiction.   Two men of Bempstone hundred had burned down a house in Allerton.   One of them was caught redhanded and taken to the tourn, which was then being held at High Bridge, and there before the under-sheriff, who was presiding in the sheriff's place, the offender turned approver and appealed his accomplice who was actually there present in the tourn.   The under-sheriff thereupon empanelled a jury on his own authority, without a royal writ, which found the accused guilty, and he was hanged out of hand.   The approver was sent to Ivelchester Jail, and was also convicted and hanged later. For exceeding his powers by trying and hanging an indicted felon, the under-sheriff was fined a mark by the justices in eyre.[3]

Such judicial power, then, as the sheriff had in the tourn was over the petty offences—encroachments on public land, the removal of boundary marks, division of watercourse, brewing or baking contrary to government regulations, dishonest weights and measures, the tricks of the trade practised by tanners, curriers, butchers, and tailors.   For dealing with such matters no royal writ was needed.   More particularly the supervision of the local police system was the business of the tourn : has hue and cry been properly raised and duly followed up ? Have the watches commanded by the archbishop's assize of 1242 been duly observed ?   It was in the tourn that the ward penny was exacted,

[1] *Pat. Roll Cal.*, July 23, 1280, p. 392.   [2] K.B., 27/244, Rex, m. 12.
[3] Ass. R., 759, m. 30.

and that inquiry was made into the observance of the curious custom of the ward staff,[1] which survived into the eighteenth century in some hundreds as an archaic and meaningless ceremonial. Generally speaking, the jurisdiction of the thirteenth-century sheriff in the tourn corresponds to the work done by a nineteenth-century justice of the peace before county and district councils had come into existence. And closely related to the inquiries as to hue and cry and watch and ward were the inquiries into the frank-pledges.

The system of frank-pledges has been often described.[2] Each village or borough south of Yorkshire and east of Wales was divided into tithings—groups nominally of ten men, actually of numbers ranging from four to thirty. In the south-west a man was in a given tithing by virtue of the place of his dwelling; in the midlands and the eastern counties he was formally adopted into a group which was personal and not territorial, a kind of family, named after the chief tithing man. The tithing formed a body of collective guarantors for the good conduct of each member, and all persons were bound by law to be enrolled in a tithing at the age of twelve, unless, like free tenants, domestic servants, women, and clergy, they were already guaranteed by lord, freehold, master, or order. The 1217 reissue of Magna Carta had provided that the sheriff in his Michaelmas tourn should hold a view of frank-pledge : ' see, that is, that our peace is kept and that the tithings be full, according to custom, and that he take no more for his trouble than the sheriff used to take in the time of our grandfather, king Henry.' [3]

When the number of villages in the average hundred is considered, as well as the amount of other business to be got through on the day of the tourn, it becomes probable that the sheriff's share in this business would be confined to inquiry and supervision ; that he would not in person correct the old roll and swear in the new members. Any one who has had practical experience of the working of a coal and clothing club, for instance, in a village to-day, will know how much time is needed for this

[1] L.T.R. Misc. Roll, 6/13, 6/14 (Hundred of Branch and Dole).
[2] See, for instance, W. A. Morris, *The Frankpledge System.*
[3] Stubbs, *Charters*, p. 343.

kind of checking of lists and dealing with the personal details that are involved. All available thirteenth-century evidence confirms this presumption. Not only in those liberties referred to in 1217, where the lord of a manor held a view of frank-pledge for his own unfree tenants, but also for those villages where the view was still in the king's hands, it appears that the preliminary work of checking and enrolling was done locally, village by village, by the hundred bailiff, acting, of course, as the sheriff's agent. In the Essex hundreds in 1274 the jurors complain of the exactions of the hundred bailiffs at the view of frank-pledge, and of the sheriffs at the tourn.[1] In the royal hundred of South Erpingham, Norfolk, the hundred bailiff is charged with holding ' all the leets [2] of the hundred ' twice a year instead of once, as Magna Carta had provided.[3] The articles of Kirkby's Quest in 1285 distinguish between payments made at the view of frank-pledge and at the tourn.[4] The double system is very clearly revealed in the description given in 1279 of the Earl of Gloucester's Oxfordshire hundred of Chadlington, where the view is held in each vill by the bailiffs of the earl, whilst the sheriff holds the tourn for the whole hundred.[5] The sheriff at his tourn, then, receives the reports of the bailiff as to the state of the tithings, and the cert-money and tithing-pence that they have collected in the different villages. From those villages where the lord of the manor has view of frank-pledge he will not receive these last payments. The relation of the sheriff's tourn to these private views is not uniform ; the Hundred Rolls and the Placita Quo Warranto reveal a great variety of arrangements. There are those villages where the view is held by the lord of the manor in the presence of the king's bailiff, that is, the hundred bailiff or some other deputy of the sheriff who takes a fixed or variable part of the profits of the view.[6] There are other villages where the bailiff is present but takes no payment ; [7] there are others where it is said that the lord must give notice to the bailiff, who can come or not as he

---

[1] R.H., I, 136 ff., 146 ff. [2] The local name for view of frank-pledge : see below.
[3] R.H., I, 514.   [4] Chron. Petroburg. (C.S.), p. 105.
[5] R.H., II, 725–747 (under heading Forinsecum).
[6] P.Q.W., 721, 722, 724 ; R.H., II, 275, 186.
[7] P.Q.W., 723, R.H. II, 275, 186.

likes ; [1] and there are others where he is not entitled to be present at all. [2] In some the lord makes a payment at the tourn which represents the profits of his view. In some villages, it seems, attendance at the lord's view exempts the villagers from attendance at the tourn ; there are others when the reeve and four men are bound to attend the tourn, although a view has already been held in their village. [3] In one village of Barford hundred, Beds, all the residents of Barford Manor attend their lord's view on Hockday (the second Tuesday after Easter), and the tithing lists are revised and every one present pays a penny, and the absent are amerced, and for this the lord pays the lump sum of four shillings a year to the king. But besides this, every man in his frank-pledge is also bound to attend the king's hundred of Barford once a year, to present the other articles of the view there and to pay the said sum of money to the king's bailiff. [4]

In this case the lord claims nothing beyond the strict frank-pledge functions, but in a great number of places when a man claimed a view he was claiming also the right to receive presentments—to administer, in fact, those articles which the sheriff administered in his tourn, [5] the articles which the lord of Barford called ' the other articles of the view '. Those who held such sessions of their courts were later described as having leet jurisdiction, for the word *leet* found so frequently in the Norfolk Hundred Rolls as the equivalent of *bortreming* in Suffolk, *tremur* in Devonshire, and *lawday* in Sussex and elsewhere [6] comes to oust all other terms for this kind of manorial tourn. Yet even when the articles of the tourn or of the leet had been administered to the villagers in a private view of frank-pledge they might still have to send representatives to the tourn. Somehow or other the indictments of pleas of the crown must be recorded, and unless there was a coroner on the spot some way of reporting presentments to a royal agent must be found. Thus though J. Peverel, for instance, holds the view of frank-pledge in Torring,

---

[1] *P.Q.W.*, 10, 302 ; *Cal. Ch. R.*, I, 199, 122.
[2] *P.Q.W.*, 3, 242 ; *R.H.*, I, 496, II, 189.
[3] *P.Q.W.*, 248, 259, 292, 298, 299, 345, 505, 759.   [4] Ibid., 47.
[5] Maitland, *Sel. Pleas in Manorial Courts*, xxix, xxxv.
[6] *R.H.* I, 484, etc. ; II, 147 ; I, 92 ; II, 103, etc. *The Trymming day* is a sixteenth-century form in Bedfordshire.

he takes no amends for the trespasses presented there, but sends them on to the hundred court, where the penalties are imposed.[1] In various Huntingdonshire hundreds it is stated that the reeve and four men of a vill, as well as the freemen, attend the hundred court to make presentments although a view has already been held by their lord.[2] Earl Warenne holds the view without a bailiff in his soke of Gimmingham, but all his free tenants, as well as the reeves and four villeins, in eight vills of the soke used to attend the sheriff's tourn and make sworn presentments of trespasses ; now they have been withdrawn he cannot hold proper inquests concerning the keeping of the peace in those vills.[3]

There were thus endless variations in the division of labour and the division of profits between the private views of frank-pledge and the tourn in any hundred ; but right up to the end of the Middle Ages the tourn continued to be held, whether by a franchise holder or by the sheriff, in spite of the encroaching powers of the justices of the peace. Not till 1461, when one of the first statutes of Edward IV ordered the sheriffs to pass on the indictments received in the tourn to the justices of the peace, for them to take action, was it really superannuated.

Even then the 'great' or 'general' hundred lingered on by virtue of its financial aspect.[4] It has already been noted that much of the customary revenue of the hundred was paid in at the tourn. This is doubtless one of the reasons why men were expected to attend it, though much of its work, as far as they were concerned, had already been done at the view of frank-pledge in their village. They came to pay the assised rents, the ward-silver, the horderesgyft, the 'tourn money', the lathescot, the hidage, the sheriff's aid, and the like.[5] They might also bring the cert-money or the tithing-penny or the head-money or the wapentake fine on behalf of those who were not present. The bailiffs brought the profits of the royal views in the hundred ; the stewards of lords who had the view brought the compositions

---

[1] *P.Q.W.*, 757 ; cf. *P.Q.W.*, 259.   [2] Ibid., 292, 295, 298, 299.
[3] *R.H.*, I, 496.
[4] 'Head money' was still paid in Malmesbury hundred in 1872. 'Wroth silver'—called *warth*, or ward-silver on the Patent Roll of 1270—is still paid in Knightlow hundred at Martinmas. See Plate IV, facing p. 126.
[5] See, for instance, *R.H.*, I, 97, 223 ; II, 12, 132 ; *P.Q.W.*, 293.

paid by some at least in return for that privilege. Some paid
the farm of their hundred at the sheriff's tourn.[1] When to these
receipts were added the fines and amercements arising out of
the police and judicial business done there—fines for breaking the
assize of ale, for not keeping watches, for not being in a tithing—
it is easily understood that the profits of the tourns might form a
considerable item in the sheriff's accounts.

V. THE SHERIFF'S COLLEAGUES: THE CORONERS AND THE CONSTABLES

At this point, before turning to consider the body of
subordinates who worked under the sheriff, we ought to notice
his colleagues in the shire : the men who in an emergency could
act in his place. Obscure as their origin still is, we know that
from 1194 at least there had been in every county two, three, or
four men whose business it was ' to keep the pleas of the crown '.
Their work was well defined by custom by 1274, and we can see
to what extent they limited the sheriff's powers, and to what
extent they acted with him. In case of his sudden death or some
legal disqualification they might have to act without him.

Socially speaking, the coroners were of the same type as the
sheriffs ; they were country gentlemen, and they sometimes
became sheriffs themselves. Their position was different, however, in that they were elected in the county court, instead of
being appointed in the Exchequer, and that they served for life
or until they were past their work. A Dorset coroner had to be
replaced in 1255 because he had gone blind. On other occasions
the county was ordered to make a fresh election because they had
chosen a man whose substance was not sufficient to sustain the
office.

This method of appointment, making the coroner entirely
independent of the sheriff, fitted them particularly well to act
as a check on him in their especial sphere of activity—the keeping
a record of all crimes and other occurrences that involved crown
rights in the shire. Thus they had to be present at the execution

[1] *R.H.*, I, 227, 230, 234.

of red-handed thieves in private courts, at outlawries and at appeals of crime in the county court, and at presentments of crimes, whether in the tourn or the county court ; and on the news of any sudden death, of the finding of treasure or the occurrence of a valuable wreck, they had to proceed to the scene of the event and hold an inquest of men of the four nearest townships and record the findings on their rolls.

It was the coroners' rolls, and not the sheriff's, that formed the legal record upon which the king's justices acted. They had to be produced at the general eyre, and the lands of the coroners and their heirs could be seized if they were not available. The grandson of a Lancashire coroner petitioned the king in 1292 for protection against such treatment in future eyres, for his grandfather's rolls had all been stolen or destroyed in a border raid when the village and manor-house had been burned by the Scots. Any eyre roll shows their importance, for the ' pleas of the crown ' always open with a long series of entries copied from the coroners' rolls since last the justices held their eyre in the county, forming a chronicle of deaths by misadventure, of murders, of outlawries, of treasure found, of wrecks, and of other such incidents affecting the rights of the crown. The action taken had to be reported, the fines and penalties inflicted, the value of felons' goods and of the deodand or dumb cause of death, for all of which the sheriff was mainly responsible ; thus the coroner's record was of the first importance in checking his zeal and honesty. No record of such things made without his co-operation was accepted ; when in June 1274 the sheriff was ordered to inquire in full county court whether Robert fitz Gernon had been outlawed, and if so, when and why, he returned that he had not been able to hold the inquest at the first county court after receiving the writ because no coroner was present there.[1] At an earlier date the oral record of the county court of Lincolnshire had been overridden by the coroners' rolls, which led to the county's being amerced at two hundred pounds.[2]

Thus it was with an indispensable record that the Lincolnshire coroner was tampering when, according to the jurors of 1274, two

[1] *Cal. Misc. Inq.*, p. 582.   [2] *Sel. Pleas of Crown* (S.S.), p. 16.

Jews had stolen a poke of wool worth four marks and their theft
had been written on the coroners' roll, and William of Holgate
' fraudulently extracted ' the case from the roll in return for forty
shillings, which the Jews gave him.[1] A similar charge is brought
against a Norfolk coroner.[2]

Most of the complaints recorded by the jurors, however, are
connected with the occasional inquests that the coroners were
bound to hold, then as now, when a sudden death occurred. By
their oath the coroners were pledged to come at once when summoned, and hold the inquest without a fee. Again and again the
jurors of 1274 allege that they either have refused to hold the
inquest or have demanded payment before they would come. A
boy died by misadventure in Sutton village and the Lincolnshire
coroner would not come for ten days to view the body, so that it
was torn by dogs and birds.[3] The knights who bring a joint
verdict for nine of the Norfolk hundreds have twenty-four such
charges against their coroner.[4] In Northants a coroner took
6s. 8d. from four men whose little boys had found two dead bodies
in a wood and in their ignorance had omitted to raise the hue and
cry as law required.[5] Ten charges of extorting fees are brought
in one hundred against a Derbyshire coroner.[6] The coroner of
the geldable hundreds of Suffolk is said to have come to Mendham to view a corpse found in the Waveney, and, having
summoned the country-side to the spot, to have refused to hold
the inquest. The hundred bailiff then dragged the body ashore,
and got the Norfolk coroner to come across the river and hold
the inquest, which found the Prior of Mendham guilty of the
death, and by this false charge twenty-four marks were extorted
from the prior, of which the Norfolk coroner only pocketed one
mark.[7] It is not only in the Hundred Rolls that these complaints
of the coroners' slackness are found. In 1285 a jury of Devonshire knights report how a dead man lay unburied for eight days
in Axminster, at fair time, and the coroner absolutely refused to
come and view the body.[8]

Another duty that devolved upon the coroners was to deliver

[1] *R.H.*, I, 313. [2] Ibid., I, 481. [3] Ibid., I, 308. [4] Ibid., I, 481–2.
[5] Ibid., II, 9. [6] Ibid., II, 293. [7] Ibid., II, 187. [8] Ass. Roll 194.

a fugitive from sanctuary. A runaway always made for the nearest church, and there he was free from arrest, and there he had to stay till the coroner came and solemnly bade him abjure the realm and make his way to such-and-such a seaport, staff in hand, bareheaded and barefooted, keeping strictly to the king's highway, on which he was safe from attack, till he reached the sea. Once across the sea he might never return unless pardoned. Here again the coroners held up the country-side to ransom. A felon who had taken sanctuary in Fosdyke Church remained there for forty days, to the great annoyance of the villagers, who were morally bound to feed him and legally bound to prevent his escape, and though they offered the Lincolnshire coroner 6s. 8d., he held out for 13s. 4d.[1] It was not the coroner, however, but the constable of Banbury Castle, who was to blame when a gang of men attacked a properly certified felon who was going seawards, dragged him off the king's highway, and slew him.[2]

Besides county coroners there were many coroners of liberties. Henry of Helhoughton, of whom the Suffolk jurors have many complaints, was coroner of the eight and a half hundreds of St. Edmunds. His will is preserved, and along with legacies to his wife and children, to servants, to the parish clergy, and to the friars, he leaves to St. Edmund's shrine his charger, with its trappings, to atone for all the trespasses committed by him against the saint. Probably his conscience was less burdened by the extortion of irregular fees from the Suffolk villagers than by his failure to pass an adequate proportion of them on to St. Edmund's house. Much smaller liberties also had coroners: Lothingland hundred in Suffolk; Rochford hundred, Essex; Lifton hundred, Devon; and the hundred of Wye in Kent, for instance.[3]

Other shire officials who were parallel rather than subordinate to the sheriff were the escheators and the constables of castles, the escheator's work belongs to the feudal aspect of the shire and will be considered later.[4] Constables were put in charge of those castles which were not in the sheriff's keeping, and to judge from the Hundred Rolls they had considerable independent powers and were occasionally very oppressive. Hugh of Dennington,

---

[1] *R.H.*, I, 308. [2] Ibid., II, 33. [3] Ibid., I, 76; II, 169, 180. [4] See below, pp. 199 ff.

constable of Orford Castle in Suffolk, is accused of imprisoning
men who were carrying royal writs, of making encroachments on
the king's highway and in Orford market-place, of taking bribes
from felons, of torturing a prisoner to death and having him
buried secretly without view of the coroners, of hindering an Ely
bailiff from doing the king's work in Orford, of levying market
dues unjustly from merchants coming into Orford, and otherwise exercising his functions outside the castle precincts.[1] His
ingenuity was surpassed, however, by the man in charge of
Scarborough Castle, who scattered corn under the castle walls,
and when the pigs of the townsfolk climbed up the slopes to eat
it drove them into the castle.[2] It seems clear from what is said
of the constables of Dover and Canterbury castles [3] that the office
was essentially military, but that the constables' military powers
could readily be exploited in time of peace so as to extort money,
goods, and services from the town and the surrounding district.
Occasionally—in Essex, for instance—he may have acted with or
for the sheriff ; as a rule, however, he must have been in direct
touch with the hundred as organized for military purposes.[4]

The county keepers of the peace, or *custodes pacis*, were still
regarded so much as emergency officials that there is no reference
to them in the Hundred Rolls. Appointed to keep order in each
county in the unsettled state of the country after the battle of
Lewes, their functions had been largely military ; for the time
being the forces of the shire seem to have been at their disposal
rather than under the sheriff. But in 1274 it was not yet dis-
cernible that these military police captains were eventually going
to oust the sheriff from his pride of place, though three years
later, when the knights of the shire were ordered to elect as
custos pacis for their county some knight who was not going with
the king on the Welsh wars, with power to hold inquests into the
keeping of the peace, some hint of the coming transformation
from commander to justice might have been discerned.

VI. The Sheriff's Subordinates

The county staff of officials was large. When in 1258 the

[1] *R.H.*, II, 188, 191, 199. [2] Ibid., I, 131. [3] Ibid., I, 209, 210. [4] See below, pp. 188 ff.

barons demanded a close scrutiny of local government they
desired the inquiry to cover ' all bailiffs, greater, middling and
less, and all their dependents within and without liberties ',
and, in more technical terms, ' sheriffs, under-sheriffs, itinerant
serjeants, serjeants of hundreds, bedels, sub-bedels, bailiffs of
liberties, and all bailiffs whatsoever '.[1] For the selection of all
these, except the bailiffs of liberties, the sheriff was held responsible ; in 1221 the knights of Shropshire observe that at least
twelve of his nominees are unsatisfactory : ' Their removal
would benefit both the king and the county '.[2] In 1258 the king
made the sheriffs swear that they would not have more serjeants
than were needed for the work of the shire, and that they would
only employ men whose good faith they could answer for.[3]

Some of the sheriff's staff served him throughout the county ;
the activities of others were localized in a hundred or group of
hundreds. Of those whose sphere of action is the whole shire the
most important were the under-sheriff and the sheriff's clerk and
receiver. The sheriff could apparently obtain leave to appoint
an under-sheriff with full power to discharge any of his functions
and act as his substitute on any occasion. Power to do this is
expressly given in some appointments. As mentioned in the
Hundred Rolls, under-sheriffs are found doing almost anything
that a sheriff could do. An under-sheriff in Wiltshire takes
charge of the prisoners in Salisbury Castle, takes distresses, and
holds a hundred court.[4] An under-sheriff in Devonshire collects
royal dues on behalf of his chief.[5] Roger of Kelvedon, one of the
chief villains of the piece in Essex, is charged, as under-sheriff,
with the most various offences in seven different hundreds. An
under-sheriff later in the reign is mentioned as holding the county
court of Staffordshire. The under-sheriff of Huntingdonshire
attends to witness the paying of homage to the Abbot of Peterborough in 1289. The under-sheriff of Somerset takes fees and
gloves when he does his business at Wells, and he has a clerk of
his own. Under-sheriffs render account at the Exchequer on
behalf of their principal, and writs addressed to the sheriff are

[1] M. Paris, *Chron. Maj.*, R.S., VI, 397.   [2] *Sel. Pleas of Crown* (S.S.), p. 110.
[3] Hennings, *England under Henry III*, p. 203.   [4] *R.H.*, II, 256, 271.
[5] Ibid., I, 87.

delivered into their keeping by the justices. But though the under-sheriff has all these powers, he is as yet far removed from the under-sheriff of the eighteenth century, who does all the work of the office, leaving to the sheriff only the honorary functions.

The sheriff's clerks are constantly mentioned, both in the Hundred Rolls and elsewhere. It is obvious that the business-like methods expected at head-quarters must have involved a heavy amount of clerical work in the county : to draw up the records and accounts which the sheriff had to produce at the Exchequer, the notes needed for his own use, the rolls of courts, and the copies of writs which he had to pass on to hundred bailiffs and bailiffs of liberties must have occupied several scribes for all their time. It must be remembered that the average country squire of the thirteenth century, and thus the average sheriff, could neither read nor write. A statute of 1298 asserts that many sheriffs are wholly lay persons, and that others, though they are lettered, put so much faith in their clerks as to leave the carrying out of writs to them entirely, so that it is possible for them to forge false returns.[1] The position of the clerk of an illiterate sheriff must have been both highly confidential and highly influential.

Under the general description of clerical, two main kinds of activity are included : the financial and the legal work. The sheriff's 'clerk and receiver' is frequently mentioned in the Exchequer records, and the Hundred Rolls mention several times the receiver of the king's debts in the shire.[2] From early in the reign of Henry III there was one clerk assigned to this most important task in every shire, receiving all the moneys paid in and acting head of what is sometimes called the exchequer in the castle. It is this type of clerk who is charged by the jurors with collecting payments and not giving receipts, and with levying amounts in excess of the Twentieth.[3] The clerks to whom sheriffs tended to leave too free a hand in the receiving and returning of writs had functions more like those of chancery officials. It is they who are accused of taking bribes to remove men's names from panels of jurors and from lists of persons

[1] *Stat. Realm*, I, 213.   [2] *Stat. Realm*, I, 130 ; II, 92, 95.   [3] *R.H.*, I, 144 ; II, 190.

indicted in the tourn.[1]   Such clerks were responsible for keeping
the rolls of the tourn and the county court.   In 1268 a commissioner sent down to Suffolk reports how ' I found the sheriff's
clerk, and asked him what he had collected from the town, and
he refused to give any information without the sheriff's leave and
said if I wanted to see the rolls I must go to Norwich '—where
the sheriff's office was and the archives were stored.   The clerks
who spent most of their time in the castle and who had so much
information were people worth placating.   A man who came to
the castle of York to reclaim a beast in pound there was coerced
into signing away a piece of land to Robert of Foxoles—this by
the power of Robert's brother John, clerk in the said castle.[2]
The most remarkable charge brought against a sheriff's clerk
belongs to a later date than the inquest of 1274.   A north-country
woman who was indicted of murder before the coroners by her
own account hid from justice ' not for fear of the charge but
because the sheriff's clerk, Simon of Wakefield, threatened that
when he had her in Newcastle Gaol he would rape her and pull
out all her teeth, the sheriff being then absent in London ' ; but
when the sheriff returned she surrendered herself to the king's
prison, the more willingly as the sheriff had dismissed Simon
from his office.[3]   Though the clerks were dismissible by the
sheriffs, and entirely subordinate to them, it seems very probable
that they had the strong position that the permanent civil servant
has to-day over against his political superiors.   They knew the
ropes thoroughly and were, in fact, professionals.   A series of
charges brought against Devonshire officials in Kirkby's Quest of
1285 reveals the fact that one clerk had held office under four sheriffs
of Devon, one under three, and three under two.[4]   A sheriff without much force of character might be as dependent upon his clerk
as a bench of county justices is on the justices' clerk to-day.

After these comparatively stationary officials at county
head-quarters come the bailiffs errant—the travelling staff who
carried the sheriff's commands up and down the county.   Such
men as Robert del Duffhus, bailiff errant in Suffolk, or Roger
North, serjeant itinerant in Norfolk, are found acting all over

[1] Ibid., I, 448.   [2] Ibid., I, 118.   [3] *Cal. Misc. Inq.*, p. 538.   [4] Ass. R., 194, m. 2.

the shire. A great part of their work was the conveying and execution of writs, and this varied according to the orders contained in the writs. They levied distresses, driving off beasts with the officials of the hundred and taking and selling goods of an inanimate kind. They collected dues on occasion ; they summoned juries and attached persons to appear in court. They handed over writs to the bailiffs of liberties where they might not enter ; but on occasion they had to act because the bailiffs of the liberties had failed to do the work. In a formulary for the use of a sheriff of the thirteenth century there is the formula for returning to the justices : ' Not omitting because of the liberty of X, I have sent my bailiff errant to distrain so and so, but he has been forcibly prevented from executing the writ.'

These roving bailiffs, whilst as indispensable to the sheriff as his clerk, also served the private litigant, and probably drew part of their emoluments for the execution of writs from the persons whose work they were doing. If they were ' riding bailiffs ' they also took fodder and lodging for their horses—a practice carefully limited by law in the wapentakes of Lancashire and Cheshire, but a constant source of grumbling all over England. The sheriff himself was limited to five horses, for himself and four attendants, when he demanded hospitality, according to the new oath of 1258.

The office was sometimes granted by the king direct ; a bailiff errant for Northamptonshire was so appointed in 1332. Three years later the sheriff of Norfolk and Suffolk petitioned parliament against the granting of such an office for life ; the sheriffs, he says, are responsible for the behaviour of these bailiffs and ought to be free to appoint or dismiss them at his will. This was probably the normal practice, and in some cases the sheriff appointed hundred bailiffs to do the work, as well as their jobs in their own hundreds.

So much for the county staff. Of the localized officials, little is known as yet of the activities of those bailiffs of ridings, rapes, and lasts to whom occasional reference is made in the Hundred Rolls.[1] The lesser unit of primary significance is the hundred, and it is to its staff and its government that we must now turn.

[1] *R.H.*, I, 118, 130, 201, 236 ; II, 205, 209.

CHAPTER X

THE HUNDRED AND THE HUNDRED BAILIFF

I. Royal and Private Hundreds

' Of the farms of hundreds and wapentakes.'—c. 5.

' How many hundreds and wapentakes are now in the king's hands and how many in the hands of others . . . and how much each is worth a year ? '—c. 6.

' What sheriffs have delivered hundreds or wapentakes at high farms to bailiffs who used extortion to raise those farms ? '—c. 18.

EVERY shire in England was subdivided into hundreds or wapentakes, and though the sheriff was responsible for the whole shire the degree and the directness of his control of any one hundred depended on the answer to this last question— Who was the lord of the hundred ?   Though the Hundred Rolls themselves are not complete enough to give the answer for all England, other records, notably the *Nomina Villarum* of 1316, fill the gap.   We are thus able to state with assurance that when Edward I became king there were something like 628 hundreds in England, and that of these 270 were royal and 358 in private hands.[1]   The map at the end of the volume makes the distribution clear.   Broadly speaking, the royal hundred is thickest in the eastern midlands and the private hundreds in the south and south-west.   There are no private hundreds in Buckinghamshire, in Warwickshire, or in Cambridgeshire outside the Isle of Ely ; only one in Lincolnshire, one in Bedfordshire and one in Leicester-shire.   In Devonshire thirty-three out of thirty-five hundreds are private, in Oxfordshire twelve out of fourteen, in Somerset thirty-six out of forty ; in Sussex all are in private hands.

To attempt to determine how long these hundreds had been

[1] See Appendix IV.

held by subjects is to plunge into the sea of uncertainties of which Richard fitz Neal speaks. There is good reason to think that some hundreds had never been in the king's hands ; the rights of the Bishop of Worcester in Worcestershire, for instance, are probably older than the hundredal system itself, and the same may be true of the two hundreds of the Isle of Ely. By 1066 it is possible that at least one hundred of the English wapentakes and hundreds were held by subjects. Only in Essex, Norfolk, and Suffolk does Domesday Book tell us much about lay lords of hundreds, and there may well have been many of them in the western counties, in view of the Conqueror's well-known policy of imitating the concessions of his predecessors.

As soon as an official roll of royal charters is found, under Richard I, records of the grant of private hundreds are frequent. Fifty-five such grants are recorded under John, 108 under Henry III. The Hundred Rolls frequently narrate the history of a hundred, and often the statements of the jurors are confirmed by a stray record. It is clear that Henry II saw no inconsistency between the extension of the scope of royal jurisdiction and the granting of hundreds, with their courts, to subjects. He can be shown to have made at least fifty-two grants of hundreds, and the list is certainly not complete.

To what extent did such a grant take the government of a hundred out of the king's hands ? Or, to put it another way, to what extent was the sheriff excluded by such a grant from acting in the hundred ? It all depended on the terms of the charter. If the king had granted ' whatever the sheriff has in the king's hundreds ', or if he had granted ' return of writs ', the sheriff would not normally enter the hundred. His duty would end when his bailiff errant or other messenger had handed over the king's commands to the officials of the lord of the hundred. But a great many lords had much more restricted rights. In Devon, for example, out of thirty-three private hundreds only two— Lifton and Plympton—had return of writs. In Wilts, out of twenty-eight private hundreds, sixteen had return of writs, ten having religious and six secular lords. In Chalk hundred, held by the Abbess of Wilton, though she had the return of writs, the sheriff held his tourn twice a year.   The sheriff's responsibility was certainly not limited to the royal hundreds.   He had constantly to report, either to the king's justices or to the Exchequer officials, what he had been doing with regard to residents in private hundreds ; he would have to account for money due from them, and he would then have in some way to see that the king's commands were obeyed there.   Rents or dues payable to the king from the hundred, presentments of royal pleas made at the tourn or the leets of the private hundred would pass through his hands.   In a few instances the officials of a private hundred dealt direct with the Exchequer, but for administration and legal purposes the sheriff was the indispensable means in all but the very most exalted liberties.

The conditions on which a lord held a hundred varied widely. He might hold it in free alms, as Buckland Abbey held Roborough hundred, Devon, or the Bishop of Bath held the hundreds of Winterstoke and Cheddar in Somerset.   He might hold it along with a manor, by knight service, as the Bishop of Salisbury held Underditch hundred, Wilts.[1]   He might hold it on a lease for a term of years, as Thomas le Grete received Munslow hundred, Shropshire, in 1261 for three years ; or for life, as Walter de Pedwardin received Bradford hundred in the same county in 1267 ; or during pleasure, as Ralph of Ufford held Samford hundred, Suffolk, in 1274.[2]   But the most typical tenure was fee-farm : the lord, that is, inherited the hundred by the ordinary laws governing the descent of land, and he paid a fixed annual farm or rent for it, either to the sheriff or at the royal Exchequer. Now and then an Exchequer roll notes that this or that hundred has been taken into the king's hands because its farm is in arrears ; in 1273, for instance, the Earl of Lincoln's wapentake of Staincliff in Yorkshire was so taken over, but the arrears must soon have been paid up, for the earl's bailiff was, as we saw, taking a very high line about his lord's rights there in 1275.   The application of ordinary land law to the tenure of a hundred is constantly illustrated in the Hundred Rolls, whose jurors often give us a long piece of family history in answering this article.   Bullingdon

[1] *R.H.*, II, 279.   [2] Ibid., II, 189.

and Northgate hundreds outside Oxford were granted by King
John, together with the manor of Headington, to Thomas Basset
in 1203, at a farm of twenty-three pounds a year, to be held as
one knight's fee. They descended first to his eldest daughter,
Philippa, Countess of Warwick, who died childless in 1265, and
whose tombstone, once in Oseney Abbey, may be seen to-day in
the cathedral church of Oxford ; then to her three nieces. Hugh
of Pleshy, the husband of one of them, bought out the other two
coheiresses, and was holding the manor and the two hundreds in
1274.[1] In 1281, after his wife's death, he granted it to the king,
who was holding it when the Quo Warranto Pleas were held in
1285. Kinwardstone hundred, Wiltshire, granted by Henry II
to John Marshal at a farm of twenty-eight pounds a year,
descended to William, Earl Marshal, who married Eleanor sister
of Henry III ; she brought it with her to her second husband
Simon de Montfort, and was holding it as his widow in 1275. On
her death it reverted to the Marshal family, represented by
Gilbert de Clare, great nephew of William Marshal, who was
holding it when the justices held the Quo Warranto Pleas in
Wiltshire in 1281.

Again, hundreds change hands like lands. The Countess of
Devon in 1276 gave her hundreds of High Worth and Cricklade
to the infamous Adam de Stratton, who held them till his disgrace
in 1291. John and Clemence Lestrange were enfeoffed of the
hundreds of Launditch and South Greenhoe in Norfolk in 1295
by John Lestrange, who inherited it, through a series of ancestors,
from Durant le Strange, to whom Floald fitz Alan, the vassal of
William I, had granted it for a payment of six pounds a year to
the Fitz Alans and 48s. 6d. a year payable as farm to the sheriff at
Norwich Castle.[2] Barstable hundred in Essex, granted by
Henry I to the Fitzgerold family, descended to Margery Sutton,
who in 1242, with her second husband, conveyed it by fine to her
daughter Gundred and her husband William Giffard, who were
the holders in 1274. Before 1281, however, they had made it
over to their son, Robert Giffard, who in that year surrendered it
to the king, in the Exchequer, in the presence of his father and

[1] R.H., II, 30. [2] Ibid., I, 434, 436 ; Cal. Inq., IV, 208.

mother, together with the charters of Henry I and II, thus becoming quit both of the duties of lord of the hundred and of the obligation to pay the farm of twenty-five marks annually at the Exchequer.[1]

The application of the rule of equal partitioning amongst heiresses resulted sometimes in complicated divisions of hundredal rights.   William Marshal's first wife inherited Flitt hundred in Bedfordshire from her father Baldwin de Bethune to whom Richard I had given it.   On her death it was confirmed to William Marshal on his second marriage with Eleanor of England, on whose death in 1274 it passed to Isabel de Mohun, his great-niece.   When Isabel's granddaughter died childless the hundred was shared among various cousins, in 1329 it was being held by five coheirs in the proportions of one-quarter, one-quarter, one-quarter, one-eighth, and one-eighth.[2]

Such a situation forces upon one the question : What was the exact position of the lord of a hundred ?   Though such joint lordships were exceptional no one thought them extraordinary. In one county, Kent, we are told again and again that the lord-ship of a hundred was shared by two, three, or four lords. Twenty-three of the seventy Kentish hundreds have two lords, two have three lords, and two have four lords.   We have no reason to think that these hundreds, some of them very small indeed, had two or three bailiffs apiece ; in fact, we can be pretty sure that some of them were thrown together for adminis-trative purposes, like the seven hundreds of Windsor in Berkshire, which had three lords and one bailiff.   The division of lordship means division of the profits of the hundred, whatever they were, and some agreement about the appointment of a bailiff.   There is no doubt that a hundred was regarded primarily as a source of revenue rather than a source of political prestige or public authority.   The Kentish fractions of one-third and two-thirds that recur so frequently are in all probability simply the primitive third penny of the pleas, common to both Anglo-Saxon and Frankish law as the perquisites of the presiding official, in contrast to the two-thirds that went to the remoter authority.   In the

[1] *R.H.*, I, 154 ; *Pat. Roll. Cal.*, 453 (1281).   [2] *Plac. Quo War.*, p. 54.

majority of cases the lord of the hundred seems to be little more than a sleeping partner, drawing his share of the profits of government, but leaving his officials, as we shall see, very much under the orders of the sheriff in actual governmental work.

The revenue arising from a hundred, called its 'value' in Article 5 of the inquest of 1274, consisted of the profits of the hundred court, that is, the pleas or judicial payments and the perquisites or customary payments made every year at stated terms, and also called the 'assized rents' of the hundred, together with any other fiscal privileges granted by royal charter or ancient custom to the lord of the hundred. The inquests held by the escheator on the death of a tenant-in-chief often give more detailed accounts of the value of hundreds than do the returns of 1274–5. Alton hundred, in Hampshire, was worth in 1274 four pounds a year, which included sheriff's tourn, tithing-penny, and suit, as well as twenty shillings a year by the pleas and perquisites of the three-weekly court. The hundred of Blithing in Suffolk brought in £3 6s. 1d. from assized rents, £1 9s. 0½d. from view of frank-pledge, ten shillings toll, and twenty-nine shillings from the pleas of the court, together with that of Wangford hundred. The value of Framland wapentake, Leicestershire, in 1319, included the customary payments called Palefredselver or Beauver, Wakyngselver, Shirrefstoth, and Fraunkplegage. In 1272 the value of Paling hundred, Sussex, was £6 6s. 5d. per annum ; forty shillings from pleas and perquisites of the court, thirty shillings paid by the bailiff for his office, 56s. 5d. of 'common fine'. Such statements could be multiplied many times. Unless the lord had very great privileges a hundred was not as profitable as an estate, but the revenue it brought in was not to be despised.

The jurors were asked to report not only on the value of the hundreds and on their farms, but also on the raising of farms by the sheriff. The Suffolk jurors, for instance, estimate the value of the eight and a half hundreds of St. Edmund at seventy-two pounds, and they then state that the farms have been increased by recent abbots by over thirty pounds.[1] These cannot be farms

---

[1] *R.H.*, II, 151, 155.

payable by the lord of the hundred to the king ; those would never be raised by the tenant. Moreover, we know that the eight and a half hundreds were held without payment in frank-almoign. The farms which are raised by sheriffs in royal hundreds and by lords in private hundreds are the sums payable by the hundred bailiff for his office ; from the lord's point of view they go to make up the value of the hundred. Thus the jurors of Blofield hundred, Norfolk, report that William de St. Omer pays a farm of twelve pounds to the king and farms out the bailiwick—the office of hundred bailiff—for eighteen pounds.[1] A succession of Kentish sheriffs, between 1248 and 1272, have raised the farms of Bridge hundred by five marks in the aggregate.[2] William de Lisle, the villain of Matthew Paris's story, has raised the farm of Guilsborough hundred, Northamptonshire, year by year, from two pounds to five pounds.[3] What reason or pretext existed for these changes ?

The farm payable by a hundred bailiff to the sheriff or to his lord represented a rough estimate of the income that the bailiff hoped to make out of the incidental fees and profits arising out of the work he did in the hundred, less that margin which made it worth his while to take on the job. As a rule, though as we shall see shortly there were exceptions, the local government official did not draw a salary as does the policeman or postmaster of to-day. On the contrary, he paid so much a year for the office. Even to-day, in some small villages, the postmistress may want the position rather for the custom it may bring to her little shop than for the nominal salary attached. In the thirteenth century the hundred bailiff expected to make a profit on the farm he paid for his office, and it followed that if the farm were raised he would be more likely to extort irregular fees or bribes from those with whom he had dealings. Thus both sheriffs and lords of liberties are blamed by the jurors for inducing oppression, as to-day Whitehall is held responsible for the unprogressive policy of local government officials. William of Plumstead, they say, whom Robert of Tattershall has appointed bailiff of his hundred of Freebridge in Norfolk, extorts ' unlimited sums ' from the men

<hr />

[1] Ibid., I, 512.   [2] Ibid., I, 202.   [3] Ibid., II, 7.

of the hundred in order to cover the farm he pays for his office.[1] As we have seen, there is another side to the question. Undoubtedly some of the bailiff's perquisites arose as commissions on work done ; and if the business increased, and the bailiff had more to do, or had to employ assistants, the profits of the office might increase out of all proportion. In that case, the sheriff or the lord, as the case might be, was quite justified in raising the farm. It is also highly probable that the Exchequer might in fact be compelling the sheriff to raise farms of hundreds by the general policy of demanding and securing stricter administration which marked the reign of Henry III.

The profits, then, of government in the private hundred were shared in varying proportions between the officials, the lord of the hundred, and the king, except in those most highly privileged hundreds where the king had made over all the royal revenues to the lord of the hundred. But the methods and the responsibility of government was not left entirely to the lord, even in those great liberties. The framework of administration, the routine of government, was the same within liberties and without ; the writs served by whose soever bailiffs were the king's writs ; the business done at the six-monthly courts was the king's business ; the bailiffs, though the servants of bishop or magnate, were yet the king's bailiffs. In the typical private hundred the subordination of the hundred bailiff to the sheriff in administrative and fiscal matters, always tacitly assumed, is sometimes explicitly stated, as in an agreement between two ecclesiastical magnates in Devonshire. The hundred of Axminster had been granted in 1247 by Reginald Mohun to the local abbey of Newnham. The manor of Uplyme within this hundred was held by the Abbot of Glastonbury, who enjoyed return of writs and freedom from suit to shire and hundred in all his lands, by royal grant. In a charter of about 1250, witnessed by the sheriff of Devon, the Abbot of Newnham recognized the Abbot of Glastonbury's freedom from suit to Axminster hundred court, but he made the proviso that if the Glastonbury officials should fail to execute the king's commands, as passed on to them by the sheriff of Devon, and if the

1 R.H., I, 542.

PLATE V

BAILIFF OR BEDEL WITH ROD

sheriff should then complain to the Abbot of Newnham as lord of the hundred, then the hundred bailiff, ' as the sheriff's bailiff, not as our bailiff ', might enter the manor of Uplyme and demand execution of the king's writ.[1]

Whether the hundred were royal or private it was an integral part of the royal system of administration controlled by the sheriff.

II. The Bailiff's Appointment and Tenure of Office

' *Concerning sheriffs who have delivered hundreds or wapentakes to bailiffs who have been oppressive and extortionate.*'—c. 18.

The activities of the hundred bailiff are written large all over the returns of 1274–5, but there is little direct information as to the method of his appointment or the duration of his tenure of office. These must have varied widely, not merely as between royal and private hundreds, but as between east and west, north and south. In Lancashire, for instance, as in Somerset and Cornwall, we find hereditary hundred bailiffs; the office is attached to the tenure of a piece of land. In Somerset the bailiwick of Andersfield hundred is hereditary,[2] and it is the same in the hundreds of Brent, Barrow, Whitley, Bath, Bempston, Abdick, Winterstoke, and North Curry. All the wapentakes of Lancashire and all the hundreds of Cornwall have ' bailiffs of fee ', to use the medieval expression ; and there are instances in Devon (Cliston and Budleigh), Dorset (Beaminster), Wilts (Calne), Derbyshire (Appletree), Essex (Waltham), and Bedfordshire (Willey). Jocelin of Brakelond tells of a claim made to a hereditary bailiwick in Corsford hundred, Suffolk, which Abbot Samson refused to recognize, just as Henry III's justices later refused to allow the claim of the Longswords to a hereditary shrievalty in Wiltshire. The arrangement is almost certainly an archaic survival; in Cornwall the association of the office with a certain holding of land can be traced unbrokenly from Domesday to the eighteenth century. In a few Devonshire hundreds and in one Northants hundred the lord himself acted as bailiff. In Amounderness, Lancashire, on the other hand, the bailiff's

---

[1] Bodl. MS., Wood, 1, fo. 213d.   [2] Coram Rege R., 297 (Trin. Term), m. 1.

work became so heavy in the thirteenth century, with the clearing of the forests and the increase of population, that the hereditary serjeant farmed out the office to an official who was prepared to give his whole time to it.[1]

Where there was no such vested interest the appointment must have been matter for a special contract. A few such contracts may still be read. Among the copious records of St. Edmund's Abbey there are indentures between the abbot and the bailiffs of the seven hundreds, belonging to the early part of Henry VI's reign.[2] The bailiff agrees to pay a farm varying from £6 13s. 4d. in Risbridge hundred to thirty-five pounds in Blackbourne (a double hundred), and is given office for periods of one to five years. He undertakes to hold courts, keep rolls, levy fines and amercements of the king's courts and the Exchequer, and account for them at the Exchequer. Felons' goods and waifs and strays are excepted from his perquisites. He promises not to sublet his office. These indentures are late, but the form is probably traditional; also they concern private hundreds. Three thirteenth-century contracts between a sheriff of Essex and Herts and the bailiffs of royal hundreds in those counties may be seen in the Bodleian Library, dating from the year 1292. In these the bailiff enters into a bond to pay the sheriff the farm of the hundred at Colchester Castle (£5 6s. 8d. for the half-year for Chafford hundred, eleven pounds for Chelmsford), and to keep the hundred duly, serving the sheriff and the king faithfully, levying the king's debts and safeguarding his interests. Six guarantors, with the bailiff, append their seals.[3] Similar contracts are recorded on the rolls of the county of Cheshire for 1391 and later years concerning the hundred of Wirral, whose bailiffs undertake to pay ten pounds a year as the farm of that hundred.[4] Some legal security for the bailiff's honesty must have been necessary, and every appointment of a hundred bailiff probably entailed a sealed contract.

Besides this, however, the bailiff had to take a formal oath to

---

[1] Coram Rege R., 297 (Trin. Term), m. 1.   [2] B.M. Add. MS. 14848, ff. 43–4.
[3] Bodleian Charters, Essex 182, 189 ; Herts 7b. One is printed by Morant, *History of Essex*, I, 76, Note F.
[4] Stewart Brown, *Hundred of Wirral*, pp. 177·9.

execute the king's commands similar to that administered to the sheriff. Whether the hundred were royal or private its bailiff was the sworn bailiff, the *ballivus juratus*, and the oath was publicly taken. It may sometimes have been taken twice over : the rolls of Gresley hundred, Derbyshire, record how Walter de Scroweston was made bailiff on 5th June 1302 to exercise the office of hundredor, and to levy the lord's debts, and to answer for them faithfully, and took the oath there in the hundred court.[1] In Berkeley hundred, Gloucestershire, the hundred bailiff was elected annually in the hundred court down to 1900. Other records show that the bailiff had to take an oath to the sheriff, which was administered in the county court. In Worcestershire the bailiff of Oswaldslaw hundred delivered the letters patent of the Bishop of Worcester appointing him to the sheriff of Worcestershire before being sworn in in full county court.[2] There was a good practical reason for this publicity. A statute of 1315 laid it down that hundredors who executed the king's writs should be ' known and sworn in full county ',[3] the need for which regulation is brought out by one of the returns of 1275. A Wiltshire jury complains that certain free tenants of the hundred of Thornhill were summoned to an inquest at Salisbury Castle, twenty-five leagues away, the other side of the county. As the summons was delivered by a stranger who had not been sworn to the office they took the risk of ignoring it and were heavily amerced by the sheriff in consequence.[4] Thornhill was a royal hundred, but the same rule applied in private hundreds ; the Earl of Gloucester's bailiff of Hasilor hundred, Dorset, had to be sworn to the sheriff.[5] On the other hand, the jurors of Underditch hundred complain that the Bishop of Salisbury's bailiff of that hundred, who executes the king's writs there, does *not* take an oath to the sheriff, whereby justice is obstructed.[6] Another story from the Hundred Rolls illustrates the need of some distinctive mark of office. A ship had been wrecked off the coast of Lincolnshire, and the sailors, suspecting the natives of a desire to carry off the barrels of oil and wine which were

[1] Duchy of Lancaster Court Rolls, 43/484, m.3d. [2] *Monasticon*, I, 612.
[3] *Stat. Realm*, I, 175. [4] *R.H.*, II, 276.
[5] *Feudal Aids*, II, 23. [6] *R.H.*, II, 280.

strewing the sands, demanded ' who is the bailiff in these parts ? ' Whereupon William de Walton, ' for a joke ', said ' I am ', and at their request arrested a would-be thief and took security from him, only to be himself arrested when the real bailiff turned up in a state of righteous indignation and carried off to Lincoln, where he had to pay one hundred shillings to recover his liberty.[1]

Some idea of the ceremony of swearing-in may be got from the custumal of Fordwich, a seignorial borough, where it is said that the newly-appointed bailiff had to take an oath before the mayor and community to be faithful to the king and to his lord, the Abbot of St. Augustine's, and to exercise the office of bailiff faithfully and maintain its dignity, and the white rod was handed to him and the commonalty was exhorted to obey him.[2] This white rod, or staff, borne by the hundred bailiff, like other local government officials, served both as a badge of office and as a symbol of authority. In the pictures you may know a bailiff by his rod.[3] The bailiff of Ermington hundred, Devon, paid his annual farm of forty shillings to his lord for ' bearing the rod '.[4] In 1344 Richard Giffard, bailiff of the same hundred, came with his white staff to attach the Abbot of Buckfastleigh for encroaching on John Stonor's fishery, and the abbot took the staff away from him—an infringement of his dignity which led to a lawsuit.[5] It was contempt of the king to break an official's staff of office. Hardy's readers will recall how the two timid constables of Casterbridge who ' didn't want the folk to notice them as law-officers ' pushed their ' gover'ment staves ' up the water-pipe when the town was in an uproar over the Skimmington ride.

In the royal hundreds, where the bailiff was responsible to the sheriff, presumably the sheriff chose him. In the 358 private hundreds of 1274, where the hundred bailiff was responsible both to his lord and to the sheriff, though in many cases we can be pretty sure that his lord appointed him, this is not always certain. In Gloucestershire, for instance, in 1248, Adam Joye was hundred bailiff not only for the hundred of Pucklechurch,

---

[1] R.H., I, 268.

[2] Black Book of St. Augustine's, p. 152. See also bailiff's oath in Court Baron [S.S.], p. 77.

[3] See accompanying illustration, from MS. Royal 6 E. VI, fo. 194.

[4] Ministers' Accts., 827 33.   [5] Year Book, 20 Ed., III, I, 236–56.

held by the Bishop of Bath, but also for Langley hundred, held by Fulk fitzWarin ; Thornbury, held by the Earl of Gloucester ; and Grumbald's Ash, Agmead, and Swineshead, which were still in the king's hands.[1] Who had first nominated him for office ? Again, in Berkshire in 1268 the royal hundreds of Charlton, Bray, Cookham, Ripplesmere, and Beynherst shared their bailiff with the Bishop of Winchester's hundred of Wargrave and the Bishop of Salisbury's hundred of Sunning.[2] In such cases it seems the more probable that the lords of private hundreds accepted the sheriff's nominees. The jurors of 1274 speak of the sheriff of Norfolk as letting Earl Warenne's hundreds of Gallow and Brothercross to extortionate bailiffs.[3] That there was a risk of divided loyalties is suggested by the orders sent to the sheriff of Gloucester in 1287 not to employ as hundred bailiffs men who during their term of office were also stewards of seignorial liberties ; [4] and in the Gloucestershire eyre of 1287 it appears that the grouping of 1248 has been abandoned.

In the royal hundreds a sheriff often transferred his subordinates from one hundred to another, though by his official oath he was bound not to employ any man who had served under the sheriff of another shire. William Bowyer, bailiff of the rape of Lewes in 1275, had been bailiff of the rape of Pevensey in 1271. In Norfolk Thomas de Snitterton was bailiff in turn of Gallow and Brothercross, of Guiltcross and Shropham, and of Smethdon and Freebridge hundreds, whilst Geoffrey de Harpole was bailiff of nine hundreds between the years 1238 and 1274 and Andrew Wascelin of six in the period of 1236–44. In the six royal bailiwicks of Cambridgeshire, in the years 1259–99, there are excellent instances both of long tenure of office and of transfers from one bailiwick to another. One bailiff held the bailiwick of the Chesterton group of hundreds from 1261–99. Nicholas Orfyk, bailiff of Armingford hundred in 1274, was bailiff of Radfield and Cheveley from 1286–99. And so on with the other hundreds : periods of fourteen years' service in one bailiwick, followed by service in another, are quite normal. In Herefordshire, according to the Hundred Rolls, Roger Ive was bailiff of Webtree hundred,

---

[1] Ass. R., 274. [2] Ibid., 42. [3] *R.H.*, I, 453. [4] *Plac. Quo War.*, 265.

under six sheriffs, for something like twenty years.[1] Thomas of Wyketoft was appointed bailiff of Kirton wapentake by three successive sheriffs of Lincolnshire.[2] Men with this kind of record may fairly be considered professional local government officials.

How did a whole-time bailiff make his living? In a few exceptional cases he may have received a salary, instead of paying a farm to his employer. This was apparently regarded as the ideal method in the king's proclamation of 1258, which embodies the views of some at least in the baronial party: 'We will pay our bailiffs from our own resources,' Henry is made to say, ' so that they shall not have occasion to take anything from other people.'[3] This was not found practicable in the long run. The hundred bailiff was, in fact, expected to make his fair profit on the sum he paid by way of farm out of the work he did, whether by perquisites or by customary fees, varying according to the locality. In 1286 it was stated that the bedel of the three royal hundreds of Swanborough, Roborough, and Stodfold had nothing fixed belonging to his office except what the men of the hundred gave of their own free will, which amounted to twenty shillings a year,[4] which was what he paid for his office. In two of the Suffolk hundreds it is said that certain holdings contributed to the bailiff's farm,[5] and probably the Wiltshire contributions were made in the same way. In a few instances there is mention of a small holding of land that went with the office: a survival, it would seem, of the *reveland* of Domesday Book. The bailiff of Clavering hundred, Norfolk, had a rood of land in Wheatacre called Gildescote, which belonged to the bailiwick and was worth a penny a year.[6] In some of the northern counties the bailiff's right to exact hospitality, or *puture*, was of considerable value. A temporary hundred bailiff in Hampshire had twenty shillings a year ' for his robe ', and a bushel of wheat weekly; this is a salary.[7] One of the commonest complaints against the officials of the hundred was that they took men's sheaves in autumn. They appear to have claimed corn from the harvest-field as a

[1] *R.H.*, I, 187. [2] Ibid., I, 307.
[3] *Royal Letters* (R.S.), II, 130. See also Stubbs' *Charters*, p. 386.
[4] *Cal. Misc. Inq.*, No. 350. [5] *R.H.*, II, 147, 179.
[6] Ass. R., 562, m.5d. [7] *Fine R. Cal.*, 1356–68, p. 279.

perquisite, and as early as 1254 the justices in eyre were regularly inquiring into their abuse of this custom, together with the allied practice of holding scotales. It seems that the barley acquired by such high-handed means was brewed into ale which the villagers were then compelled to buy from the bailiffs at fancy prices : a form of compulsory revelry probably even more unpopular with the brewsters and alewives than with the rest of the village. The jurors of Stottesdon hundred, Salop, allege that all the bailiffs of Shropshire have been oppressing the people by taking their sheaves for the last twenty-five years.[1] A Hertfordshire bailiff made scotale and sold it to the men of his bailiwick for a penny a gallon when it was only worth a half penny,[2] whilst the bailiffs of Bath hundred refused to allow any one else in their bailiwick to sell ale so long as any of their scotale was left.[3] In Hinckford hundred, Essex, the price was twopence a gallon, and if any man failed to turn up at the bailiff's ' tavern ' he was expected to pay sixpence—for washing the dishes ! [4]

Other perquisites were in the nature of commissions on work done. The rent levied for the king in Wye hundred amounted to 14s. 3d., of which the bedel had threepence for his labour in collecting it.[5] The hundred bailiff of Whitley, Somerset, kept some of the beasts which he took as distresses.[6] In North Curry, Somerset, the hundred bailiff had fourpence for every prisoner in the ' Stockhouse ', a hundred penny from every man or boy ' entering the assize ', presumably at view of frank-pledge, and at Christmas two white loaves, as much ale as he liked while daylight lasted, a good dish of beef with mustard, a ' browis ' of chickens, a cheese, fire to cook his dinner, and two candles after dark.[7] A Yorkshire bailiff took fourpence for every distraint he made in levying the king's debts,[8] and when in 1320 the people of Kent petitioned parliament to be relieved of paying threehalfpence for every sixpence or eightpence they pay in green wax debts, the answer simply was : ' All bailiffs do this.' [9]

Moreover, in addition to the commission on doing the king's

---

[1] *R.H.*, II, 109.   [2] *Ass. R.* 323, m.49.   [3] *Ass. R.* 759, m.43d.
[4] *Ass. R.* 242, m.79.   [5] *Battle Custumals* (C.S.), pp. 124–5.
[6] *Bodl. MS.*, Wood 1, fo. 201.   [7] *H. M. C. Wells' MSS.* (1907), p. 332.
[8] *Cal. Misc. Inq.*, No. 501.   [9] *Rot. Parl.*, I, 377.

work, it is plain that the bailiff claimed his share of the fees paid by the folk of the hundred who needed his professional services, whether in serving writs, in taking distresses, or in summoning or attaching the neighbours whom they were suing. A large proportion of the livelihood of the bailiffs must have come from such fees, hardly distinguishable from modern tips. To increase these regular, recognized payments by applying pressure would be very easy ; the transition from tip to bribe is as natural as that from fee to tip, and no doubt the country-folk, like travellers to-day, made it more difficult for each other by offering larger and larger *douceurs* : ' To do my business first ' ; ' To strike my name off that list ' ; ' To back me up in the hundred court ' ; ' To let me have back my cows quickly ' ; ' To persuade the sheriff to allow me bail ' ; and so forth. Every hundred verdict will supply examples of the pretexts on which the hundred bailiffs took the pence and shillings of the villagers, and there must have been few who did not deserve the title of ' extortionate '. ' The wapentake of Kirton is worth ten pounds to the sheriff, but it is worth at least five pounds more to the under-bailiffs, which they get out of the men of the wapentake by their acts of extortion ; but if the tenants of the wapentake were justly treated, it would not be worth more than 13s. 4d.' [1] No doubt this is an exaggerated statement, but the feeling was general.

What was the social standing of the hundred bailiff ? It is not altogether easy to place him : as with the sheriff, reformers desired that he should be a solid and substantial person. Hundred bailiffs, it would seem, were drawn from the class from which lords chose their stewards, some being landholders and some clerks. Apart from their work we know little of them. They figure alongside other freemen as witnesses of transfers of land, the enfranchisement of villeins and so on. Occasionally, when a justice in eyre fines one it appears that he is ' poor ', and his fine is reduced or remitted ; this is recorded of William Leverer, who worked in Cambridgeshire for twenty-seven years under a long succession of sheriffs. Roger de Chaldeford, who was bailiff of Witham hundred, Essex, in 1272, and is mentioned fifteen times

[1] *R.H.*, I, 305.

in the Hundred Rolls, gave evidence in 1289 as to the age of Thomas Filiol: ' He knows that Thomas is over twenty-two years of age, because twenty-four years ago, when Roger was hundredor of Witham, he used to often go to the house of Thomas's father.' [1] Yet even here it seems highly probable that the visits to the older Filiol's house were official rather than social in character.

III. THE BAILIFF'S WORK AND HIS ASSISTANTS

The work of the hundred bailiff was almost entirely subordinate. He was largely occupied in carrying out the sheriff's orders. Nevertheless he had in most cases bought his office, he had in practice a pretty free hand in carrying out those orders, and in most districts he had a number of assistants to help in the work. As we have seen, the size of the hundreds varied greatly, but the normal hundred bailiff would certainly have from ten to twenty villages under him, and he might well have more, since the grouping of two or three hundreds together was very common. The eighteen royal hundreds of Buckinghamshire, for instance, were under six bailiffs ; the fourteen royal hundreds of Cambridgeshire also formed six bailiwicks ; and in Norfolk and Oxfordshire, to take only two counties, private hundreds went in pairs also. A list of bailiffs for the West Riding of Yorkshire in 1280 gives a chief bailiff for each pair of wapentakes, with a sub-bailiff under him for one of them.[2] Such lists usually name only the chief bailiff. The number of the staff of a hundred would thus vary according to its size. The Hundred Rolls mention besides the ' master bailiff ', clerks, bedels (a word used sometimes for the hundred bailiff himself), sub-bedels, serjeants, cacherels, or catchpolls, and sub-bailiffs. In Blackbourne hundred, Suffolk, for example, there is mention of John Margot, bedel of Hugh the hundred bailiff.[3] There are also summoners or messengers, who often are bound to carry writs and summons in the hundred as the service by which they hold their land, as in Blything hundred, Suffolk, where twelve acres in Stoneover are held by the service

[1] *Cal. Inq.*, II, 450.   [2] Ass. R. 1078, m.41.   [3] *R.H.*, II, 199.

of a halfpenny and of making summons and distraints at the command of the hundred bailiff.[1] Another tenant in the same hundred is bound to provide a house wherein thieves might be guarded.[2] Quite a number of odd jobs might be done by these tenants in petty serjeanty : one man might hold his land by the service of selling the beasts taken as distresses, another by the service of guarding and hanging thieves, another by collecting dues and making summons and attachments.[3] Though not appointed by the hundred bailiff they would take their orders from him. Such part-timers were especially frequent in the west. In Cheshire the summons to the hundred court were carried by messengers, who bore a special wooden ball which they passed on to the next messenger at the parish boundaries. In some instances the subordinate's functions were limited to one village, in some he moved at large in the hundred like the sheriff's bailiff errant in the shire.[4]

The number of the hundred bailiff's colleagues is not seldom a subject for complaint : the more there were of them the more had the men of the hundred to find for their upkeep. In Forehoe hundred, Norfolk, the whole community of the hundred complains to the king that whereas once there was one chief bailiff and his clerk (unmounted) and two cacherels, now, although a third of the hundred is under seignorial administration, the bailiff, his clerk, and a cacherel are all mounted, and there are three grooms and a cacherel on foot as well.[5] So in Bassetlaw, Notts, six serjeants on foot have been replaced by three riding bedels with two grooms and three bedels on foot, all of whom oppress the country-side grievously, taking hay in haytime and sheaves in autumn and oats at sowing time, thus raising twenty-three marks a year for the use of their master and his bailiff.[6] Here, as in Amounderness, an increase of population may afford a good excuse, but the villagers do not think so. In Holeford hundred, Gloucestershire, the jurors protest against the multitude of bailiffs—the chief bailiff, they say, has his sub-bailiff, and he again has others, and they beg for a remedy.[7] The same tale

[1] R·H., II, 147.   [2] Ibid., II, 147.
[3] Cal. Inq., II, 39 ; R.H., II, 169, 179.   [4] Ibid., II, 148, 198.
[5] Extract H.R., 4, m.3.   [6] R.H., II, 307.   [7] Ibid., I, 372.

comes from Tickhill, Yorkshire,[1] and from Salford in Lancashire,[2] and from Wormlow, Herefordshire.[3]

The country-side might protest against the increase of mounted sub-bailiffs, whose horses had to be kept at their expense, but it is only fair to the officials to recognize that the increase of the sheriff's work was bound to increase that of the hundredors also. The serving of writs and the collection of green wax debts, for instance, demanded not merely the bodily activity of messengers but also clerical skill. The system of checking receipts and endorsing returns enjoined from Westminster meant that the sheriff also expected formal replies to his mandates. The keeping of rolls of the hundred courts was usual ; lists of fines and amercements imposed in them had to be kept : and the rolls bear the marks of the pen that ticked off a name when the business was wound up.[4] The records of the sheriff's tourn might have to be produced for the coroners as well as for the sheriff. All this meant, in any good-sized hundred, heavy work and skilled work, and though some hundred bailiffs did their own clerical work, many had clerks, who are constantly mentioned in the Hundred Rolls. A local priest may frequently have acted. In 1286 the parson of Birlingham Church was sworn clerk of Pershore hundred, and was therefore reckoned a royal official by the judges who held the great inquiry of 1290.[5] Others, like the clerk of Babergh hundred,[6] and three others mentioned in the Suffolk hundred rolls, became hundred bailiffs at a later date. The offences they are charged with are connected with the levying of money ; one Essex hundred clerk got money from a villager by pretending that he had to contribute to the twentieth.[7] Simon Cubaud, the clerk of Blything hundred in Suffolk, is accused of taking bribes from a number of indicted persons ' to help them against the sheriff ' ; presumably either by altering the roll of indictments or by getting a jury packed for them.[8]

The rolls of courts and of debts, the sheriff's mandates, the tallies, and the money must have been stowed in some safe place.

[1] *R.H.*, I, 113.   [2] Ass. R., 436, m.1d.
[3] Ass. R., 300 c, m.25d.   [4] *See* Frontispiece.   [5] Ass. R., 541 A, m.31.
[6] William de Boxford (*R.H.*, II, 145), bailiff in 1286.
[7] *R.H.*, I, 145.   [8] Ibid., II, 149 ; cf. *R.H.*, I. 139

It is probable that many a hundred bailiff had his hundred office, whether in his own house or elsewhere, where his records could be kept and the stationary part of his work could be carried on. The only trace of such an office that I have found is on the rolls of Milton hundred in Kent. This large hundred had various peculiarities which differentiate it from other Kentish and other royal hundreds. The hundred court met here on Thursdays, but there are frequent references on the rolls of business done on intervening Saturdays at a place called the shop—*schopa de Middleton*.[1] On the eve of Passion Sunday 1290, for instance, twenty-four villagers from five of the vills of the hundred were ordered to appear there to serve on an inquest, bringing their seals with them to seal the verdict they should then give, as to the guilt of a man accused of stealing wool. The business to be done at the shop is generally the holding of an inquest; it is only recorded on the court roll because it arises out of some lawsuit or other judicial business; but it seems highly probable that the shop was in fact the hundred office and was used for many other purposes as well.

The cacherels and bedels appear mainly in what might be called field-work. In distraining beasts especially numbers would be needed, all the more if resistance were anticipated; the mere work of driving the cattle might be more than one man's job. In the long lawsuit between the Abbot of Burton and his villeins in 1280 the bailiffs of three wapentakes between them took 27 boars, 40 oxen, 50 cows, 506 sheep and 77 pigs as distresses.[2] Enough stories are told of 'rescues' of beasts to explain why the bailiff of Kinwardstone hundred thought it best to employ two bedels in distraining Matthew de Columbers.[3] It is mainly in connection with distraining, attaching criminals and making up juries that these underlings in the hundred are mentioned. Apart from those who were discharging serjeanties, they appear to have been appointed by, and responsible to, the hundred bailiff. There are few examples of insubordination recorded, but one Suffolk hundredor, who stands out in the jurors' returns as the only man for the last twenty-six years who

---

[1] Court Rolls, 181/74, mm. 4-7. [2] Burton Cartulary, fo. 88.
[3] R.H, II., 260.

has not paid a higher farm for Babergh hundred, sacked his under-bailiff for misconduct during his chief's illness.[1]

The duties of a hundredor are well summed up in an inquest of the year 1323 for one of the Lancashire wapentakes. They are defined as ' Making execution of the mandates of the king's courts by writs and summons, and of summons of the king's Exchequer by precept of the sheriff ; executing the judgements of the county court and of the wapentake ; executing summons, attachments, and distraints by command of the sheriff, and also executing the commands of the sheriff's tourns.'[2] The hundredor of North Curry, Somerset, had to receive and execute the king's writs in the hundred, and guard the prisoners in the ' stockhouse '.[3] His hundred belonged to the church of Wells, which had extensive liberties. Only in the Bury St. Edmunds indentures are any judicial duties specified ; they provide that the hundred bailiff is ' to hold hundreds, leets, and tourns, to certify inquests to the seneschal, to levy fines and amercements, to keep rolls, and to hear pleas of contracts between the value of 6s. 8d. and 39s. $11\frac{3}{4}d$.' Where one lord had many private hundreds the seneschal often held the hundred courts, but in the royal hundreds it was normally the duty of the hundredor, for it is stated as a remarkable fact in 1285 that in Bedfordshire the hundred bailiffs do *not* hold pleas in the hundreds.[4]

In the performance of his executive duties the hundred bailiff was almost entirely under the sheriff's orders. In the charges of misconduct brought against him in 1274–5 it is not uncommon to find the profits of oppression had been shared between sheriff, bailiff, and sub-bailiff. But in some matters it would seem the officials of the hundred retained more initiative than in others. Most of the charges of concealment of felonies, unjust accusation of innocent persons, and release of criminals seem to be laid at the sheriff's door, and, as we have seen, it rested with him to give or to refuse bail. But the attaching and distraining of parties was carried out by the subordinates, and before the prisoner reached the jail or the beast the pound, the bailiff's

---

[1] *R.H.*, II, 146. [2] *Lanc Inq.*, II, 160.
[3] *H.M.C. Rep on Wells* MSS. (1907), p. 332. [4] *R.H.*, I, 8 (Kirkby's Quest.)

discretionary powers had come into play. There are long lists of charges in hundred after hundred against bailiffs who attached men and let them go again in payment of half a mark, of his girdle and his axe, his gloves, his surcoat, and the like. It was the ' satellites ' of the sheriff who arrested Richard of Dodemonston by night, and led him about from wood to wood, with such threats that he paid them three marks to be taken to Bridgnorth Castle without being beheaded first,[1] but it was the bedels of Stottesden hundred who extorted money from the merchants of Bridgnorth on the king's highway before they allowed them to go freely on their way.[2] It was, above all, in taking distresses that the lesser official took his advantage. An Essex villager tried in vain to recover the horse by which he had been distrained ; it was too useful to the hundred bailiff, who rode it to death and then left it in the stables of a local squire.[3] On another occasion four horses were kept by the bailiff so long that their owner got no work from them all through the ploughing season. Another bailiff took a horse on a false pretext and used it for five days in carting his hay, and even after that it had to be redeemed by a payment of eighteenpence. A Suffolk landholder was distrained by all his beasts and chattels, simply to induce him to give up the title-deeds of a holding about which he was at law.[4] The charges against the hundred bailiffs of St. Edmunds under this heading are monotonous and interminable [5] : cows, horses, ploughs, clothes, corn, pots and pans, and household goods were all taken by way of unjust distresses '.

Another executive job where the hundred bailiff seems generally to have had a free hand was in the making up of juries. He may have had detailed instructions from the sheriff if a jury was to be packed, but as a rule he was free to include or to exempt any freeman, and he made large sums that way. The bailiffs of Pimhill hundred, Salop, systematically levied one shilling or sixpence on every township where they had to empanel a jury.[6] A Worcestershire bailiff made twenty shillings by letting off men from serving on one particular assize of Darrein Presentment.[7]

---

[1] *R.H.*, II, 89.   [2] Ibid.   [3] Ibid., I, 136.   [4] Ibid., II, 144.
[5] Ibid., II, 155-8.   [6] Ibid., II, 105.   [7] *R.H.*, II, 105.

The sub-bailiff of a Sussex hundred summoned four men to sit on an inquest at Horsham, which they attended, but the day of the inquest was that on which the county court sat, and whilst they were doing their duty at Horsham the sheriff was amercing them for not being at Chichester. Altogether they had to pay six shillings for not being in two places at once.[1] A freeman of Cambridgeshire complained to the commissioners that he was constantly being put on juries in different places on the same day.[2] The bailiff of Barstable hundred, Essex, took threepence from one man, fourpence from another, when he was making up panels, to let them off and put less clever people in their place.[3] The bailiff of Avelund wapentake, Lincolnshire, took two shillings from a deaf and dumb man that he might be free from serving on assizes.[4] Another Sussex bailiff summoned thirty men when he needed twelve for the jury, and made the other eighteen pay fivepence or sixpence a head for their exemption.[5] But the most vivid picture we have of the local bureaucrat enjoying the power of this function conferred comes not from the Hundred Rolls but from those of the eyre of Hertford four years later. ' John of Balham is convicted of having caused all the free tenants of Hatfield, to the number of eighty and more, to come before the king's justice at Waltham Cross to make a recognition in a certain assize, and when they were come he said to them, " Now you know what the bailiffs of the lord king can do ", and that was all he did.'[6]

The returns of 1274–5 amply justify the new rules laid down in 1285 for those who empanelled juries. ' Whereas sheriffs, hundredors, and bailiffs of liberties have been accustomed to put on juries men who are ailing, decrepit, permanently or temporarily incapable, and strangers to the county, or else to get together an unbridled multitude of jurors in order to obtain money from them to be let off, so that the rich escape and only poor men act ; henceforth not more than twenty-four men are to be summoned ; none over seventy years of age or being a chronic invalid is to be

[1] Ibid., II, 215.   [2] Cambs. H.R. (unprinted), No. 3, m.2.
[3] R.H., I, 138.   [4] Ibid., I, 257.   [5] Ibid., II, 215.
[6] Ass. R., 323, m. 47.

called upon, and only those worth twenty shillings in the shire or forty shillings outside it may serve.'[1]

The executive functions of the hundred bailiff shade off imperceptibly into his fiscal functions : when he is distraining and attaching, as often as not it is in connexion with the levying of the king's debts. It is here that his dependence upon the sheriff will be most frequently enforced. There must, of course, be a clear understanding as to what share of the money collected is the perquisite of the bailiff, and what he pays over to his chief ; as we have seen, the distribution varies widely, and the contracts differ from county to county and from hundred to hundred. As the intermediary between the sheriff and the villagers, the hundredor is liable to a double fire of abuse. A poet of Edward's reign draws a picture of the brutal and blustering master bailiff ' raving like a boar ', who comes in to collect the debt and carries off all the contents of a man's house by way of distress :

> Then there comes the bedel, a boastful tale to tell ;
>   ' Hand me out your money which is due by the green wax,
> Your name is written in my writ, and that you know full well ! '
>   More than ten times over have I to pay my tax.

> When the day of payment comes I have to sell my mare ;
>   So grievous is the green wax, it hardly can be thought ;
> The bedels they hunt us, as hounds hunt a hare,
>   For they escape unpunished, and we are always caught.[2]

He might well have been writing of Richard le Brun, bailiff of Dengie hundred, Essex, who came by night to the house of Parnel of Asheldham on the Monday after Martinmas 1271 with a band of followers, and said to Parnel's husband, ' Churl, where is your money ? Hand it over, or you shall die ! ' to which Parnel and her husband replied : ' We have no money.' So the bailiff and his men beat them, and bound them with cords till the blood ran, and carried off the whole of their household stores, which the jurors enumerate in detail, from the eleven ells of russet cloth worth tenpence an ell to the pig lying in pickle— linen sheets, tallow, cheese, butter, corn, pease, hides, carcasses,

---

[1] *Stat. Realm*, I, 89.
[2] ' Song of the Husbandman ', in Wright, *Pol. Songs* (C.S.), p. 151.

wax, and other small matters, to the total value of four pounds. The villagers of Dengie hundred were rightly indignant ; four different juries reported the outrage, backing up the widow's own complaint, which was enrolled on their verdict, for though three years had passed and her husband was dead, the goods had not been restored, though it had been proved that the king had no claim on them.[1]

The villagers had to complain not only that the bailiffs were violent and high-handed, but also that they were often compelled to make a payment twice over, once to the subordinate and once to the sheriff. On the other hand, the sheriff would assert at the Exchequer that he had not received the money from his subordinate, and the bailiff was had up before the barons for the matter to be settled there. In 1250, for instance, the Exchequer ordered up a jury from Rochford hundred to testify that sixty shillings in oats and in money was paid over to the hundred bailiff—part for scutage and part for the aid on marrying the king's eldest daughter Margaret.[2] A Devonshire bailiff who collected the amercements imposed by the justices in eyre had not given the debtors their receipts, so that the Exchequer was still issuing green wax summons against them.[3] Ten years later the Devonshire folk were still complaining of this practice of re-exaction of ' old estreats '.[4] The bailiff of a Wiltshire hundred was accused in 1275 of collecting ten shillings twice over from one village ; of levying twenty shillings from another which was amerced at ten shillings ; of collecting a fine imposed in the court of King's Bench which had already been paid once, but giving no receipt for it, so that it was collected a third time by a special collector, who also gave no receipt. The unfortunate litigant had finally to go in person to the Exchequer and pay it a fourth time before he could obtain the tally of quittance.[5] If a special official was appointed to collect the outstanding debts to the king in a county, or to levy some occasional tax or aid, he, like the sheriff, might issue commands to the hundred bailiffs which they would have to execute. Certainly, from the point of view of the Exchequer, the primary

---

[1] *R.H.*, I, 136–7, 142.   [2] Exchequer Inquisitions, E 143, 1/1.
[3] *R.H.*, I, 70.   [4] Ibid., I, 84 (Kirkby's Quest).   [5] Ibid., II, 256.

function of a hundred bailiff was to levy the moneys due to the king in his hundred.

These moneys, it will be remembered, included the ancient fixed customary charges on land as well as the new occasional impositions on persons. It was these customary rents, with the profits of the hundred court, which made up the 'value' of a hundred, whether to the king or to its private lord. In a royal hundred they went, as a rule, towards the farm of the shire paid in by the sheriff at the Exchequer. In many private hundreds the lord kept them, as, for example, in Hurstingstone hundred, Hunts, where the 'sheriff's aid, wardpenny, pontage, and wood hire', which were collected on the Abbot of Ramsey's manors by his hundred bailiff, were retained by the abbot as part of the regalian rights bestowed on him by a succession of royal charters. The aid once payable for the upkeep of the king's sheriff, and the commutations for the service of watch and ward and of bridge-building at the royal command, were now paid to the church, and whilst the crown thereby acquired merit the church thereby accepted responsibility, though the revenue probably suffered. The Abbot of Ramsey, however, paid a farm of eight pounds a year at the Exchequer for Hurstingstone hundred.[1] Where the most sweeping fiscal privileges had been granted to lords of private hundreds, as at Peterborough, Reading, or Bury St. Edmunds, even occasional revenue, like the amercements of the eyres, might be retained by them. Nor did these three abbots pay any farm at the Exchequer. In 1292 the only payments received at Westminster from the eight and a half hundreds of St. Edmund in Suffolk were those for deodands and treasure-trove ; a few payments for writs and juries ; and amercements paid by persons who were living within the abbot's hundreds but were not the abbot's tenants.[2] All the other 'royal dues' collected by the bailiffs, even the *murdrum* fine, stayed in Suffolk and went to the upkeep of the great Benedictine house at Bury and the government of West Suffolk.

Such extensive fiscal privileges were not, however, typical.

[1] *Monasticon*, II, 572.
[2] Harl. MS., 645, fo. 26b ; cf. Harl. MS., 1708, fo. 4d. (Reading).

The average bailiff of a private hundred had a double responsibility, accounting to his lord for some of his receipts and to the sheriff for others. Thomas Silvester, of whose adventures at Exeter Castle we have already heard, came ' to render his account at the King's Exchequer in the same castle ' for his tenure of office as bailiff of the lord king, of the Countess of Albemarle, and of Simon of Montacute in the hundred of Wonford.[1] Simon of Montacute held the chief manor of this hundred from the countess, and was bound to appoint a bailiff to collect the king's debts in the hundred, receiving the summons and estreats of the Exchequer from the sheriff, who did not enter the hundred himself unless the bailiff failed in his duty.[2] The hundred was worth five pounds a year to its lady in 1274–5, apart from those sums which the bailiff collected and paid over to the sheriff.[3] On the other hand, at a later date the bailiff of another Devonshire hundred protested that the sheriff was trying to make him collect part of a common amercement within the hundred, and account for it to him, contrary to custom. The bailiff complained to his lord, a Buckinghamshire squire, that ' that was never don hebeffore ' ; the machinery of the private hundred was being unfairly exploited to save the king's pocket. The end of the lawsuit which followed this dispute has not been traced.[4]

The Hundred Rolls illustrate copiously the extortion and oppression of the hundred bailiff, wringing money from the poor folk on every conceivable pretext. Of the forty-eight officials mentioned in the returns for Essex as being concerned in the collection of the king's debts, twenty are hundred bailiffs and fifteen more are subordinate officials of the hundred. Only seven belong to the county staff ; clearly the bulk of the royal revenue passed through the hands of the hundred officials. What happened to the money after they had paid it was often unknown to the country-side, though one Essex village alleged that the bailiffs kept back eightpence which they ought to have paid over to the sheriff in his tourn ; [5] in any case, they were more interested in the wrongs done to them than in frauds committed by the bailiffs

[1] *State Trials*, C.S., pp. 51–2.   [2] *R.H.*, I, 84 (Kirkby's Quest).
[3] Ibid., I, 86.   [4] *Stonor Letters* (C.S.), II, 106.   [5] *R.H.*, I, 147.

on the sheriff or on the king. To get some notion of this we have to leave the Hundred Rolls and look at the accounts of hundred bailiffs as enrolled on Exchequer records or as preserved among the archives of the lords of private hundreds. A great many of these survive. In some of the private hundreds of the west—those, for instance, of Winchester or of Glastonbury, where the same bailiffs looked after the manors and the hundreds of their lords—the estate accounts are confused with the government accounts. In the liberties of Bury St. Edmunds and of Ely the distinction is well marked. As a Bury register says: ' The seneschal's office is to keep the liberty that belongs to the crown and to execute the king's writs ; he is not to intermeddle with the manors except by the special command of the abbot.' [1] In the hundreds of East Meon and of Crondall, Hampshire, on the other hand, heriots and entry fines are entered along with the hundredal perquisites proper.[2] This, no doubt, is because the church of Winchester was landlord as well as ruler of every rood of land within the hundred : the hundred and manor were, in fact, conterminous.

Setting aside these manorialized hundreds a few typical accounts may be examined. The four and a half Chiltern hundreds in Oxfordshire (not to be confused with the three Chiltern hundreds of Parliamentary fame in Buckinghamshire), which were held in 1275 by the king's first cousin, Edmund of Cornwall, reverted to the crown on his death in 1300. Their accounts for the year 1309 are extant. The hundred bailiff accounts for the assized rents, namely hidage and warpenny (£6 9s. 3d.) ; for the cert-money paid at the view of frank-pledge in twenty-four villages (£3 7s.) ; for the profits of the three-weekly hundred courts (£9 16s. 7d.) ; and for the perquisites of the leets (£5 6s. 3d.) : a total of £25 1s. 1d. Another Oxfordshire hundred, that of Chadlington, produced £24 11s. 7¼d., which was made up by cert-money, ward-silver, hidage, the profits of the view, and the pleas and perquisites of the three-weekly courts. The fixed rents in this hundred remained unchanged from 1279 to 1327, and probably much longer.

[1] *Pinchbeck Register*, fo. 152.   [2] Baigent, *Crondal Records*, pp. 53–4, 142–8.

These accounts do not show what part, if any, of these receipts was paid over to the sheriff, and they do not record those collections of occasional royal debts which the hundred bailiff makes by the sheriff's command.   The sheriff's accounts for twenty hundreds of Dorset in the year 1258 give a more comprehensive view of the system.   From all twenty hundreds the sheriff receives certain fixed payments at his tourn ; in thirteen hundreds he has the perquisites of the tourn ; in the seven royal hundreds a due called St. Michael's gift is paid, and in two of them a due called austage ; and the perquisites of the hundred courts are paid in from the seven royal hundreds.   In those seven private hundreds where the sheriff did not hold his tourn the fixed rents must have been collected by the hundred bailiffs and paid over to him.[1]   A Norfolk account of 1237 shows the bailiffs of royal hundreds paying their farms to the sheriff, and the bailiffs of various other lords paying over to him the due known as sheriff's aid ; whilst from the highly privileged hundreds of the Bishop of Ely (Mitford) and the Abbot of Ramsey (Clackclose) no payment at all is recorded.[2]   The bailiff of the hundred of Wirral, Cheshire, accounts for waifs and strays ; for half the perquisites of the hundred court (he retains the other half) ; and for the farm which he owes.[3]   In Wilts, in 1265, the sheriff receives the perquisites of the courts of the twelve royal hundreds ; the profits of his tourn in twenty hundreds ; the tithing penny of eleven hundreds ; and sheriff's aid in eighteen hundreds.   These examples are enough to show that very little can be taken for granted with regard to the revenues of a hundred ; we cannot affirm under what headings they will be classified, who will levy them, or how they will be divided between the sheriff, the bailiff, and the lord of the hundred if it is not royal.   How often the sheriff had difficulties in getting in the king's revenue from the hundreds it is hard to say.   We do not often meet with a statement like that on the memoranda roll of the Exchequer for 1276, which shows that the sheriff of Northants was in arrears for the sums due from the private or, as they are called,

---

[1] L.T.R. Misc. R., 6/5.　　　　　　　　　　[2] Ibid., 5/67.
[3] Stewart Brown, *Hundred of Wirral*, p. 175.

the ' free ' hundreds of his shire.   The bailiffs of these hundreds were behind both in rents and fiscal payments and in the pleas and perquisites for 1272–4 ; if they were people of substance they were to be distrained to pay what is due, but if not, their lords were to be distrained.[1]   This mandate of the barons of the Exchequer brings out clearly the fiscal responsibility of the bailiff to the sheriff, who dealt with him directly, only referring to his lord when other means of coercion were inadequate.

It is characteristic of English institutions that the longest-lived element in hundredal organization should be the fiscal rights associated with the tenure of the hundred.   Long after the three-weekly court had become extinct over the great part of England the six-monthly sessions were held for the collection of the ancient customary dues and the cert-money.   The payments known as the customs of the hundred in Domesday Book, as the hundred pennies in the south-west, as hundred geld in the midlands, as hundred scot in East Anglia, and as hundred silver on the Welsh marches, and as ' assized rents ' almost everywhere, figure at considerable length in the Commonwealth survey of crown lands in 1651, and a few survived into the nineteenth century.   Hundred silver was a rent-charge paid in some of the villages of Dodingtree hundred in Worcestershire up to 1893, and ' wroth-silver ', once ward silver, is still paid to the lord of the hundred of Knightlow, Warwickshire, at Martinmas.[2]

The fiscal activities of the hundred bailiff brought him into close contact with most of the residents in his hundred ; on occasion into conflict.   Cases are on record of hundred bailiffs slain by those who resisted them in the exercise of their office ; [3] of hundred bailiffs imprisoned from three to eight days ; [4] whilst the Essex hundred rolls relate how one man was fined 10s. 8d. because he refused to say who had beaten a hundred bailiff.[5] But the bailiffs had not to go round the villages to collect all the money they levied : these were ' geldable at the hundred ' also, and it is to the hundred court that we must now turn.

---

[1] Mem. R.L.T.R., 49, m.9.   [2] See Plate IV
[3] *R.H.*, I, 79.   [4] Ibid., II, 311 ; cf. Ibid., II, 173.   [5] Ibid., I, 147.

IV. THE HUNDRED COURT AND THE VIEW OF FRANK-PLEDGE

Though the sheriff was ultimately responsible for the due holding of hundred courts, in practice most of the business concerned with these was in the bailiff's hands. A manual for holders of courts written about 1269 gives the form to be used by a seneschal directing the bailiff of a private hundred to summon, ' according to local custom ', those who owe suit to the hundred and those who have business there, so that all may be ready for prompt action on the day when the seneschal arrives.[1] But in some liberties the bailiff had a freer hand than this, and, in most royal hundreds, he would settle for himself the time and place for all the ordinary sessions of the court.

It is unlikely that formal summons were required for these ordinary sessions. The suitors were expected to come without a summons ; all that was necessary was that they should know the place and time. Parties to a suit had to be properly summoned ; for the two great or general hundreds proper notice had to be given in due form. The free tenants of Henbury hundred complained that they had only had two or three days' summons instead of eight, according to old custom, under the last two bailiffs of the hundred.[2] In the Bedfordshire Hundred Rolls a story of the villagers' refusal to carry the summons to the ' great court ', the date of which a seneschal wished to put before Michaelmas instead of after, to suit his convenience—' I am leaving the county, and I don't know when I shall be here again '—illustrates the tenacity with which the country-side clung to precedent, though it concerns a manorial court and not a hundred.[3] It also suggests, what is probably true, that the summons would be actually carried by men who held their land by that service,[4] like the Cheshire summoners who carried a pierced oaken ball fastened to an iron bar which was passed from hand to hand on the outskirts of each village, and so carried through the hundred. A special summons was also sent out when a writ of right was to be pleaded in a hundred or thieves were to be tried.

[1] *Court Baron* (S.S.), pp. 69–70.
[2] *R.H.*, I, 168.
[3] Ibid., I, 8.
[4] e.g. Ibid., II, 179, 147.

The ordinary hundred court was held every three weeks in the reign of Edward I. In the tenth century a month had been the legal interval, but more frequent sessions must have become common, in spite of Henry I's command to the sheriffs to keep the old custom and not to summon extra courts, for Henry III declared that in his grandfather's time hundreds and wapentakes had met every fortnight, and they were certainly doing so under John. In 1234 a decree was issued that henceforth, between the two tourns recognized by Magna Carta, the hundred courts were to meet every three weeks instead of fortnightly. ' These hundreds,' it adds, ' are not those two to which a general summons is issued. They need only be attended by plaintiffs and their opponents and by those suitors who hold the pleas and make the judgements, unless it should be necessary to hold an inquest into a man's death or treasure-trove or some other plea of the crown, when the four neighbouring vills must also come.' [1] Such was the law laid down by the Council in 1234 ; how far was it observed ?

The evidence is scanty for Henry III's reign. In 1226 the Bishop of Chichester's steward complains that the bishop's servants have to attend the Arundel hundred courts ' almost every week ' to defend the bishop's poor tenants ; this may be rhetorical.[2] Figures supplied to the Exchequer by various sheriffs in the years 1258–9 and 1264–5 show that eight courts in the year had been held in the royal hundreds of Somerset and Dorset, and some ten or eleven in the Wiltshire hundreds, instead of the seventeen which a three-weekly interval entails. At both these periods, however, the baronial control of the government may well have been upsetting the normal course of local government. In the reign of Edward himself we can look at the actual rolls of the courts.[3] In the Countess of Albemarle's hundred of High Worth, Wiltshire, the court met fourteen times a year in the period 1275–7, at intervals varying from a fortnight to forty-six days. This long gap occurred each year in the Christmas holidays. The countess's seneschal held the court on any day of the week

---

[1] Hennings, *England under Henry III*, pp. 192–3.
[2] *Royal Letters* (R.S.), II. 356.
[3] See Appendix V for list of Hundred Court Rolls extant.

but Sunday. The Abbot of Battle's hundred of Wye in Kent met fifteen times in the year 1284–5, on different days of the week, but roughly at three-weekly intervals, with vacations at Christmas and at harvest time. In the Abbot of Ramsey's hundred of Clackclose, Norfolk, in the same year, there were seventeen sessions, and the same is true of the Berkshire hundreds of Cookham and Bray, and the Abbess of Wilton's hundred of Chalk, which sat at three-weekly intervals with a short harvest vacation, on Wednesdays in the winter and on Thursdays in the summer. The royal hundred of Milton met seventeen times in the years 1289–91, always on Thursdays, except for the Hocktide court on a Monday. Three weeks was also the regular interval for the Derbyshire hundred of Appletree and the Cambridgeshire hundred of Wisbeach in the latter years of Edward's reign, for the Lancashire wapentakes of Lonsdale, Amounderness, and Salford under Edward II.

The general practice, then, seems to have accorded with the decree of 1234, but there is reason to think that a longer interval was common in the west country. According to the Hundred Rolls, the royal hundred of Shebbeare in Devon met every month [1]; in 1292, as in 1258, the sheriffs of Somerset and Dorset had only seven or eight courts to account for in the royal hundreds of Somerset and Dorset for nine months of the year, and in 1333 the hundred courts of Cornwall met once a month, whilst in Cogdean hundred, Dorset, there were only six courts in the year in Edward I's reign. In Sussex it is highly probable that courts were held as in the fifteenth century, when the three-weekly court was that of the lathe, and the hundred courts met only twice a year,[2] for the sessions that corresponded to the village view of frank-pledge in the eastern counties. A joint tourn for the whole rape or last was certainly held in the fourteenth century, and in 1335 it is stated the hundreds of the rape of Hastings meet only twice a year.

Custom prescribed not only the intervals but the sites of the hundred courts, and the complaints were bitter when the places

---

[1] *R.H.*, I, 78.
[2] C. Dawson, *Hastings Castle*, pp. 350 ff; B.M. Add. Rolls 31598, etc.

were altered. Bailiffs complained that they were not allowed
to hold the court in some particular spot, and the suitors complained that they were being expected to go to distant and inconvenient places. In 1202–3 there was a lively quarrel as to the
place where the hundred of Pershore should meet. Ever since
Domesday this hundred had been shared between the abbots of
Westminster and Pershore in the proportion of two-thirds and
one-third. It seems that the court had usually sat in the *atrium*
or churchyard of Pershore Abbey, and in 1202 the Abbot of
Westminster complained that the Abbot of Pershore had dispossessed him of his freehold by removing the seat of the hundred.
Apparently the fixture, whether house or benches, which had been
used by the bailiff had been removed, and a corpse had been buried
on the site. The Abbot of Pershore, while acknowledging the
other abbot's right to hold the court in the churchyard, disclaimed
responsibility for the funeral and put the blame on the bishop's
dean, who later excommunicated the bailiff, as the Abbot of
Westminster indignantly said, ' for holding the hundred in the
authorized, proper, and accustomed place '. The end of the
dispute is unknown.[1] A hundred years later the abbots of
Ramsey and Dereham were similarly wrangling as to where the
court of Clackclose hundred should be held. The Ramsey bailiff
was ' maliciously ' persisting in holding it at the park gates of
Dereham.[2] The rolls of the hundred court show that it was held
in thirteen different places in the hundred,[3] and the jurors of
1274–5 record the abbot's protest against those of his neighbours
who prevented his bailiffs from holding the hundred in their
villages.[4] There was a standing dispute, going back at least as
early as 1197, between the Clares and the Abbot of Bury St.
Edmunds as to whether the hundred court of Risbridge ought to
be held in the earl's manor of Hundon. Similar complaints of
magnates who obstruct the holding of the hundred court on their
lands come from the Norfolk hundreds of North Greenhoe, North
Erpingham, and Loddon, from the Berkshire hundred of Ock, and

---

[1] *Curia Regis Rolls*, II, 93, 248. Dr. G. G. Coulton has kindly directed me
to many other examples of the use of *atrium* for churchyard.
[2] *Chron. Ram.* (R. S.), pp. 394–5.
[3] Ault, *Court Rolls of Ramsey Abbey*, pp. 145–169.   [4] *R.H.*, I, 519.

from the Yorkshire hundred of Langbaurgh, where the angry gentleman forcibly ejected the king's bailiff.[1]

Complaints from the suitors are generally traceable to administrative adjustments. In 1274 the three Wiltshire hundreds of Stodfold, Swanborough, and Roborough were in process of being fused into the one modern hundred of Swan-borough, and the Stodfold suitors complained that they have to attend courts held three leagues outside their hundred, whilst the Swanborough suitors protested against having to go to courts in Stodfold hundred.[2] However justifiable, such changes were contrary to Magna Carta, unless the rule about ancient and customary sites was only applicable to the meetings of the tourn. Exactly the same thing was happening in Berkshire, where the suitors of Hildeslaw hundred objected to attending courts in Shrivenham hundred, which had almost completely absorbed its old partner.[3] The jurors of Aswardby wapentake in Lincolnshire complained that the court was ' cried ' in Lafford market too late in the day, and was held at out-of-the-way places at untimely hours so that in the last three years as much as one hundred shillings had been made out of the poor suitors' fines for non-attendance.[4] On the other hand, the manor of Morburn paid the bailiff of Normancross hundred a fee not to hold the hundred in Morburn, so that a court might be too near as well as too far.[5]

In the thirteenth century the hundred court often met in a village, and presumably under cover. The keeping of records necessitated a table and seats, and the suitors certainly had benches in some courts, though these might of course be in the open. It was probably the officials who desired cover ; the sheriff of Cambridgeshire expected the villagers of Stow to build a house for him to hold his tourn in.[6] But the old sites of the hundreds, on barrows and dikes, at fords and cross-roads and under trees, were still in use, and if the bailiff had a shelter it may well be that some had to stay outside. The common pasture called La Hore-thorn, which gave its name to Horethorne hundred in Somerset,

[1] *R.H.*, II, 172 ; I, 473, 496, 526, 541 ; I, 19 ; I, 128. [2] Ibid., II, 274, 275.
[3] Ibid., I, 15. [4] Ibid., I, 427.
[5] Crowland Acct. R., Ad. 34, m. 2 (Queens' Coll. MSS.). [6] Ass. R., 85.

was still in existence in 1263. The hundred of Cleyley in Northants met at Cleyley spring in Furtho parish. Another Northants hundred, Fawsley, used to be held at a thorn-tree in Newnham.[1] The hundred of Armingford met near the ford where the Ermine Street crossed the Rhee. The hundred of Cashio was held by the Abbot of St. Albans under the ash-tree in the monastery court when it was not held on Nomansland Common near the gallows place. The Bishop of Winchester's hundred of Waltham met at the Wolfpit in 1270 and long after. In 1278 the jurors of Edwinstree hundred, Herts, presented that the site of the hundred, a place called Edwinstree, was ' the king's place ', and was always held by the sheriff for the time being, who paid one penny for it at the Exchequer.[2] Wormelow Tump in Herefordshire, an open piece of rising ground where four roads meet, gives its name to the hundred that used to sit there. Knightlow Hill in Warwickshire, as we have seen, still is used once a year for the ceremony that represents the old hundred court, and the Hundred House at Great Witley which now stands at the meeting-place of the roads from Tenbury, Bromyard, Worcester and Stourport, is probably near the site of the tree which gave its name to Doddingtree hundred. Hill-tops, fords, cross-roads were marked out as inevitably for such 'moots as the market town is to-day for agricultural reunions.

How large was the attendance at these courts ? The decree of 1234 speaks of those who were bound to be present, to hold the pleas, and make the judgements. There is an abundance of evidence that well before 1272 the obligation of attendance at the three-weekly court, as at the county court, had been attached to specific holdings,[3] and that the tenants of these were the suitors or doomsmen who made up the irreducible minimum. In the wapentake districts a distinction is traceable between suitors and doomsmen. In Lonsdale wapentake, Lancashire, for instance there were sixteen or more suitors, but twelve was the standard number of doomsmen in Cheshire, Lancashire,[4] and very possibly Derby and Notts also. In 1292 ten doomsmen are mentioned by

---

[1] Ass. R., 614 B, m. 47d. [2] Ass. R., 323, m. 5.
[3] See, for instance, R.H., I, 250.
[4] Farrer, Lanc. Inq., III, 145 ff. ; E.H.R., XLI, 33-4.

name in the rolls of Appletree hundred, Derbyshire, and the hundred jurors of 1275 say that there are only twelve suitors to the wapentake of Thurgarton and Lye, but the extortionate bailiffs are compelling all the freemen of the wapentakes to come to the court or pay a fine.[1]   This reads like an attempt to extend into Notts the 'wapentake fine' mentioned constantly in the Yorkshire hundred rolls,[2] a well-established practice whereby a large number of persons commuted their duty of attendance for the greater part of the year for a lump sum payment, and attended only one county court, one riding court, and one wapentake court.[3]   Where commutation was regularly granted, the distinction between the doomsmen who gave the judgements from those who were only liable to be called up might harden.   In fact, the twelve doomsmen or lawmen are well-known features of the Danelaw districts of England, and elsewhere such specialization is not found.

Presumably every holder of a court had a list of the suitors who were bound to be present, both at the three-weekly courts and at the six-monthly 'great hundreds', but few such lists survive.   In 1252 twenty-one suits were owed to Hurstington hundred, Hunts—a large hundred.[4]   Probably the sixty-four sokemen belonging to Clackclose hundred when Edward the Confessor granted it to Ramsey [5] were the suitors to that hundred ; in 1282 it possessed at least thirty-six suitors, by the record of attendances or rather of excuses for non-attendance on its rolls. The entry ' So and so essoins himself of common suit ' supplies one absent suitor's name, but we can never tell if our list is complete.   In 1255 it is stated that nineteen suits are owed to the three-weekly sessions of Over, in Shropshire,[6] and that Seisdon hundred in Staffordshire had fifteen suitors to the three-weekly courts and twenty-five to the tourn.[7]   There were twelve suitors of Cashio hundred, Herts, in 1260, five of whom were represented by attorneys when the plea was held which was recorded on the rolls of the king's court.[8]   In Witchford hundred

---

[1] R.H., II, 312.   [2] Ibid., I, 108 ff., under de sectis.
[3] P.Q.W., 191, 196, 199 ; and see Kirkby's Quest in Surtees Soc. public., 49.
[4] Monasticon, II, 579.   [5] Hist. Ram., R.S., p. 160.
[6] R.H., I, 74.   [7] Will. Salt. Arch. Soc., VI, 110–7.   [8] C.R.R., 167, m. 15.

in the Isle of Ely the names of sixty-seven suitors are given in 1366–7 ; twenty-six of them paid down a lump sum to be quit of attendance for the year. In 1275–7 something like 270 names of persons owing suit are recorded on the rolls of High Worth hundred, Wilts. In the survey of St. Edmund's hundreds, held at the end of the twelfth century by Abbot Samson's orders, the double hundred of Blackbourne is said to have eighty-two suitors, the single hundred of Thedwastry sixty-one, whilst the largest number of suits owed from any one village is five.[1]

This Bury survey brings out very clearly the fact that the duty of attendance might be shared or exercised in turn by a number of men. In one case it describes six men as owing two suits ; in others all the sokemen take turns in discharging the obligation. In Kent the holdings from which suit is due are called hundred lands, and the returns of 1274–5 show that where they have been divided the responsibility is split.[2] The same tale is told repeatedly by the Suffolk jurors. In Risbridge hundred one man is said to have owed one-quarter of a suit, one one-sixth, and one one-eighth ; in Carlford hundred two-thirds of a suit is mentioned, in Blything one-half.[3] The subdivision of holdings which had to supply one suitor was producing much friction under Henry III and the baronial opposition secured, in the Provisions of October, 1259, that no extra suit should be demanded if such a division took place.[4] This clause, re-enacted in the Statutes of Marlborough, was being disobeyed in 1274 by the bailiffs of North Erpingham hundred in Norfolk, who were distraining all the holders of a divided tenement to come in person to the hundred court, and fining them for non-attendance, when only the eldest was bound to come.[5] In Gallow hundred, also in Norfolk, the jurors say that seventeen men are being compelled to attend the court where formerly only one owed suit.[6] The blame sometimes lay with the tenants ; it was up to them to come to a friendly agreement when the division of the land took place. The obvious plan was for one person to accept the personal obligation and the others to make proportionate

---

[1] Camb. Univ. Lib., Add. MS. 6006, ff. 81 et seq.
[2] *R.H.*, I, 221 ; cf. Ass. R., 362, m. 11.   [3] Ibid., II, 172, 188, 147 .
[4] Stubbs, *Charters*, p. 390 (2).   [5] *R.H.*, I, 498.   [6] Ibid., I, 455.

money contributions. In Hartismere hundred it is said that a certain holding in Oakley used to contribute 3½d. a year to make up a suit due to the hundred court.[1] But the chronicle of Peterborough mentions three tenants of the abbey who rendered three suits in place of one because they could never come to a family agreement [2] on the subject, and the story does not stand alone.

The figures given above indicate that the size of a hundred court varied greatly, quite apart from the geographical extent of the hundred. Twelve seems to be the minimum number of suitors, and seventy to eighty the maximum, if we except High Worth. The contrast it presents is so startling as to suggest that the names recorded are those of men discharging a suit by turns. In Suffolk, as we have seen, this was quite common in the twelfth century, and a Ramsey cartulary describes how it worked in a Cambridgeshire manor. ' The tenants of Chatteris paid suit to Witchford hundred and to the county court by two of the said tenants, and this in turn ; namely those who came to one shire and hundred on one day were then quit until all their neighbours had likewise in turn been to shire and hundred.' [3] This system may well have persisted longer in the West than in the eastern counties, where the division of the obligation had become so well marked by 1275. It is quite possible, then, that an ordinary session of High Worth hundred would be no more crowded than that of Clackclose or Thedwastry.

In reckoning up the numbers present we have to allow, however, not only for suitors but for litigants ; people who came on their own business and not because they were compelled to come. In the list which opens any record of a hundred court there are generally more essoins, or excuses for absence, from persons who have a case before the court than from those who owe suit. Allowing for these people, we should probably not be far wrong in visualizing an assembly of some forty or fifty persons at the three-weekly court of a hundred of the reign of Edward I which was neither very large nor very small ; and only the officials and the suitors would have to stay till the business was finished. The bailiff of Kiftsgate hundred, Gloucestershire, had a

---

[1] *R.H.*, II, 193. [2] *Chron. Petroburg* (C.S.), p. 154. [3] *Monasticon*, II, 578.

man amerced for not answering to his name when he had already left the hundred court and was a bowshot away.[1]

At the ' law hundred '—the general or great hundred of Michaelmas and Easter, when the sheriff appeared to hold his tourn—a much larger crowd was due to appear. Vinogradoff has shown that two kinds of obligation were recognized—the tenurial and the communal. The vill or township, as such, had to be represented by the reeve and four men—normally villeins—on certain occasions, and the great six-monthly courts were among them. A large number of agreements are recorded between the lord of a village and the lord of a hundred in which such an obligation is acknowledged ; for instance, for Crondall hundred (Hants), Tewkesbury hundred (Gloucestershire), Bullingdon hundred (Oxon), Portbury hundred (Somerset), Waltham hundred (Essex), for dates between 1220 and 1283. A typical agreement, of the date 1230, provides that all the Abbot of Glastonbury's men in Idmaston over the age of twelve shall attend the Martin-mas and Hockday courts of Alderbury hundred, Wilts, shepherds, ploughmen, and carters being excepted, and those who are in the abbot's mainpast (eating his bread), unless they have a plea in the hundred court.[2]

The ordinary hundred court might also be enlarged, or ' afforced ', as the expression went, to deal with cases of a particular sort, and very often an agreement about suit mentions these occasions. According to the jurors of Hoo hundred, Kent, ' Thomas Malemains used to come to the hundred court of Hoo to hear the king's writ and to help to give judgement of blood, life and limb, together with others of the hundred.'[3] The lord of Cocker hundred in Somerset releases the men of the Prior of Montacute from all obligation to attend his hundred, ' saving when the king's writ is to be pleaded in the hundred court, or robbers are to be hanged '. Similar agreements are extant for South Damerham hundred in Wilts, for Keynsham hundred, Somerset, for Whitchurch hundred, Dorset, and for Kingston hundred, Surrey, and it is always stipulated that for such special occasion a special summons, and a ' reasonable summons ', is

[1] *R.H.*, I, 174.   [2] Bodl. MS., Wood, I, fo. 100.   [3] *R.H.*, I, 220.

PLATE VI

THIEF HANGING

ASSAULT AND BATTERY

SERJEANT OR CLERK IN THE
EYRE OF NOTTINGHAM, 1280

necessary.   Such an occasion is recorded in the Bishop of Ely's hundred of Wisbeach on 10th June 1305 ; the king's writ of right is read, ordering the bishop at once to do right to one of his tenants, failing which the sheriff will have to take action ; and the order goes out that all free tenants are to be summoned to the next court for the hearing of the case.   In the second contingency, the judging of thieves, it was probably thought desirable that there should be as many responsible persons present as possible, so that the matter could be duly presented when the time came for recording the pleas of the crown in the tourn or in the county. It was certainly desirable to secure the presence of the coroner himself if the trial issued in an execution.   In 1200 a woman thief, caught with the stolen property on her, was drowned in the presence of the Kentish coroners ; in 1302, on the other hand, a man who was caught in Bodmin market with a stolen horse was condemned and hanged in a hastily assembled court without the coroner's presence, and although he had been caught red-handed and admitted the theft, the justices in eyre rebuked the court severely.   ' You went to judgement on a man who acknowledged that he was a felon without presentment by the coroner who can bear record, when your court is not a court of record, and this you cannot deny.' [1]

Two conflicting motives on the part of the crown were here at work.   This summary justice on the red-handed thief was, as Maitland says, ' ridding England of more malefactors than the king's court could hang '.   It was not desirable in the interests of order to forbid the local court, whether a seignorial court or a royal hundred, to deal with the criminal ' taken with the manner ', as Costard says in *Love's Labour's Lost*. The liberty of the gallows, like other liberties, might be made to serve the king's turn.   The jurors of 1275 complained that the Abbot of Glastonbury had been interfering to prevent the thieves condemned in Warminster hundred from being hanged on the gallows at Alkmere, ' where they ought of old custom to be hanged '.[2]   In Northumberland and Yorkshire old custom, probably of Danish origin, allowed the injured party to recover his stolen goods by the process of acting

---

[1] *Year Books* 30–31 E I [R.S.], p. 502.   [2] *R.H.*, II, 277.

himself as executioner of the court's judgement on the thief.
'So soon as anyone is taken with the mainour [the stolen pro-
perty] he shall straightway be beheaded, and he from whom the
goods were stolen may have his chattels as a reward for beheading
him.' [1] The king's judges would approve such conduct. But this
decollation had to be done in the presence of the king's bailiff, for
the hundred or wapentake or the baron's court was not a court of
record ; its rolls had no force in a royal court, and the oral witness
of the suitors needed a visit from the sheriff, armed with a writ of
recordari facias, to be transformed into legal evidence. Such
informal methods, if unchecked, would leave too wide an opening
for the loss of royal perquisites. The felon's goods which should
have figured on the sheriff's accounts at the Exchequer would be
quietly annexed by some one else, unless the king's coroner were
present to record the case and to note the value of the dead man's
property. When two hundreds were contending for the right to
hang a man, like Totnor and Felborough hundreds in Kent,[2]
it was because the archbishop would not, in the interests of his
church tamely surrender to the lords of Felborough hundred the
perquisites arising from the hanging of one of his tenants.

It is possible that where the hundred was still in the king's
hand the presence of the coroner was not required. The account
of the hanging of thieves in the royal hundreds of Aloesbridge and
Ham in 1279 makes no reference to the coroner, but speaks only
of the king's bailiff who holds the courts and of the king's gallows,
on which the thief should be hanged when the hundred has
judged him.[3] But the lords of private hundreds took risks if
they drowned, hanged, or beheaded the red-handed criminal
without an official witness. In some hundreds the problem was
simplified by the possession of a private coroner ; Lifton in
Devon, Holderness in Yorkshire, Rochford and Waltham in
Essex had their own coroners.[4] So had the city of Salisbury,
where John Down was appealed before them by a weaver of the
city for having on his person ' two coverlets worth 6s. 8d., two
sheets worth two shillings, a hanging worth eightpence, a towel

---

[1] Pollock and Maitland, II, 496.   [2] *R.H.*, I, 210 ; cf. *Monasticon*, II, 81-3.
[3] *P.Q.W.*, 341-2.   [4] *R.H.*, I, 75, 109 ; Ass. R., 233.

worth sixpence, a thread covering worth sixpence, and a blanket worth sixpence, stolen from him two days before '. So he was hanged, as the coroners' roll is there to testify to-day.[1]

In considering the size of a hundred court we have been led to discuss its business. Apart from these occasional demands upon them, what kind of cases would chiefly occupy the suitors or doomsmen ? There is no doubt that the judicial importance of the hundred court was on the wane, that it had less to do under Edward I than it had had under Henry II, and that it would have still less to do under Edward III. All the same, it had plenty of work to do, some of it interesting work, for a good while after 1275.[2] Men could still be appealed of theft or murder in the hundred, though as a rule the sheriff and coroners would come by royal command to make a record of the charge and so transfer the case to a higher court. But to make that record the co-operation of the suitors was indispensable, for they had witnessed the appeal. An appeal of murder made in an Oxfordshire hundred in 1226 and thus transferred is noted by Bracton.[3] The Kentish Hundred Rolls mention a bailiff of Barclay hundred who caused a man to be appealed in his court of the theft of a pig.[4] The greater liberties were the most tenacious of such pleas ; as late as 1235 Bracton notes that a duel was waged in Clackclose hundred between an approver and the man he had appealed of theft, but such a duel had long been held irregular and the hundred was amerced because such an appeal ought to be judged before a royal justice.[5] Nevertheless five years later the Prior of Ely was still claiming to hear and to terminate appeals, whether by the duel or otherwise, in his Suffolk hundred of Thredling,[6] and the Abbot of St. Albans maintained his right to have duels fought in his hundred of Cashio.[7] On the other hand, a duel might be the outcome of a writ of right, and a duel to settle a plea of land could be lawfully waged in a hundred as late as 1290.

In the twelfth century cases concerning land had frequently

---

[1] *Select Coroners' Rolls* (S.S.), p. 107.
[2] Thirty cases or more were determined at each three-weekly court at Berkeley Hundred at the end of the sixteenth century. *Berkeley* MSS., III, 16.
[3] *Bracton's Notebook*, case 1711.   [4] *R.H.*, I, 114.
[5] *Bracton's Notebook*, case 1159.   [6] Ass. R., 818, m. 49.
[7] *Curia Regis R.*, II, 56.

been settled in a hundred court, even without a writ of right. By the thirteenth century much fewer cases would be heard there without a writ. Where lords of private hundreds had the return of writs we see clearly how exceptional are their privileges. In the Ely hundreds of Norfolk and Suffolk, according to a record of 1226, the sheriffs sent on to the bishop's bailiffs the king's writs, and they held in those hundreds the pleas which the sheriffs held by writ in the county court.[1] In Worcestershire the sheriff recognized in 1258 that the bishop's bailiffs could hold in his hundred of Oswaldslaw the pleas which the sheriff held in the county court, and only if they failed in their duty would the plea come to the county court.[2] Denise of Wyrmdale, it seems, was fully justified in protesting against the false judgement of Milton hundred, which had dispossessed her of her dower without a royal writ by an irregular inquest.[3] Incidental processes arising out of a lawsuit concerning land, like the holding of inquests or the viewing of boundaries, might be held in a hundred court it is true, and royal grants or private transfers of land might be published there. Amongst the profits of royal hundred courts in 1236 are noted fees for such transactions, and in 1271 the hundred bailiff of Hemlingford hundred, Warwickshire, puts his seal to certain charters which Osbert of Clinton has published in the hundred court. Again, men do fealty for their land in the hundred court or are formally enfeoffed with it there. All this is in the old tradition, but when it comes to actual litigation over freehold nothing can be done in the hundred without the king's writ of right.

On the other hand, claims for services arising out of land tenure may be heard in the hundred court, and are recorded on the rolls of Appletree and Milton hundreds. One such case that came up in Wisbeach hundred in 1302 has a special interest. A landlord was claiming homage, fealty and rent from his tenant Roger Baker, and had begun in the regular way by distraining his beasts. The holding had recently been transferred and Roger was apparently ignorant of the changes made in the law by the

---

[1] *Monasticon*, I, 489 ; cf. *R.H.*, I, 479.
[2] *Monasticon*, I, 611.
[3] Ass. R., 362, m. 6.

statute of *Quia Emptores*. ' Why should I pay homage and fealty to John Aleyn,' he protests, ' when he himself alleges that the land was held of him by another man ? Does he expect to get the services twice over ? ' But by the new law the intermediary tenant had dropped out as soon as he made over the land to Roger, and John Aleyn was in his rights in applying direct to Roger for the sixpence rent and the other services owed from the holding.[1] A similar plea in Mitford hundred in 1311 was taken to the king's courts.[2]

The ordinary business of the three-weekly hundred court is summarized in 1234 as consisting of pleas of battery and brawls that do not amount to felony, of the wounding and maiming of beasts, and of debts that can be collected without a royal writ.[3] This summary is confirmed by the surviving records of thirteenth-century hundred courts, whether court rolls or lists of profits.[4] A simple case of battery is that of John Thresher, attacked and beaten by three men in Rushmore wood on St. Lawrence's Day 1284. They acknowledge their deed and offer 6s. 8d. as damages, and the hundred court of Chalk amerces them at eightpence for their trespass against the king. Trespass is the plea that recurs most frequently ; it was a legal form that had developed very rapidly since 1234 and was freely used in complaints not only of battery but of all kinds of violence. Thus in Appletree hundred in 1303 Walter son of Robert complains that Nigel de Bures came with four horses and other beasts to the common pasture called La Haye in Bearwardcote and depastured and destroyed it so that Walter suffered twenty shillings damage. In Milton hundred, in 1290, Robert Kite charges Stephen Winter with trespass and *hamsoken*, for coming into his garden at Eaststreet on the first Saturday in August, and breaking down his walls and hedges there, picking and carrying off his roses, and doing other outrageous things against the peace. It is a trespass when a fishmonger sells a whiting, price one penny, to Andrina Smith of Milton and then sells the same fish to Alice Barber and sends

---

[1] Wisbeach Hundred Court Rolls, Ely Diocesan Registry.
[2] *Year Book*, 5 Ed. II (S.S.), p. 87.   [3] *Bracton's Notebook*, case 1110.
[4] See frontispiece for roll of Milton Hundred Court ; for representation of battery, see Plate VI.

Andrina a worse fish. In Clackclose hundred, in July 1284, John Malkin charges Maud atte Hythe and her son Edmund with beating his pig till it had eight wounds, and egging on the dogs till they bit off the pig's tail; and Robert Steward charges two of his neighbours with carrying off his hay, by force of arms and against the peace. The most remarkable plea of trespass is that of John, son of Gerard, in Wisbeach hundred. He had entrusted a valuable bitch—a *licista*, or cross between a wolf and a hound— to a neighbour of his at Tydd, and this Thomas, ' contrary to the custom of the country ', had, he alleges, failed to shut her up in the breeding season so that her progeny were hopeless mongrels.

After trespass the commonest pleas are those of debt. There is less variety in these ; under the statute issued at Gloucester in 1278 only sums below forty shillings could be claimed in the local courts, with the result that debts of 39s. 11½d. recur in the rolls with monotonous regularity. But it is these monotonous cases that account for the survival of the three-weekly court into the fifteenth century ; for many it must have served the purpose that county courts serve to-day, and it was a place where debts were put on record as well as exacted.

Detention of chattels is another heading under which cases are recorded, very often cases of breach of contract. A defendant is accused of withholding from the plaintiff twelve shillings rent due for two acres of land leased from Easter to Michaelmas. Another is withholding 38s. 7d., the balance due on the purchase of sixty-three sheep sold for 105s. 3d. In another case oats bought in advance have not been delivered ; the response is that the plaintiff failed to produce the money on the day appointed. The executor of a will refuses to pay over two marks to the lessees of the lands he is administering. A lady claims a missal worth twenty shillings, a manual worth 6s. 8d., and two rolls of songs worth sixpence and twopence respectively which were snatched from her on the king's highway between Boughton and her home at Wereham on Easter Day 1282. The court gives judgement that the books be returned to her and that she receive twenty shillings as damages. Agnes Carpenter accuses Avice Young of keeping a brass pot worth six shillings, a towel worth eightpence, and a dish worth one shilling, which had been pawned with her for two shillings in December 1286. The sequel is interesting; the court orders Avice to 'make her law', that is, to clear herself by an oath in the old form, and because in the middle of her oath she took her left hand off the book and put her right hand on it instead she loses her case. The archaic technicalities which have been ousted from the king's court by the jury of trial are still in force in the old local courts.

A sea-captain of Dunwich in June 1290 brings a plea against some men of Milton hundred who having agreed to purchase his ship's cargo failed to pay the price on the set day, so that by this delay and the low tide the ship was held up and twenty-men lay idle, to their great loss. Closely allied to such bargain-breaking are cases such as that brought in Wisbeach hundred by Richard Baker against Thomas Fisher for seducing from his service a man who had agreed to work for him from Michaelmas 1304 to Easter 1305, by which Richard had lost half a mark. Such cases are sometimes called pleas of convention; the agreements enforced were, however, almost certainly unwritten. Like the borough court, the court of the hundred was discharging a most useful function in registering the verbal contracts of small folk, in enforcing them by the infliction of penalties for their breach, and in furthering the loveday, or agreement out of court, by which such a dispute was often ended. In this respect they had the advantage over the king's courts. There was another matter in which the local courts gave a remedy where the king's courts gave none—in slander suits. In Wisbeach hundred court in 1306 Walter Tolmer asserted that John Nunne had maliciously defamed him before the justices of Trailbaston at Ely so that he had been forced to appear before them and had lost a horse in going and returning; whilst another man complained that he had lost a bargain because one of his neighbours called him a 'false man', and a third that he had been accused of speaking ill of the bailiff.

Such are the matters on which the suitors of the hundred court had to give judgement, and the rolls make it clear that their co-operation was real and not merely nominal. Those who are familiar with the rolls of other courts may, however, ask at this point what need there was for a hundred court, since many seignorial courts could deal with practically every kind of plea described above.   It was unusual for every resident in a hundred to be a tenant of the lord of the hundred, whether king or subject, and a very large proportion of the freeholders in any given hundred must have been tenants of a lord whose court was competent to deal with such pleas as were heard in the hundred. Moreover, the records of such courts show that the lords clung to such jurisdiction, and objected to their tenants seeking for justice in the hundred court.   It is possible that tenants sometimes wilfully sought the hundred rather than their lord's court, but there were cases where they had no choice.   If two litigants in a hundred were men of two different lords neither would consent to appear in the court of a strange lord ; the hundred court would have to be the tribunal for all such disputes, just as, by Henry I's decree, the men of two different lords in one shire were to seek justice in the shire court.[1]

Criminal and civil jurisdiction was not the only function of the three-weekly hundred court.   In some hundreds inquiries were held every three weeks into the keeping of the assizes of bread and ale and measures ; in some presentments were made by the tithing men of the villages.   The hundred bailiff might be sworn in there.   Letters of attorney were read there, by which a man appointed a standing proxy for himself as suitor, a privilege secured under the statute of Merton.   Various transactions requiring publicity took place there ; the transfer of lands by the witness of the hundred, as in old days ; the proclamation of royal letters or statutes, like, for instance, the second Statutes of Westminster with their rules for sheriffs and bailiffs, or of orders for the keeping of watch and ward.[2]   On occasion the sheriff or the coroners held inquests there into matters on which the king required information, or the sheriff might come to make a record for the royal courts.   On 30th July 1303 Appletree hundred refused to make such a record because the sheriff had sent a clerk instead of coming himself.

[1] Stubbs, *Charters*, p. 122.   [2] See frontispiece.

The way in which business was conducted varied locally. In the royal hundreds the bailiff normally presided, as the Hundred Rolls indicate;[1] in private hundreds it was sometimes the bailiff and sometimes the seneschal of the lord who held the court. The bailiff was bound to be present in any case; in cases of assault the wounds had to be shown to him, he had to certify that litigants had been summoned and pledges given, and he sometimes acted as a pledge himself. At Appletree a suitor is charged with giving the bailiff the lie in the presence of the seneschal and the hundred. In Wye hundred, in 1275, the seneschal and his underlings take turns in holding the courts. Proceedings begin with the calling of suitors' names and the presentation of essoins or excuses for absentees. Then comes the regular business: appeals, pleadings, wagers of law, recognitions of debts, reports that a case has been settled out of court, requests for leave to make such a settlement. The clerk is steadily noting down judgements and commands; this man is to be distrained to appear at the next court; this one is amerced; an inquest is to be summoned; so much is to be paid for having the aid of the court.[2] Two or three members of the court are selected to assess or 'affeer' the amount to be paid by all who have been amerced, so that the rule in Magna Carta about reasonable amercements may be observed. In Burntree hundred, Gloucestershire, the jurors complain that there are no affeerors, but that men are amerced at the will of the hundred bailiff.[3] In the Ely hundreds the affeerors seem also to have collected the money, acting under the hundred bailiff.

Whoever held the three-weekly courts of the hundred, its Michaelmas and Easter sessions, called the sheriff's tourns, were not held by the hundred bailiff. On the other hand, as we have seen, he had preliminary work to do in connexion with the tourn. The Essex hundred rolls, to go no farther, make it clear that the bailiffs held the views of frank-pledge which preceded the sheriff's tourn. We have seen that there is reason to believe that these were held in the different villages of the hundred, and not all at one place. The old lists would be produced and checked up, the

---

[1] e.g. *R.H.*, I, 202–5   [2] See frontispiece.   [3] *R.H.*, I, 169.

names of dead men crossed out and the new members sworn in. The twelve-year-old put his hand upon the book and repeated, ' I will be a lawful man and bear loyalty to our lord the king and his heirs, and to my lord and his heirs, and I will be justiciable to my chief tithing man, so help me God and the saints.' At the same time he swore neither to be a thief nor a helper of thieves and was thus sworn in to the duty of keeping the peace ; he then kissed the book and paid his penny and was enrolled on the tithing lists. New tithing men were, if necessary, appointed or elected ; and it is possible that they made preliminary reports or presentments for their villages, both of breaches of the assize of bread and ale and of more serious offences. They also paid a penny for each member of their tithing, and this head money was what made the view a profitable privilege for a private holder. For, as we have seen, the view was not held by the hundred bailiff in every village ; in many villages he merely attended whilst it was held by a seignorial bailiff, collected a fee or took notes of presentments, whilst from other vills he was excluded altogether. There is a good account of the procedure followed in a Norfolk village in 1281 : ' The view of frank-pledge in Banham ought to be held by the lord's bailiff, the king's bailiff (of the hundred of Guiltcross) being present, and taking no payment, but hearing the secret presentments. All fines for breaking the assize of bread and ale or of measures or other things belonging to the articles of the view shall go to the lord of the hundred. Thieves taken with the mainour shall be judged in the presence of the king's bailiff, and all other persons indicted (at the view) shall be delivered by the lord's bailiff to the king's bailiff and taken to Norwich prison by the lord's homagers.' [1]

No doubt there was an infinite variety of relationships between private views and the tourn, but the part played by the hundred bailiff is fairly clear. He had to collect the information required by the sheriff and be able to give satisfactory answers to the question ' Are the tithings all full ? ' He could also, almost certainly, bring reports of presentments from the vills to be recorded or represented in the tourn. His preliminary work must

[1] *Norfolk Archaeology*, XIV, 33.

have been indispensable in saving time and trouble at the tourns, and his importance is duly reflected in the Hundred Rolls, where he is accused of fining men for default, for being out of frank-pledge, for making wrong presentments, and for resisting the holding of the view in their houses; and above all of exacting more than the due amount of cert-money and of head money.[1]

In those private hundreds where the sheriff was not admitted to hold his tourn the lord might hold a similar court twice a year for the hundred himself, or he might, if his tenure were sufficiently ancient, split up the work of the tourn into a number of separate lawdays for his different manors. The rolls of Clackclose hundred show that though the Michaelmas and Easter courts were held in obedience to Magna Carta at the old site which gave its name to the hundred, no special business was done at those two dates; [2] the business of the leet or tourn was done in the separate manors of the hundred, either by the lord of the hundred, or by the lord of the manor if sufficiently privileged. On the other hand, the *law court* held in the manor of Wye did not render unnecessary the holding of the *law hundred* of Wye in the same week; the Bishop of Wells held 'his lawful tourn' in Winterstoke hundred, Somerset, in which the presentments of the tithing men of the separate villages were duly checked by the sworn body of freemen, and the Abbot of Malmesbury appears to have held both lawdays in the villages and tourns in the hundred of Malmesbury. No safe generalization can be made about the tourn in private hands. Sussex also has its own peculiarities; the three-weekly court was held for the whole rape, and at Easter and Michaelmas a law hundred was held in each hundred by the lord of the hundred if it was private, by the sheriff if it was royal, followed by a sheriff's tourn for the whole rape. As to the riding courts of Lincolnshire and Yorkshire, there were certainly 'great courts' there also; but at present little is known of their rules and customs.

---

[1] *R.H.*, I, 136, 146, 147 ; cf. Ass. R., 242, m. 89.
[2] Ault, *Court Rolls of Ramsey Abbey*, p. xliv.

V. The Hundred as a Police and Military Unit

The hundred bailiff's duties of arresting and detaining the accused and of preparing criminal business for the hundred court would to-day be classed as police functions, but the police organization of the hundred was not in his control. It was, in fact, barely distinguishable from the military organization of the hundred ; one official, the high constable, was responsible for both, and he was not responsible to the hundred bailiff nor, as a rule, to the sheriff. The keeping of the king's peace had an organization of its own, though within the familiar framework of vill, hundred, and shire. This partly explains why the returns of 1274–5, apart from information on the upkeep of castles, the conduct of their keepers, and the provision of military supplies by the sheriff, throw little light on military organization. In so far as the king depended on feudal machinery for his forces, the hundred was not at all, and the shire very little concerned, but on those occasions when military demands were made on the subject, not on the tenant, the communal obligation was enforced by communal means.

At least since 1181, when Henry II had prescribed in the Assize of Arms the weapons that ' the community of freemen ' ought to bear,[1] there had been some provision for periodic inspection of the equipment and personnel of the forces of the shire. These freemen, with or without the quilted tunics and iron head-pieces prescribed by the assize, formed the body on whom the king had to depend no less for keeping the peace than for the defence of the realm. Hubert Walter, Richard I's right-hand man, had laid down rules for the swearing-in of all persons over the age of fifteen for the keeping of the peace and the assistance of the sheriff to the utmost of their power—*pro posse suo*—and the body of men thus sworn in under the supervision of specially appointed knights came to be known as the *posse comitatus*.[2] John kept up the system of inspection of arms and carried the organization further ; in 1204–5, on the pretext of a threatened French invasion, he ordered the universal administra-

[1] Stubbs, *Charters*, p. 183. [2] Ibid., p. 257–8.

tion of the oath of fealty to those over twelve years of age, for
the common defence of the realm and for the keeping of the peace,
and provided that in every county chief constables should supervise the armed forces of the shire, and below them a constable in
every hundred and a constable in every town, each being responsible for leading the forces of his own district.   The head constable
of the shire was to be responsible for keeping lists of the constables
of the hundreds and also of the men sworn to arms in each
district.[1]

The invasion of 1205 was a false alarm ; but the regulations
for that year give the broad outline of the methods whereby the
national levy was organized and supervised throughout the
thirteenth century, down to the time when it was overhauled by
Edward I.   Henry III confirmed John's arrangements in 1230,
and in 1242, during his absence in France,[2] the scale of require-
ments was revised by his minister, the Archbishop of York,
villeins as well as freemen being definitely included among the
armed forces of the shire.   To the chief constable of each hundred
was now added one or two constables in each village, who were
to be responsible for assembling the sworn men for the inspection
or ' view of arms ' to be held in each hundred by the sheriff,
assisted by two specially appointed knights of the shire.   It is
again clearly stated that the same force which is to defend the
realm is responsible for keeping the watch and following up the
hue and cry.   To the *posse comitatus*, on which the sheriff can
call for support against a recalcitrant franchise-holder, corresponds the *posse hundredi*, and the constables who are the local
militia officers are also the local policemen.   The village constable
is also the village keeper of the peace.

In each hundred, then, there was a high constable bound to
have lists of the men available for defence in his hundred, and
of their equipment, which varied according to their wealth.
Edward I added to his functions in 1285 the duty of inspecting
these arms twice a year.   In each village was one constable or
more, normally concerned rather with police than with military

---

[1] *Gervase of Canterbury* (R.S.), II, 96–7.
[2] Stubbs, following Matthew Paris, misdates this document by ten years,
in *Charters*, p. 363–5.   See *Close Roll Col.*, pp. 482–4 (20th May, 1242).

affairs. He embodied the communal responsibility; it was to him that the coroner assigned the duty of guarding a criminal who had taken sanctuary, after his confession and before his abjuration of the realm, and the community shared with him the responsibility for an escape. But above the constables of hundred and vill there had to be a shire authority to keep them up to the mark in police and military matters, and this authority was normally the sheriff. John's high constable of the shire disappeared; not till Tudor times did the lord lieutenant definitely take the whole system over from the sheriff. Regulations issued in 1253 make it clear that the sheriff was expected to keep records of the 'views of arms'. In that year a special commissioner inspected the working of the system in four of the eastern counties, both within liberties and without, and the questions asked as to the keeping of watches, the following of the hue and cry, and the hosting of strangers, along with the inspection of armour, make it once more evident that military and police organization were one, and that the sheriff was responsible for its working. It was he who inquired at his tourn, as the justices inquired in the eyre, if the watches were being properly kept. It was he who, assisted it may be by special knights, inspected the arms and musters of the hundreds periodically. It was he who summoned the sworn men in time of danger, whether of invasion or of gangs of robbers, as in 1224 the sheriff of Salop was ordered to bring a force against Fawkes de Bréauté, in revolt against the king, and in 1264 the sheriffs of Norfolk, Suffolk, Essex, Wiltshire, Cambridgeshire, and Huntingdonshire were ordered to muster their sworn men to defend the sea-coast against an anticipated French invasion organized by Queen Eleanor. On occasion, however, special powers were given to the constable of some important castle. In 1265 the constable of Bristol Castle was given charge of the forces of Bristol town and of four hundreds of Somerset and Gloucestershire, whilst the sheriffs of two counties were ordered to back him up. For actual military operations it would obviously be better for some one with less onerous civil duties than the sheriffs to take charge, though as late as 1277 sheriffs were leading contingents to the Welsh wars in person.

In the twelve months before the battle of Lewes, when in most counties the average countryman must have been distracted by uncertainty as to whether he had better recognize the king's nominee or the barons' nominee as sheriff, the emergency officials called the keepers of the peace in each shire seem to have had control of the police and the militia. William Marshal, *custos pacis* for Northants, appointed the constables of the hundred, and called up men for the defence of the town when Edward marched to besiege it in the spring of 1264. The assembly held under the walls of the town in the Cow-meadow, at which he addressed the community of the shire on behalf of Simon de Montfort and was followed up by other speakers, cannot have been a' regular shire-moot and may well have been a grand muster of the *jurati ad arma*.[1] It seems clear that the system, described in Domesday Book, was still in force, by which those who did not serve paid the expenses of those who did ; the levies who were guarding the sea-coast in September 1264 were being supported out of the county funds ; and in 1265, after Evesham, the hundreds were being called upon to supply men or money for carrying on the struggle. Seven men of Rochford hundred went off with the hundred bailiff to buy exemption for the whole hundred from military service, and they had to pay ten marks to be quit.[2]

One episode of the baronial wars reported by the jurors of 1275 illustrates both the obligations of the hundred and the unhappy lot of the villager caught between the rival forces. Gilbert of Clare, who had helped Simon de Montfort to win the battle of Lewes and then changed sides and helped Edward to win the battle of Evesham, was lord of Tonbridge Castle in Kent. Immediately after Evesham the constable of Dover Castle, a baronial nominee, but possessing full royal authority, called up the levies of some twelve Kentish hundreds to besiege Tonbridge Castle : in most cases four or six men came, in some the whole hundred levy ; but later the officials of Gilbert of Clare compelled either the whole hundred or individuals who had been at the siege to pay fines amounting in all to nearly one hundred and fifty

[1] Hunter, *Rotuli Selecti*, 153–7, 166, 194.   [2] Morant, *Essex*, I, 302.

pounds for their attack upon his castle when he was with the king.[1]

Edward I brought the system up to date by his Statutes of Winchester in 1285, providing that travelling justices should inquire into the enforcement of both its police and its military regulations. He also made use, for his Welsh wars, of the system of arraying—picking, that is—a certain number from the available pool, training them and grouping them in units of twenties and hundreds, under vintenars and centenars as section and company commanders. Early in the fourteenth century we begin to have muster rolls and lists of arms of these semi-armed and semi-trained bands for Cambridge, Norfolk, and Sussex. The responsibility of the hundred for finding the arms and the expenses of their contingent and the responsibility of the village constables for the custody of the communal arms comes out clearly from these lists. But once the equipped quota was ready all the military responsibility rested with the centenars and vintenars, and the system of array was supervised not by the sheriffs but by those *custodes pacis* who were also inquiring into the observance of the police clauses of the Statute of Winchester.

The forces thus provided were only bound to serve in England. Edward II's attempt in 1322 to use the national levies in his Scottish wars provoked a vehement protest at the time, and led later to the passing of the statute of 1327, which laid it down that no man should be compelled to go out of his own shire save in the event of ' the sudden coming of strange enemies '. Henceforth the forces of the shire might be a pool for recruiting overseas armies, but none but volunteers might be employed in them. Right down to the days when Elizabeth's lord lieutenants mustered the county levies for their march to London in the Armada year, and when the Sussex fencible men stood to arms against the scare of Napoleon's landing on the south coast, the hundred was the unit for home defence, but only for home defence.

There is no precise statement as to the method of appointing the village constables. They were very probably elected by their own villages, as were the borsholders in Kent.[2] They

[1] *R.H.*, I, 201–227.　　　　　　　　[2] P.R.O. Court Rolls 182/1.

were sometimes, if not always, sworn in in the hundred court, and it was at the tourn that they had to give account for watches not kept. In Appletree hundred the fines for watches not kept averaged forty shillings a year about 1297.[1] In Wiltshire, where the tithing, not the vill, was the police unit, it is the tithing-men who render account to the sheriff for their failure to keep watch in the royal hundred of Branch and Dole,[2] and in Milton hundred, Kent, it is the borsholders of the hundred who are charged with not keeping the watches according to the king's statutes, as they had been charged to do in full hundred.[3]

The constable, whether in a military or in a police capacity, represents the fusion of popular and royal government more completely than any other local government official. Elected by the township, as it would seem, he is the embodiment of communal responsibility ; but he is also the embodiment of royal authority. This is illustrated in the numerous references to the *custodes pacis* in the records of the state trials of 1290–3, for this title is not yet specialized, and applies as much to the village constable as to the county knight who inquires into the observance of the Statute of Winchester. Both are keepers of the king's peace and royal servants. The most forcible example of the constable's status is to be found on a jail delivery roll of the year 1295.

William of Hendred, a descendant of that Berkshire gentleman who changed estates with William de Lisle, was brought before the king's justices at Northampton charged with murdering the Rector of Brampton in the churchyard. The cause of the quarrel is not stated, but the parson's servants pursued the murderer with hue and cry, caught him, and put him in the keeping of the village constables and tithing-men. Somehow or other he escaped from their custody after one hour and took sanctuary in the church of Stoke Daubeny, but after forty days, as the coroner would not permit him to abjure the realm, he had to surrender to justice. To the charge of murder was added that of jail-breaking. ' The tithing-men and constables, by reason

[1] Duchy of Lancaster Court Rolls, 43/482, m.5d. ; *Inq. P.M.*, III, 300.
[2] L.T.R. Misc. R., 6/13, 6/14.
[3] P.R.O. Court Rolls, 181/75, m.1. Cf. frontispiece.

and authority of their office as keepers of the king's peace, have power to attach criminals for felony,' says the record, ' and as he was in the king's arrest, so when he escaped he was manifestly breaking the king's prison.' [1] So, on that charge, he is hanged. The communal responsibility of the tenants of the manor is strong enough for them to arrest their lord ; whilst the official dignity attaching to the king's *custodes pacis* is sufficient to constitute escape from their keeping the felonious act of jail-breaking.

[1] Gaol Delivery Roll, 95, m.6.

CHAPTER XI

THE FEUDAL ASPECT OF THE SHIRE

I THE KING'S ESTATES AND HIS TENANTS

*' What demesne manors the lord king has in each county ?
What manors in ancient demesne, once in his hands, are now held
by others ? Concerning the lord king's fiefs and tenants-in-chief ;
and concerning the tenants in ancient demesne, both free sokemen
and villeins.'—cc. 1–4.*

THESE four articles come first of the inquest. They link
it up with the Domesday Survey, but they are in fact far
less comprehensive in scope than the questions asked in
1086. The government officials of 1274 could refer at will not
only to Domesday Book but also to a series of later inquests
into feudal holdings throughout the country, made from time to
time for the purpose of checking up the services and payments
due from the king's tenants. The inquiries quoted above were,
no doubt, of use in bringing such earlier surveys up to date, but
their main purpose was to detect any local usurpations or
encroachments upon the king's rights as the first landlord in
the realm. No questions were asked as to the lands of any except
tenants-in-chief ; it was the inquest of 1279, with its categorical
inquiries as to sub-tenants, their holdings and their status, which
was the true equivalent of Domesday, and of 1279, sad to say, in
spite of the fragments of returns which are still being brought
to light at the Record Office, there is not even a complete record
for seven counties. Edward I's Domesday Book was never
compiled, and the rats have devoured the greater part of the
material from which it might have been made.

The first two questions concern only a small part of the
soil of England : the land actually, or formerly held by the
king. The conditions revealed differ widely from county to

195

county. In 1086, when the king was the largest landed pro-
prietor in the county, the crown lands or royal manors had
been much thicker in some shires than in others. Between
1086 and 1274 large numbers of William I's demesne manors had
been granted away, and though others had escheated, or fallen
in to the crown, by forfeiture or for lack of heirs, many of these
had been granted out again. The manors held by the crown in
1066 were technically known as *Ancient Demesne*, and whether
they were still in the king's hands or were held by a subject,
those dwelling on them, the 'tenants in ancient demesne',
enjoyed certain customary privileges of their own, some of which
were unknown elsewhere. They were, for instance, free from
jury-service and from trial by combat, outside the manor.[1]
Moreover, even when he had granted them away, the king retained
a special interest in these manors and special rights over the
tenants on them—a fact that accounts for the presence of the
article as to ancient demesne manors no longer in the king's
hands.

Examples of ancient demesne manors in Edward's hands in
1274 were Brill in Buckinghamshire, Milton or Middleton in
Kent, Wighton in Norfolk, and Cookham and Bray in Berkshire,
whilst ancient demesne manors held by subjects were Tavistock
in Devon and Folsham in Norfolk. The hundred of Milton,
called in Domesday a half-lathe, formed a great block of crown
lands. In 1275 the jurors declared that the manor and the
whole hundred was the king's demesne, though it was being
held for life by John de Burgh.[2] Another great block of crown
lands, where the tenants-in-chief were very small people indeed,
is recorded in the hundred of Lothingland in Suffolk. Here,
although the manor of Lothingland had been granted by Henry III
to Devorguilla of Balliol in exchange for her share, as coheiress,
of the Earldom of Chester, a number of lesser vills remained in
the king's hands. The list of the small folk who held, or had
formerly held, of the king in chief in this corner of Suffolk fills
eight and a half pages of the printed volume, including such
people as Thomas of Alton, who held three acres of land by the

---

[1] See Vinogradoff, *Villeinage in England*, pp. 89–126.   [2] *R.H.*, I, 208.

service of sixpence and one fowl a year, Lena of the Lone House, who holds one cottage for one penny a year, and John Sepey who renders a halfpenny a year for one rood of land.[1]   A similar, though much shorter, list of small tenants-in-chief is given for Brill, but the Lincolnshire gentleman who holds three knight's fees worth twenty pounds a year each and pays thirty shillings of sheriff's aid [2] is a more typical tenant-in-chief, and his like are to be found in most counties, though it is only where the original returns have been preserved that we get full details about them.

The most cursory comparison of the Hundred Rolls with Domesday Book makes it evident that the kings have been granting manors away lavishly in the intervening two hundred years.   In Bedfordshire, for instance, William I had five manors in 1086 ; not one of these was in the king's hands in 1275.   The jurors record grants of eight manors by the king, one of which had come to the crown by escheat ; one of these manors had been granted out as part of the marriage portion of Henry III's sister Eleanor, and one was the borough of Bedford, which had been granted to the burgesses of Bedford at a fixed farm.   In 1316 there were no manors in the king's hands in Bedfordshire. The crown lands had always been very unequally distributed. In 1086 the king had had no manors in Shropshire, and close on 120 in Norfolk, whilst in Yorkshire he held land in over 400 villages.   They were fairly evenly distributed in the old West Saxon kingdom.   In Devonshire there were in 1086 some seventy manors in royal hands, of which twenty-one had been held by Edward the Confessor, twelve by his wife Edith, fifteen by Harold Godwinson, and six by his brother Leofric.   In 1316 only one manor was still held by the crown.   The jurors of 1275 have a long tale to tell of grants in Devon, adding more historical details than had been asked for.   Tavistock, they say, was held by King Ethelred, Axmouth by King Athelstan, Beer and Seaton were given to the monks of Sherborne by him, and Crediton had been given to the bishopric of Exeter long before the Norman Conquest.[3]   After that epoch there are grants to report made

[1] Ibid., II, 169.   [2] Ibid., I, 148..   [3] Ibid., I, 63, 67, 68.

by Henry I, Henry II, John, and Henry III ; regrants, as of Kerswell, the chief manor of Haytor hundred, held from the time of the Conquest, as they say, by one family till its extinction, given by John to Henry-fitz-Count, who died without heirs, and granted out a third time by Henry III to the family in occupation in 1275.[1] This history is typical in Devonshire ; nearly all the royal manors of 1086 were held in 1275 by subjects, a large number of whom were said to have held ' from the Conquest ', though Domesday does not bear out the jurors' statement. Other official records, however, back up their statements as to later dates. Shebbeare alone of all the manors held by William I remained to Edward I, with the hundred belonging to it, the manor being cared for by the escheator, whilst the sheriff had charge of the hundred. An inspection of the Norfolk hundred rolls yields much the same result ; nearly all the king's Domesday manors were in private hands by 1275.

In the histories of manors falling in and being re-granted there is frequent reference to the escheats resulting from the loss of Normandy. The vassals of John and Henry III, who held lands both sides of the Channel, had had to choose after 1204 which of their two overlords they would cleave to, and the English fiefs of those who chose the King of France for their lord escheated to the crown as ' Normans' lands '. Thus half a knight's fee in Steeple Morden, Cambridgeshire, came into the hands of Henry III ' by the escheat of the Normans ', and was re-granted by him to William de Cheny ; thus Isleworth escheated, and was given to Richard of Cornwall.[2] The jurors of Taverham in Norfolk relate that the manor of Fretenham was held by Robert Bartram, a Norman, until he bore arms against King John, and for that cause he was expelled the land, and John gave the manor to Peter de Narford, who used it so ill that John took it back and re-granted it to Roger le Poor, whose tenant was in possession in 1275.[3]

Each county, then, has its own history. From the fiscal point of view it might at times seem the wiser policy for a king to grant out the crown estates to subjects for a rent rather than

---

[1] *R.H.*, I, 71–2.   [2] Ibid., I, 50, 433.   [3] Ibid., I, 449.

to exploit them by his own officials. Edward I often drove a shrewd bargain when he granted or exchanged his lands. In many cases, on the other hand, a grant must have been made for personal or political reasons, to secure or to reward some adherent, and when this had occurred and the annual rent or farm was negligible or non-existent the kings had in effect been spending capital in place of income. The grants of the early part of Henry III's reign arouse some suspicion as to the wisdom, or possibly even the rectitude, of Hubert de Burgh ; whilst Henry III's own grants to his kinsmen testify rather to the warmth of his family feeling than to his good stewardship of the resources of the crown.

II. THE ESCHEATOR AND HIS DUTIES

' *What escheators have made waste in the lands in wardship committed to them by the king ? What escheators have taken the goods of dead persons into the king's hands unjustly ; have made false valuations of men's lands ; have, for a bribe, sold a wardship under cost ; have persuaded jurors to tell lies about the age of an heir ; have deceitfully kept wardships in their own hands ; have surveyed lands and kept them in their hands too long, have taken lands into the king's hands wrongfully ?* '—cc. 30–8.

The duties connected with the royal estates were no longer *ex-officio* the sheriff's business. Since about 1242 the responsibility for the royal manors had been taken out of his hands, and the king's estate interests, as at Shebbeare, were in the charge of his escheators. In 1275 there were two chief escheators responsible respectively for the lands north and south of the Trent. Below these two chief officials were the sub-escheators, one for each county, who are often simply called escheators in the Hundred Rolls. The sheriff was under orders to assist the escheator in the performance of his duty, as required, and a sheriff might be appointed sub-escheator in his own county— as the sheriff of Essex was in 1267, for instance. But more often the two spheres of activity were kept distinct, and the sheriff was a colleague of the sub-escheator and a subordinate of the escheator, in theory at any rate.

The articles of 1274 do not inquire into the administration of royal manors, only, as we have seen, into their tenure. The questions asked about escheators concern their work in exercising the king's rights as overlord, in especial the so-called feudal incidents of primer seisin, wardship, and escheat.

When a tenant-in-chief died feudal law gave the king the right to enter and take possession of all his lands until the next heir's title had been established. In every county where the deceased had an estate it was the duty of the local escheator to occupy the lands on the king's behalf, and administer them until the heir had been formally put in possession or other arrangements had been made. By Magna Carta he was bound, on the king's behalf, to respect the rights of the heir and keep the estate in good condition. Soon orders would come down from the Exchequer for him to hold an inquest into the holdings of the deceased, and into the title and the age of the heir. In each county where land was held the sheriff would empanel a jury, and the escheator would hold an inquest *post mortem*, as it was called, sometimes in the hundred or county court, sometimes elsewhere. A great number of the returns to these inquests are preserved in our national archives and have been calendared ; [1] they are full of valuable details of family and topographical history, of feudal tenure, and of local custom. When, as sometimes happened, circumstantial evidence was demanded as to the exact age of an heir there are curious sidelights thrown on to social life : reminiscences of old family friends who were with the father when news came of the child's birth, or of old retainers who were present at the christening. One witness, who figures in the Essex hundred rolls, is sure that a man is of age because he knew his father twenty-four years ago, when the witness was bailiff of Witham hundred and had occasion often to go to his house. Though at a later date some of the evidence becomes common form, in the thirteenth century the ' proofs of age ' appear still to be spontaneous and genuine.

[1] *Calendars of Inquisitions* (H.M.S.O.).

If the heir proved to be of full age the lands were delivered to him on his giving security to pay the lawful relief, but if he was under age they remained in the king's hands, and the escheator would normally administer them unless or until the rights of wardship were granted or sold to some other person. If lawful heirs failed the estate would be administered as the king's escheat by the escheator, until granted out again.

These various duties gave as various opportunities for peculation. The escheator might seize lands that were not held in chief of the king, and hold them until bribed to give them up. He might do waste in the lands of minors, or delay unduly to hand them over to their rightful tenant. He might defraud the king by inducing jurors to misrepresent an heir's age, or to make a false valuation or 'extent' of a manor. The returns are not as copious under the heading of escheator's misdeeds as under sheriffs', but they contain many allegations that both the king and his subjects had been defrauded by escheators. A Suffolk sub-escheator, administering the estate of the late Thomas Cors de boef, gave the widow half of her husband's tenement instead of the third that was her proper dower in law; this in return for a bribe of twenty shillings.[1] The same man had kept another manor in his hand for six months, instead of winding up the business rapidly.[2] Another, when holding the manor of Wrotham on the king's behalf, took twenty shillings from the villeins of the manor and six shillings from four men who refused to sell their late master's wood to him, and also extorted eighteen-pence from one of the four to be let off serving as village reeve.[3] This election of village officials took place, of course, in the manorial court; the holding of this during the interim period was part of the escheator's duty, and the Essex jurors complain that the sub-escheator held the court of Aveley manor twice on one day in order to extort fines from the villeins and freeholders.[4] On another Suffolk estate the escheator took seventy-one shillings from the homagers, of which he kept twenty shillings for himself, that they might have respite in paying their lord's relief.[5] At

---

[1] *R.H.*, II, 194.　　　[2] Ibid., II, 190.　　　[3] Ibid., II, 194.
[4] Ibid., I, 148.　　　　　　　　　　　　　　　　　　　[5] Ibid., II, 196.

Monks' Illeigh, a Canterbury manor, ten marks were accepted as a bribe, not to waste the property.[1] The escheator, it will be seen, was often employed in administering ecclesiastical estates during the vacancy of an abbey or bishopric. Extortions in kind are reported; the taking of carts, peacocks, and hens on one estate, of deer, goats, coneys, and underwood on another,[2] the cutting down of thirty-two oaks at Blythburgh, and of eighty oaks at Reydon, for the personal use of the escheator.[3]

Possibly the reports of 1274–5 may have contributed to the reforms of the next year, by which the Exchequer put the feudal functions of the escheator back into the sheriff's hands, over whom they had perhaps more effective control. The sheriffs were made escheators in their own shires, to account for the wardship and escheats therein to the Exchequer when they accounted for their counties. By the end of 1276 the new system was in full working order. Three stewards were appointed for the whole realm, who supervised the sheriff in the administration of the escheats and wardships, being themselves responsible for the king's demesne manors. No doubt the king gained by this arrangement; but on the evidence of the Hundred Rolls it is difficult to believe that the tenants-in-chief would find it much of an advantage to find the sheriff in the sub-escheator's place.

III. The Liberties in the Shire

' What persons claim from the king to have return or estreats of writs and other royal liberties; by what warrant and from what time ? '—c. 8.

' Who have free chases and warrens ? '—c. 11.

From the point of view of local government and administration the king's feudal rights and perquisites are of less importance than those of his subjects. The royal manors are by 1275 few and far between in most counties, as we have seen; only in four are there as many as twenty; and the feudal incidents are

---

[1] *R.H.*, II, 146. [2] Ibid., II, 190; I, 145. [3] Extract Roll No. 4, m.6d.
[4] *Stat. Realm*, I, 197; *Close Roll. Cal.*, pp. 266, 295, 296, 308.

matters of revenue concerning the central government, not the shire. But the liberties enjoyed by churches, magnates, and county gentlemen are of great and continual importance in local government. The details of right and custom, of encroachment are so complex that the local knowledge, and the up-to-date knowledge of the jurors is especially necessary to the king and especially valuable to us if we wish to get a comprehensive view of shire and hundred as working units of government in 1275.

We shall get no truthful picture of the situation if we see feudal franchises purely as strongholds resisting the royal power and the royal system of government. The antitheses between baronial and royal power, between law and privilege, between a feudal and an official type of administration, which may seem merely logical to us to-day, are anachronistic if applied to the thirteenth century. The medieval baron, the medieval sheriff, the medieval countryman simply did not see things that way. In 1275 an old man might remember the granting of the great charter by John. He would have lived through a period of struggles to adjust the government of England to the conceptions implied and expressed in that document, as modified in 1216, 1217, and 1225 ; and in Magna Carta, as in the Provisions of 1258-9, he would have found recognition alike of the established customary law, deriving by tradition from Edward the Confessor ; of the feudal conventions and rules, partly international and partly national, established and accepted by the French-speaking kings of England ; and of the system of royal officialdom, gradually built up by Anglo-Norman and Angevin kings and their army of able civil servants. The good law and good government which Edward I was sworn to uphold was as mongrel as the race he governed. The ideals and the sanctions of public conduct were both English and Norman, both feudal and bureaucratic. If Edward I was ready both to appeal to feudal law to support his claims and to honour its obligations, his subjects were just as ready to use analogies from the royal system of administration when they claimed their rights, saying that they had the same power as the sheriff, that they ought to return the king's writs, that they had power to enforce his assize of bread and ale. There were two aspects of one organic whole, not two watertight systems of local government.

Nevertheless there was a constant danger that the practices and theories of seignorial privilege might be exploited so as to lessen royal power. The baron who freely used the royal courts to establish his liberties against his equals or subordinates might turn round and assert that he held them independently of the king; and the king who swore to uphold all men's just and ancient liberties might find himself forced to go more closely into the question of title, asking, ' What *is* just ? What *is* ancient ? ' and enforcing the fundamental principle of feudalism : ' No right can exist without a duty to match it ; no privilege may be permitted that defeats common justice.'

The questions of 1274 therefore ask not only who holds a liberty, but by what warrant does he hold it, and is it contrary to the common interest ? It had yet to be laid down definitely what title would warrant the holding of a liberty, and how long usage must be to establish a right ; but before this could be determined the facts in each case must be known, and so the jurors have to report from what time the liberty had been enjoyed. Nine years before, in the general scramble after Evesham, magnates and royal clerks had snatched what they could get, and some recent titles were very dubious. The Hundred Rolls are full of tales of liberties appropriated by the great men of the winning party or their followers : ' by what warrant they know not '. Edward himself, as heir to the throne, had not been blameless. And where charters could be produced they had sometimes been crookedly obtained, as in the case of Richard de Tany, an Essex gentleman, who declared ' Theydon Mount is a fair manor lying near my manor of Stapleford ; it would suit me well ' ; and in spite of the fact that the king had already granted it to Robert Bruce, as the Chancery clerks told him, contrived that a charter granting it to himself should be thrown on the pile which were to be sealed, so that the Chancellor put the great seal to it ' in ignorance and under a misunderstanding ', along with the other charters which were being sealed for the multitude of knights to whom the king was making gifts.[1] And after the land-grabbing of 1265–6 there had followed the long series of pleas arising out of the Kenilworth settlement, so that the returns to the inquest of 1255 into rights and liberties were well out of date, and a new survey was a necessary preliminary to carrying out that policy of definition of rights so dear to the heart of Edward I. Thus the facts elicited in 1275 as to liberties claimed are, as has long been recognized, of great value. The information they give as to the working of seignorial government in the shires can be best considered under the three headings of jurisdictional, administrative, and fiscal rights.

(a) Jurisdictional Liberties : Seignorial Courts

'Concerning ancient suits withdrawn: what persons have appropriated such suits to themselves '—c. 7

'Who claim to hold pleas of vee de naam, and to have gallows and the assize of bread and ale and other things belonging to the crown ? '—c. 8.

These are the only specific references to jurisdiction. Where a man had formerly owed suit to a royal court, as one of those who made the judgements there, and now attended some seignorial court instead, the jurors were required to report the fact. This is not a new line of investigation. As early as 1240 the justices in eyre in Suffolk had been putting the same question to the eyre juries. The answers will not, of course, give a complete picture of the jurisdictional franchises of the county, for only recent changes will be noted. If the jurors of Hartismere hundred in Suffolk say that one suit owed from Mellis and another owed from Little Thornham have been withdrawn from the sheriff's tourn by the seneschals of Eye, we infer the existence of a court at Eye, but learn nothing as to its origin or nature, only that it has of late been drawing off suitors from the king's hundred. Since it is the tourn they have deserted, we gather that the lord of Eye holds the view of frank-pledge and administers in it the articles of the tourn. When the same complaint is made in the

[1] E. F. Jacob, *Baronial Reform and Rebellion*, pp. 379–80.

Abbot of Bury's hundred of Risbridge we assume that R. Pikhous, or whoever it may be who withdraws the suitors twice a year from the hundred, has his view of frank-pledge for the tenants on his own manor; a lesser liberty within the greater liberty of St. Edmund's.

Suffolk may be taken as a county in which to study the working of the various types of jurisdictional liberty familiar to the jurors of 1275. We have seen that there are two great franchises—those of St. Edmund and St. Etheldreda—within which the officials of the abbot and the prior do the work the sheriff does elsewhere. But there is a higher liberty yet; within the four crosses that mark the boundaries of the *ban-lieu* of St. Edmunds the abbot can appoint justices whose authority is above the sheriffs, and who can hold courts of the same standing as those at Westminster. From this most privileged spot even the king's marshal is excluded; as at Glastonbury, the king withdraws to a distance to hold the pleas of his royal hall—the court of the Verge as it is later called. The justices in eyre do not enter the liberty of the four crosses; when they hold their eyre for St. Edmund's liberty they sit at Catteshill, two miles away; and all writs touching land within the four crosses are handed by them to the abbot's seneschal for the abbot's justices to deal with. On the other hand, the Ely hundreds appear before the justices in eyre at Ipswich, along with those of 'the geldable'; the *ban-lieu* of St. Etheldreda is at Ely, and she has no equivalent of the four crosses in Suffolk. The franchises where the lord can appoint justices with powers equivalent to the king's—where, as the phrase goes, the king's writ does not run—are few indeed. The palatinates of Durham and the earldom of Chester with some of the Marcher lordships are the only considerable areas of this type, but several of the more ancient abbeys, like Glastonbury, Battle, and Ramsey [1] have, like Bury and Ely, a tract of land thus privileged surrounding the monastery itself. Outside these two great franchises, as we have seen, four of the Suffolk hundreds are private and six royal. Of the private hundreds, Lothingland, which has been conferred

---

[1] See W. O. Ault, *Ramsey Court Rolls*, p. xxxiii.

on the Balliols by Henry III, has some of the special judicial privileges attaching to land that had been held as ancient demesne of the crown, and it has its own private coroner.

The liberties described so far are regalian; of the order described by G. B. Adams as 'franchisal' and asserted by Bracton to be delegations of the royal authority. The justice administered is royal justice, although those who administer it are not, in the ordinary sense, royal officials. But there are other liberties revealed by the returns of 1275. In reply to the question, 'Who have used their official power maliciously against any man?' the Suffolk jurors name 136 seignorial bailiffs and underlings: men employed not by sheriffs or escheators, but by some twenty lords who hold land in Suffolk. The twenty-eight who serve St. Edmund and the fourteen who serve St. Etheldreda come under our first category, but twenty-six serve Gilbert of Clare; twenty-four serve the Earl Marshal, whose chief manor was at Framlingham, in the hundred of Lose, one of the Ely hundreds which the earl held from the Prior of Ely; ten belong to the honour of Eye; and the remainder belong to various small local lords or to great men like the Earl of Oxford or Earl Warenne, whose lands mostly lie outside Suffolk. The jurisdiction connected with these lordships may fairly be described as seignorial; it needs no royal grant to explain its origin.

The honour of Clare extended through nine counties, forming a vast nexus of feudal relationships. All the tenants of the Earl of Gloucester who held 'of the honour of Clare' were not, however, bound to attend the court held at Clare in Suffolk; the recently printed rolls of that court [1] show that the suitors came from Norfolk, Suffolk, and Essex only; to exact attendance every three weeks from men who lived farther afield would obviously have been preposterous. Both freeholders and military tenants attended the court, and the business done there included not only feudal business like the rendering of homage and fealty but also transfers of land and pleas between the earl's tenants. Cases were brought up from the smaller manorial courts of the different villages where the earl had manors, and cases were

---

[1] Ault, *Court Rolls of Ramsey Abbey*, pp. 75–110.

referred back to them for the holding of local inquests. The amount of business done may be gauged by the profits and perquisites of the court, which came to over sixty pounds in the year, and explain why such a liberty would be tenaciously defended by its lord. The Suffolk suitors to the court came from eleven villages in four different hundreds, most of them, like Clare itself, within St. Edmund's liberty ; the tenants of the honour were far more widely scattered.[1] No man would be willing to undertake regular attendance at more than one three-weekly court ; on the other hand, the tenants of the honour would have to go to shire or hundred court if they had a plea to bring against a neighbour who was not a tenant of the honour of Clare. It seems that they tried to escape the honour court in other ways as well, for twice in one year the order was enrolled that men were to be attached for impleading the earl's tenants in county and hundred and outside his liberty. This is the reverse side of the king's complaint that suitors have been stolen from his courts ; both the suit and the litigation of these stray knights and freeholders were still worth fighting for in Edward's reign.

The jurors of 1275 do not tell us much about this court at Clare, but they bring out the fact, which the court rolls hardly suggest, that its head-quarters were within the liberty of the Abbot of Bury and that disputes had arisen between the earl and the abbot as to their rival claims. Two agreements defining the limits of their judicial rights are preserved—one of 1197, another, belonging to the period 1257–62, which is mentioned more than once by the jurors of 1275 [2] and is recorded in draft form in a Bury record.[3] By it the abbot undertook to pass on to the earl the writs that he received from the sheriff touching the earl's tenants, and only to execute them if the earl's bailiffs had failed in their duty. The bailiffs, according to the jurors, refused to execute the king's suits until the abbot had countersigned them. The jurors know of no warrant except this agreement for the earl's claim to have return of writs, levying of royal debts and pleas of *vee de naam*, but if it had been duly registered as a ' final

---

[1] See map opposite.
[3] *Pinchbeck Register*, I, 432–4.

[2] *R.H.*, II, 172, 178.

PLATE VII

THE ABBOT'S TRIBUNAL, GLASTONBURY

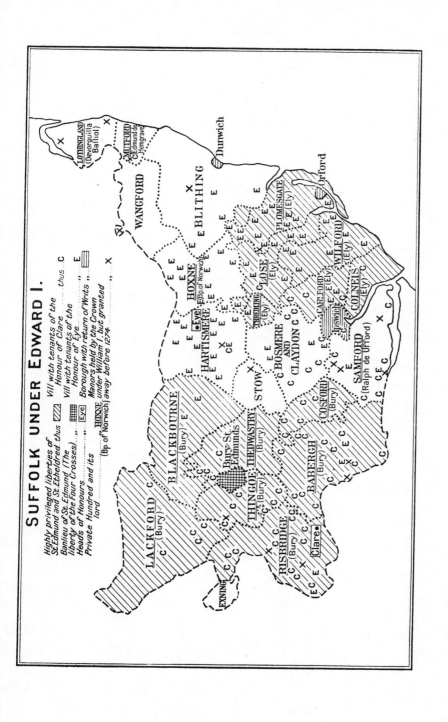

SUFFOLK UNDER EDWARD I.

Highly privileged liberties of the
St. Edmund and St. Etheldred thus ▨ · · · Vill with tenants of the
Banleu of St. Edmund (The Honour of Clare · · · · · thus C
liberty of the Four Crosses) · · · ▦ · · · Vill with tenants of the
Heads of Honours · · · · · · · · · ·🄴 · · · Honour of Eye · · · · · · E
Private Hundred and its Borough with return of Writs · · ▤
   HOXNE lord Manors held by the Crown
(Bp of Norwich) under William I, but granted
   away before 1274 · · · ×

LOTHINGLAND ×
(Devorguilla Balliol)

MUTFORD ×
C (Edmund de Hengrave)

WANGFORD

Dunwich

HOXNE
(Bp of Norwich)

BLITHING ×

E Eye

HARTISMERE

STOW

BLACKBOURNE
(Bury)

Bury St. Edmunds

LACKFORD
(Bury)

THINGOE
(Bury)

THEDWASTRY
(Bury)

EXNING

RISBRIDGE
(Bury)

Clare

COSFORD
(Bury)

BABERGH
(Bury)

BOSMERE AND CLAYDON

CARLFORD

Ipswich

SAMFORD
C (Ralph de Ufford)

COLNEIS
(Ely)

WILFORD
(Ely)

PLOMESGATE
(Ely)

LOSE
(Ely)

THREDLING
(Ely)

Orford

concord ' before the king's justices, as they say,[1] the earl might fairly claim that the king's consent had been given to this sub-delegation of regalian rights. The other rights claimed by the earl in his liberty of Clare were gallows, that is, the right to hang thieves, and the assize of bread and ale.[2]

In the north of the county, in the royal hundred of Hartis-mere, was Eye, the head of the Earl of Cornwall's honour. Complaints are brought against the seneschals of this honour, five of whom are named, by the jurors of eight hundreds. Not only the sheriff of Suffolk, from whose tourn they had drawn away suitors in three hundreds, but also the Prior of Ely had been vexed by their encroachments on his rights.[3] Nor is this surprising ; there were tenants of the honour of Eye in seventy-five Suffolk villages, scattered through thirteen hundreds, and thirty-one of these villages were within St. Etheldreda's liberty.[4] But of the proceedings of the court at Eye we know little, and even less of the earl Marshal's court at Framlingham, the most important of the ten manors he held in Suffolk.[5] Little as we know of these feudal complexes, however, we can see how they ramified through the hundredal framework of shire administration. A tenant of the honour of Clare, living in a private hundred of the St. Edmund's liberty, had to acknowledge a complicated set of rival claims and obligations ; yet it may well be that they were no more of a burden to him than are his obligations to-day to a local government elector who is also a parishioner of an ecclesiastical parish, a member of a college, of an athletic, a professional, and a political association, and finds no difficulty in reconciling these rival loyalties with the ultimate duties of national citizenship. The antithesis between ' party ' and ' state ' is no more and no less real than the antithesis between feudalism and monarchism. The courts of Clare and Eye and Framlingham might withdraw suitors from the king's hundreds and be compelled to surrender them if wrongfully withdrawn, but the right to hold such courts was secured to their lords by the custom of

---

[1] *R.H.*, II, 178 : ' The note is in the King's Court.' It is not to be found to-day.
[2] Ibid., II, 172.   [3] Ibid., II, 187, 191, 193, 194.
[4] *Cal. Inq.*, III, 477–8. See map facing p. 208.   [5] Ibid., IV, 292–3.

the land and upheld by the king's justices, and for doing justice in these courts their lords had to answer to the king.

After the four or five magnates who have really extensive judicial activities in the county come a whole army of lords of manors who hold courts for their villeins and free tenants. It was not the existence of a court but the nature of its business and the amount of its profits that interested the king's agents. But if a lord were holding pleas of *vee de naam*, that is, hearing complaints against litigants who refused to deliver up a distress to the owner when proper security was offered, and the bailiff demanded it, the jurors were asked to report it, for this was a royal plea which only the sheriff could hear without a royal writ. On the other hand, the position was less clear with regard to view of frank-pledge and the enforcement of the assize of bread and ale. In theory only a royal grant should authorize men to inquire into the observation of the king's ordinance that men should be in frank-pledge, and that bread and ale should be sold under certain conditions, but in practice these liberties were so generally exercised by lords of manors that it would be difficult for the king to take a high line about them now. The articles do not refer to frank-pledge at all, but in spite of that the returns give copious information as to views, which the Norfolk jurors call ' leets ' and the Suffolk jurors ' bortremings ',[1] from the ' trimming ' or bringing up to date, of the ' borhs ' or tithings. The *Quo Warranto* Pleas later show that with the inspection of tithings there normally went an inquiry into the articles of the tourn, leading to presentments, and it was generally taken for granted that the right to punish brewers and bakers for infringing the assize of bread and ale also went with the holding of the view,[2] though sometimes an overlord held the view and a lesser lord the assize.

How common it was for the lord of a manor to hold the view is well shown in the returns for Norfolk or Suffolk. In Norfolk the justices inquired in 1286 into some ninety cases of the exercise of this liberty, and this does not by any means cover all the instances presented in the Hundred Rolls. Two Suffolk hundreds

[1] e.g. *R.H.*, II, 186.　　　　[2] *Year Book*, Ed. II (S.S.), VIII, 182.

of the geldable may be taken as examples. In Hartismere hundred the view was held by twelve lords for their tenants in seventeen villages, and in no case is it stated that the hundred bailiff was present. In Blything hundred, also in the king's hands, twenty-one lords held the view in twenty-five villages, and in six instances the jurors add that it used formerly to be held by the king's bailiffs, whilst in at least three other instances the bailiffs attended the view and received some payment on the king's behalf. This arrangement, laid down in several charters of John and Henry III, by which all or most of the profits were retained by the lord, but a royal official took note of the proceedings, was probably meant to secure the passing on of presentments from the lord's court to the tourn or county ; as we have seen, the hundred bailiff was a liaison officer.

There might be two or three lords in one village, each having the right to hold a view for his own tenants. In such circumstances a lord sometimes summoned his tenants from three or four villages to one spot for the holding of the view, or, occasionally, a joint view was held by the officials of several lords for the whole village each lord taking the profits, whether head-money, cert-money, or amercements arising from his own tenants.[1] The village community was a unit not only for economic, but for police and petty criminal matters, and practical convenience or common sense might always triumph over feudal formalism.

The holding of the assize of bread and ale was in practice more of a fiscal than a judicial privilege. The fines imposed on brewsters for brewing contrary to the king's assize recur with such regularity on the court rolls that it is clear that the offence was winked at for the sake of the profits arising from fines : the lord was in effect taking a licensing fee. In many cases, as it turned out when the king's justices looked into the presentments of 1275, the lords who posed as enforcing the assize did not even possess a pillory and tumbril, the *judicialia* for administering the appropriate punishment to the bad baker or brewster. To pay a fine suited both parties better, and whatever the purchasers of

[1] Ault, in *Ramsey Court Rolls*, pp. 173-9, prints records of such a joint leet.

the ale and bread thought about it, there is no complaint on the subject in the Hundred Rolls. The king's justices were severe on the practice, but the records do not suggest that they put an end to it. The juries of St. Edmund's liberty report thirty-six lords, other than the abbot, as holding this privilege in the eight and a half hundreds.

We have now surveyed the whole range of judicial liberties in one county, extending from the highest judicial rights enjoyed by the Abbot of Bury within the four crosses to Thomas of Molton's right to fine an alewife in Hawkedon. Although the exercise of such a liberty is no evidence of its validity, we can say with certainty that many of those claimed in 1275 were well warranted, and had been upheld in the courts at Westminster time and again. The lord of the liberty had the right to vindicate his claim by stopping any case where it had been infringed. On the rolls of the king's courts at Westminster, not to mention the records of shire and hundred courts, is often found the entry, ' So and so claimed his court of such an one as his tenant ' or ' as a resident within his liberty ', and the bailiff or sheriff or justice surrenders the case as soon as such tenure or residence is proved. A long and vivid narrative tells how the Abbot of Bury claimed jurisdiction over two of his knights accused of treason in a joint session of the shire courts of Norfolk and Suffolk, sitting in the bishop's garden at Norwich, towards the end of Stephen's reign, and how his claim was upheld by an old knight who said that in all the fifty years that he had been attending shire courts and hundred courts he had always seen that claim honoured. So in the court rolls of Wisbeach hundred in 1302 we find the Prior of Ely claiming his court in respect of his tenants within the hundred. Here, it seems probable, the prior is content to have his tenants' cases heard in the bishop's hundred court by the ordinary procedure, provided the profits of jurisdiction are made over to him. So, on the rolls of the Curia Regis, the Earl of Warenne or the Abbot of Ramsey claim their court and withdraw the case from Westminster. Such a proceeding is the clearest evidence of the king's acceptance of that correlation of privilege and responsibility which, as the fundamental principle

of feudalism, was ingrained in the social consciousness of the
thirteenth century.

(b) Administrative Liberties

' *What persons claim to have return or estreats of writs ?* '—*c.* 8.

After the jurisdictional liberties come the executive liberties
bound up with them ; the gallows, which was the outward sign
of the right to hang thieves ; the prison, where criminals could
be kept until trial ; the pillory and tumbril for the punishment
of petty crimes. Such conveniences were sometimes shared ;
the Abbot of Tewkesbury made use of the Earl of Gloucester's
gallows, and the Abbot of Cheltenham was allowed to use the
king's gallows there.   Prisons are less frequent than gallows ; in
Suffolk the bailiffs of Eye had a prison for thieves, and the Prior
of Ely had a jail at Melton for St. Etheldreda's liberty, which is
still standing to-day, as is the bishop's prison in Ely.   There was
a third Ely jail at Dereham in the Norfolk hundred of Mitford,
where the jurors complained that men from outside the liberty
were imprisoned.[1] The possession of a jail meant responsibility,
parallel to that of the sheriff, for the keeping of prisoners till the
justices of jail delivery came ; it also meant fees and perquisites
arising from the custody of prisoners, and those opportunities for
extortion which the returns of 1274-5 make so evident.   Very
often the right to hang criminals was accompanied by the right
to take the felon's goods ; a right reserved for the crown by the
Assize of Clarendon in 1166, but granted to many lords of liberties
both by Henry II himself and by his successors.

Of all the administrative liberties, however, far and away the
most important was the right to levy royal debts and to execute
royal writs. The lord who had the estreats and summons of the
Exchequer and the return of writs could exclude the sheriff and
his staff from his lands ; such work could only be done by his
own bailiff, who, by virtue of such offices, became the king's
bailiff in the liberty under the sheriff's commands.[2] As we
have seen, it was the sheriff's duty to pass on all royal commands,

---

[1] *R.H.*, I, 461.   [2] *P.Q.W.*, 152 (Earl of Lancaster), 557 (E. Longsword).

with his own mandate to execute and report to himself; on occasion, observance is required 'on pain of the loss of your liberty'. There had to be some definite arrangement for handing over the writs; the bailiffs of Evesham and of Glastonbury Abbeys, for instance, received the king's writs at the door of the abbey; those of the Bishop of Worcester's liberty received them in the county court. At Bury St. Edmund's the seneschal received the writs from the sheriff and passed them on to the bailiffs for execution. All the manifold activities which a writ, as we have seen, could set going might thus be demanded of the officials of a liberty which had the return of writs—empanelling inquests, attaching, distraining, and so forth. A sheriff who attempted to carry out these operations by his own officials was liable to receive a sharp rap over the knuckles; the records of the greater liberties constantly include copies of severe commands from the king to the sheriff to desist from interfering with the liberty of Peterborough or St. Albans or Canterbury or whatever it may be. In 1252 Henry III commanded the sheriff of Yorkshire to uphold the rights of his ward, the young Earl of Lincoln, to return of writs in the wapentakes of Staincross and Osgoldcross; rights which were being disputed by the Abbot of St. Mary's, York. It was a well-recognized vested interest. But it might lead to delay of, and even resistance to, the king's justice; and thus the law of Bracton's time, which required the authorization of a writ *ne omittas propter libertatem* before the sheriff could enter such a liberty,[1] was amended by the Statutes of Westminster in 1275 so that the sheriff could enter the liberty without delay if the bailiffs failed to act.[2] In 1306, when Edward I renewed the grant of the liberty to the Earl of Lincoln for the term of his life, he ordered it to be put on record in the Chancery, the Wardrobe, and the Exchequer that no such franchise should be granted by him henceforth, save to his own children.[3]

The right to serve writs always included the more restricted privilege of levying moneys for the Exchequer, sometimes accompanied by the duty of accounting direct to the Exchequer. Here

---

[1] Bracton (R.S.), VI, 488.   [2] *Stat. of Realm*, I, 31 (ch. 17).
[3] *Rot. Parl.*, I, 211.

also slackness might lead to loss of the liberty; the Abbot of Peterborough is warned that ' whereas we learn that your bailiff has not levied any portion of the fine [for forest offences] we command you and your bailiff to obey upon pain of the loss of your franchise, and failing this, the sheriff shall enter and take the franchise into our hands and cause you and your bailiff to be imprisoned '.

(c) Fiscal Liberties

The privileges already described might be valued for the prestige they conferred, but they meant heavy work; as one writer says : ' *Retorna brevium* was a feather in the holder's cap, but also a thorn in his foot.' It seems probable that on the whole liberties were valued less for political than for financial reasons. It was the perquisites and profits of the courts, the fees payable for distraining or for executing writs or for levying royal debts that the lord of a liberty prized. Some portion of these perquisites no doubt stayed in the pockets of the officials, but a good proportion joined the rents and other revenues of the lord. We have seen what a large income was produced by the court of Clare. To such incidental profits special fiscal privileges might be added by grant ; such were the right to the goods of an executed felon or of a runaway outlaw, the right to confiscate waifs and strays, the right to keep wreck cast up on your fore-shore, and treasure found on your land. All these privileges are reported by the jurors. Felons' goods were a perquisite still enjoyed by the lord of Wirrall hundred in the nineteenth century. Sometimes the king had granted to a magnate the amercements imposed on the men of his liberty by the justices in eyre : the justices of either Bench, the barons of the Exchequer, the justices of the forest or of jail delivery. These amercements might be collected by the sheriff's officials and handed over to the lord. Sometimes the *murdrum* fine was also granted.

Another kind of liberty, which still survives, was a market, a commercial monopoly, with the right to take market dues and to inflict fines for false weights and measures. Tolls of different sorts might also be granted, and conversely freedom from toll imposed by other men. Any negative grant of this sort may be safely assumed to create a positive right to correspond. Quittance from shire and hundred meant the right to hold a court that could do the work of shire and hundred so far as the men of the liberty were concerned; freedom from tallage, lastage, stallage, pontage meant that the men who could have paid these dues to another authority paid them to the lord of the liberty; freedom from sheriff's aid, wardpenny, hundredpenny, borthpenny, averpenny meant that these ancient customary dues were levied by the lord of the liberty for his own use instead of being levied by the sheriffs' underlings for the king's use. Lastly, to all other possible sources of revenue may be added rights of chase and warren, which certainly had their economic as well as their sporting and legal aspect.

(d) The Obligations of the Franchise Holder

'Of those who have liberties granted to them by the kings of England and have used them as they should not; also of liberties which hinder common justice and subvert royal power.'—cc. 9, 10.

'What lords or seneschals or bailiffs of lords have not upheld the execution of the lord king's commands, or have scorned to obey them?'—c. 12.

It has already been said that these privileges involved heavy responsibilities. If the king recognized the right of a subject to draw a case from the king's court to his own, to serve his writs, or to receive sheriff's aid or felons' goods, he demanded in return that the work of government should be well done. A good earl or abbot might take a pride in doing the work well. A fifteenth-century Abbot of St. Edmund's boasted that his liberty had been 'noted and holden the most notable franchise of good rule in the land'. But another monk of the same abbey, writing at much the same date, tells how Edward the Confessor when he first granted the eight and a half hundreds to Abbot Baldwin said to him, 'Unwisely have you demanded for yourself and your successors a great and continuous labour.' Those reforms which had increased the sheriff's work had multiplied the duties of the franchise-holder also, and the community must not be allowed to suffer by the substitution of seignorial for royal officials. The jurors of 1274 were asked whether the liberties granted by the king had impeded common justice, and if they had been exercised in accordance with the terms of the grant, and further, if lords of liberties had impeded the execution of the king's commands. To this last question there are copious returns, in which the recalcitrant lord of a liberty is often bracketed with a corrupt or negligent sheriff. In Yorkshire ' almost all the sheriffs and bailiffs do this '.[1] One lord refused to allow the wapentake to be held on his land, sending out his bailiff to resist by force of arms.[2] In Wilts the Abbot of Glastonbury resisted the due execution of thieves in Warminster hundred.[3] In Lincolnshire, in Calceworth hundred, there are three cases of concerted attacks on the king's bailiffs led by seignorial officials, in resistance to distraint.[4] In Nottinghamshire seignorial bailiffs resisted the king's bailiff of Thurgarton wapentake when he came to do his office, beat him, and imprisoned him for three days.[5] John Beauchamp, lord of Boltbury, killed the hundred bailiff of Stanborough when he came to distrain for the king's debts.[6] William of Munchensy protected an indicted felon who had taken refuge in his house within the Earl of Gloucester's liberty in Cambridgeshire, and refused to hand him over to the bailiff of Wetherley hundred who came to arrest him.[7] The most flagrant defiance of royal authority recorded is that already described, of the Earl of Lincoln's bailiff in Staincliff hundred, who insulted the commissioners with vile words, threatening to arrest them if they entered his lord's liberty. Parallel to this is the case of the bailiff of Ainsty wapentake, which was held by the citizens of York ; having been removed from his office by the commissioners in 1274–5 he had been reinstated by the mayor before the justices in eyre came round in 1279.[8] In Suffolk the Earl of Gloucester's bailiffs and those of Peter de Walpole often impeded the bailiffs of Risbridge hundred by beating him,[9] and the bailiffs of Eye also resisted the hundred bailiff.[10] The government action which

[1] *R.H.*, I, 130. [2] Ibid., I, 128. [3] Ibid., II, 277.
[4] Ibid., I, 269. [5] Ibid., II, 311. [6] Ibid., I, 79.
[7] Ibid., I, 50. [8] Ibid., I, 126. [9] Ibid., II, 171. [10] Ibid., II, 148.

most often provoked this resistance was, according to the jurors, the taking of beasts, very generally, to compel payment of the king's debts. To overcome such resistance the sheriff could call on the military forces of the shire long before the statute of 1285 authorized this proceeding.[1] In 1251, for instance, the sheriff of Northants was commanded to take the forces of the shire and arrest the thieves whom the Bishop of Lincoln's officials had failed to take. Where the fault clearly lay with the official and not with the lord of the liberty less drastic methods were necessary. The returns for Holderness wapentake mention William Blaungy, who had bought the bailiwick of the wapentake from its lord, Edmund of Cornwall, as oppressing the country-side in order to raise the price he had paid.[2] The Exchequer rolls for 1275 show that Blaungy has been committed to the Fleet Prison for returning the names of dead men in writs connected with the holding of a certain inquest.[3]

The jurors are handicapped when they wish to report the abuse of privileges by their ignorance of the exact terms of the charters that had conferred them. But, in their opinion, lords are constantly going beyond their chartered liberties ; enforcing forest law outside their chases,[4] imparking the beasts of outsiders,[5] taking distresses outside the bounds of their fiefs,[6] taking tolls which their market rights do not warrant,[7] withdrawing their man from suit at the two great hundreds,[8] and holding their courts at wrong times,[9] or contrary to the custom of the realm.[10] They are also charged with impeding common justice by the reception of outlaws [11] and by the refusal to admit the king's coroner into their liberties.[12]

Both the Hundred Rolls and the returns to Kirkby's Quest ten years later give the impression that this seignorial obstructiveness, to use no harsher term, was commoner in the northern counties than in the south. Nearness to the marches and remoteness from Westminster, as in Wales, probably helped to lessen the force of the king's writ ; yet even in these far-off parts,

---

[1] *Stat. Realm*, I (c.39.)   [2] *R.H.*, II, 313.
[3] Rigg, *Exchequer of Jews*, II, 313.   [4] *R.H.*, II, 280.   [5] Ibid., II, 171.
[6] Ibid., II, 148.   [7] Ibid., I, 280.   [8] Ibid., II, 278.   [9] Ibid., II, 116.
[10] Ibid., II, 21.   [11] Ibid.   [12] Ibid., II, 96.

if the king's government stood firm, the lord of the liberty would have to yield. If the writ *ne omittas propter libertatem* was of no avail, and the sheriff found himself prevented by force from entering the liberty to carry out the king's commands, the next step was the confiscation of the liberty itself. Thus in 1268 the Exchequer rolls record that because John de Burgh and his bailiffs fail to execute the king's writs when they have received them from the sheriff within the hundred of Rochford, and also refuse to let the sheriff execute them, the king, unwilling that justice shall perish, commands the sheriff to take the liberty into the king's hands and administer it himself.[1] The same fate befell the greatest franchise holder in the land, the Bishop of Durham, though it took the full authority of the king's council in Parliament to pronounce the judgement in his case. The bishop had long defied the authority of the king, finally throwing into prison the messengers bearing the king's writs directed to him. His liberty therefore was taken into the king's hands ' because the bishop, since he holds the said liberty, issuing from and dependent upon the crown, by the king's grant, is so far the king's minister for upholding and carrying out in the king's name and in due manner what belongs to royal authority within the said liberty ; so that he ought to do justice to all and each there, and duly submit both to the lord king and his lord and his mandates, although by the said grant he receive the profits and issues thence arising. For the royal authority extends through the whole realm, both within the liberties and without.' [2]

The judgement on Antony Bek was given at the end of Edward's reign, when his life-work was complete, but in his first great parliament of 1275 the same principle had been laid down : ' Even where the king's writ does not run, as in the Marches of Wales, the king is sovereign lord and will do right to any who complains to him if the lord of the liberty is remiss.' [3] The principle logically involved in Henry II's use of the writ of right was now being applied in practice : ' Do right, or the king will do it for you.' In the past the holders of liberties had often

---

[1] Madox, *Exchequer*, p. 703.   [2] *Plac. Abbrev.*, p. 257.
[3] *Stat. Realm*, I, 31 (c. 17).

likened their position to that of royal officers : they had claimed 'whatever belongs to the sheriff'; they had acted 'as if sheriffs or hundredors'. Now Edward I retorts : 'If you have the powers of a hundredor, of a sheriff, of a royal justice, you must accept their obligations. You are my servants as much as they are, and I expect to be well served.'

CHAPTER XII

CENTRAL CONTROL

TO the knight of the shire in the thirteenth century the shire might well seem the centre of governmental activity. He still could feel that he and his fellows ran the county court ; most often the sheriff was one of themselves, and though a sheriff might come along from some other county every now and then, the custom of the shire was stronger than he, and only with the help and goodwill of the county gentry could he hold the court. The sheriff's band of underlings were mostly men of the country-side ; the coroners were chosen in the county court ; the constables of the hundreds and vills were responsible to and for their hundreds and vills. The abbot too, colleague or subordinate of the sheriff, was a local man, officially if not personally, holding by tradition as tenaciously as any squire. The earl or baron might be an absentee, and might transfer seneschals or bailiffs from some other shire to administer his liberty ; but in fact local custom ruled here also and survived even a change of landlord.

> And as in good St. Edward's days
> So must it go, Saint Use allows,
> When Norman lords ride English ways.

The country-side had accepted and incorporated many new things since 1066, slowly and obstinately ; it held to them tenaciously, and its affairs were largely administered by natives of the shire. A sheriff who came from outside might find himself, like Alan of Whiton in 1204, insulted as ' upstart ' and ' alien ' in his own county court by those who prided themselves on being gentlemen born and bred in the shire and felt that Somerset men ought to manage Somerset affairs.[1] Yet it is possible to over-emphasize the self-sufficiency of local life, socially, economically, and constitutionally. The government of the shire was inter-penetrated by outgrowths of the central government. The

[1] *Curia Regis Rolls*, III, 129.

Norman lords had ridden English ways to such purpose that at every turn of the road a signpost could be seen pointing to Westminster. The long arm of the king reached far enough to touch the humblest villager as well as the lordliest earl ; not with the capricious finger of the despot, but with the matter-of-fact rap of the royal messenger, bearing his bundle of writs. Such a budget might contain commands to the sheriff to appear before the treasurer and barons on such and such a day to make his annual account at the Exchequer ; orders to the escheator to hold an inquest into the lands and rents held in the shire by some lately deceased tenant-in-chief ; a summons to a magnate to appear before the king's justices and explain why his bailiffs had failed to execute the king's writ ; an order to the sheriff to cause a record to be made in the shire court of a plea begun there between two county gentlemen that had since been called into the king's court at Westminster ; a mandate from the justices for a jury to be ready to appear before them three weeks after Easter to give a verdict in a case of Novel Disseisin ; orders to the sheriff to call together the forces of the shire to defend the sea-coast, or to have chosen in the county court four knights to see to the assessment and collection of the fifteenth lately granted to the king, or to see that such a young gentleman assumed knighthood or paid a fine. And every such writ would contain the clause requiring the recipient to return it, endorsed, to the place whence it came.

Behind and above the local oligarchies was the king's court, organized, by 1274, in a number of departments, each with its tradition, its machinery, its *esprit de corps*. In theory at least there were no loose ends in local government ; the lazy or oppressive or corrupt official might at any moment feel the jerk that reminded him of his obligations.

Every question put to the jurors in 1274 as to the sheriff's performance of his fiscal duties implies a vigilant Exchequer, ready and able to make the sheriff pay whether he cheats king or people. Here we have good reason to know that it is not merely a question of ideals and theories ; the system works. If the sheriff comes short in one year he will have to make it up next year or later; his remotest heirs will never be quit till the shortage was made good. The lord of the liberty who has estreats of writs will not be able to protect his bailiffs if they have failed to collect the king's revenues when they received the king's commands at the hands of the sheriff; and if they have direct dealings with the Exchequer their case is no better— rather worse. The escheator who has been making hay for himself while the sun shines between the death of a tenant-in-chief and the taking of seisin by the heir will find himself accountable; if he escapes the barons of the Exchequer it will be only to fall into the hands of the justices in eyre or of some special commissioner. The coroners will have to meet the justices of jail delivery, coming to clear up the criminal business accumulated by the sheriff's tourns and coroner's inquests. The whole army of local government officials, down to sub-bailiffs, bedels, and village constables, will sooner or later be raked by the searching eyes and exhaustive catechizing of the justices in Eyre—the justices for all pleas, as they are called. And behind the itinerant justices is the king's council, ready, at a pinch, to teach an earl or baron that the king's law rules the land, as well within liberties as without.

Whichever line of local administration you follow you find the king at the end. His writs, his barons, his justices, his counsellors are there to compel acceptance of the rule of law. That is the theory: as much the theory of Henry III's reign as of his son's. Bracton had formulated all the claims that Edward made, and both of them built on the foundations laid by Henry II. ' You claim to govern yourselves; I am here to see that you govern yourselves well,' almost expresses the blending of the English and the Norman in our government. What had to be defined was the standard behind the word ' well '. Was ' good government ' in the king's interest, in that of the country-side, in that of the nobles ? The answer of Edward I was, ' In my interest,' but the barons of the fourteenth century would not allow the answer to stand, and the fifteenth century wrote in its place, ' Get yourself lordship, for thereby hang the law and the prophets.'

PART IV

THE SEQUEL TO THE INQUESTS OF 1274-5

CHAPTER XIII

ADMINISTRATIVE REFORM AND JUDICIAL ACTION

IN March 1275 the commissioners returned to Westminster, bearing their rolls with them—masses of information, far more than now survive. What good came of all this labour ? It is a question often asked to-day when a royal commission reports. The historian, the statistician, and the scientific economist pounce on the blue books and analyse and deduce ; how often is action taken upon the report ? The fate of the great Poor Law Commission of 1909-10 and of three successive commissions on the coal-mining industry should warn us against hasty condemnation of Edward I's government for slowness or inadequacy in acting upon the returns of 1274-5.

To use modern terminology, two kinds of government action were called for : where individuals had misconducted themselves, judicial action ; where the system was wrong, legislative action. The distinction is clear to us now ; it was less sharply marked in 1275, when the king's council, whether in parliament or out of parliament, had both judicial and legislative functions. It is to the administrators and judges in that body, inspired undoubtedly by the energetic personality of Edward himself, that we must attribute the prompt action taken in 1275. How far that action was effective and adequate is another matter.

On 26th December 1274 Edward had issued summons to a ' general parliament ', originally intended to be held in February, now postponed till after Easter, and had ordered every sheriff to send four of the knights of his shire who were ' more discreet in law ', as well as four or six burgesses from each of its boroughs, to be at Westminster to meet the magnates and treat with them concerning the affairs of the realm. On April 22nd this parliament began, and the chief monument of its labours is to be found in some fifty-one ' establishments ' or statutes, referred to in the law-books for centuries after as the Statutes of Westminster I. Drafted in the Council as they must have been, they were issued with the assent not only of the magnates but of the commonalty of the realm ; the burgesses and legally-minded knights had sanctioned them, and one chronicler describes them, in effect, as a bid for popularity. ' The king desiring, as was fitting, to please the people, compiled certain new statutes, which were not only in accordance with the spirit of the law, but also very much needed for the good of the whole realm.' [1]

These statutes [2] seem at first sight a mass of technicalities, baffling to those who are not ' discreet in the law ' of the thirteenth century. Stubbs, in his invaluable *Charters*, found only two of them worthy of citation. Coming to them, however, from the reports of the hundred juries of the previous six months we find ourselves on familiar ground. Again and again we recognize a well-known contingency. The ninth chapter, for instance, deals with the arrest of felons, providing for the punishment of both sheriffs and coroners who conceal felonies and fail to arrest felons, and of those lords of liberties who fail to carry out the sheriff's orders and so protect felons. The royal officials are to be imprisoned ; the lord is to lose his liberty. The fifteenth chapter deals with the sheriff's habit of allowing bail to offenders who had no lawful claim to it and of refusing it to those who were so entitled. The nineteenth chapter deals with the refusal to give quittance to those who had paid their debts to the king's Exchequer ; whilst the seventh chapter concerns the failure to pay for goods taken for the king's use, and the first chapter prescribes what hospitality the sheriff may lawfully claim on his journeys round the shire. In all, some twenty-four chapters deal with local government, and most are so nearly concerned with the type of offence reported in the Hundred Rolls that it is impossible to believe that there is no connexion. Those who

[1] Wykes (in *Annales Monastici* (R.S.), Vol. IV), p. 263.   [2] *Stat. Realm*, I, 26–39.

drew up the articles of October 11th 1274 must have had some hand in drafting the statutes approved in the parliament of April 1275. On May 28th orders were issued that the new statutes were to be proclaimed in every county court of England.

This was only the beginning of legislation on these matters. In the Michaelmas Parliament of 1275 another series of decrees, called the Statutes of the Exchequer, supplemented the existing regulations for the collecting of Exchequer debts by the sheriff and for the taking and selling of distresses. Provision was also made, as we shall see, in 1278, for inquiry into the keeping of these new statutes, with their new fresh restrictions upon the conduct of the local bureaucracy. In March 1284 came the so-called Statutes of Rhuddlan : [1] a series of elaborate regulations defining the procedure of accounting at the Exchequer and prescribing means of checking the sheriff. They were especially aimed against the practice of collecting the same sum several times over, which in 1274-5 had been a ubiquitous source of complaint ; and in order that the Exchequer might have precise and up-to-date information as to outstanding debts, an inquiry was ordered, in which the treasurer, John de Kirkby, himself took part. [2] Two or three Exchequer officials were sent to every county with a set of articles, some of them covering much the same ground as those of 1274, but all bearing on the fiscal organization of the county, and the obligations of its residents and officials towards the Exchequer. A wide invitation was extended to all who wished to complain of sheriffs and bailiffs to let the treasurer know their grievances. The official summary of the returns, long known by the name of Kirkby's Quest, is almost complete, though most of the original returns are lost. Those which survive show that the sworn knights did not mind repeating themselves, and brought charges against their sheriffs dating from the reign of Henry III. When the inquest was over—it took eighteen months—the Exchequer was in possession of up-to-date facts as to the farms of shires and hundreds, the handling of Exchequer tallies, the estreats of sheriffs and bailiffs of liberties, and other kindred matters.

[1] *Stat. Realm*, I, 69–70.   [2] See *Feudal Aids*, I, viii–xvii.

Even before Kirkby's Quest was over the sheriff's duties had been further defined by statute. The Statutes of Westminster II, published in the Easter Parliament of 1285,[1] dealt in detail, as we have already seen, with a number of the abuses revealed in the Hundred Rolls. The sheriff's power to arrest or blackmail men on a pretended indictment in the tourn was curtailed by chapter thirteen, which provided that all presentments by juries, whether in the tourn or elsewhere, should be sealed by at least twelve jurors before action was taken on them. The use made by the sheriff of approvers to obtain charges against wealthy and innocent persons must have been materially diminished by chapter twelve, which assigned a punishment for frivolous appeals, and ordered that the appellant might only be heard if he had possessions which could be forfeited in case of a false charge. The thirty-ninth chapter went thoroughly into an abuse which had been insufficiently handled in the first statutes of Westminster,[2] namely, the sheriff's delay in executing writs. The remedy was like that provided by the Statute of Rhyddlan in the case of money payments ; writs were to be delivered to the sheriff before witnesses, and he was to give a receipt for them. As the Exchequer had to supply the justices with a list of those liberties which had return of writs it was not open to the sheriff to pretend that the neglect lay with officials who were out of his control when in fact he possessed full powers. If he falsely returned that he had been prevented by force from executing a writ a penalty was provided ; the justices of assize were given power to inquire into the sheriff's non-execution of writs and to punish them if fault was proved. If, on the other hand, it was found that the fault lay with the lord of a liberty, the king reserved his punishment to himself. Other chapters provided punishment for the practice of compelling men to attend courts to answer false or malicious charges, regulated the public swearing in of bailiffs who come to be employed in taking distresses, and prohibited the empanelling on juries of men over seventy or non-resident in the shire, as well as the summoning of ' an unbridled number of jurors ' when only a few were required.[3] Property

---

[1] *Stat. Realm*, I, 71–95. [2] C. 45. [3] CC. 36, 37, 38.

qualifications were fixed for jurors who served on the possessory assizes. These rules also were to be enforced by the justices of assize.

As far as legislation went, the statutes of 1275–85 had covered practically all the administrative abuses revealed in the Hundred Rolls. What other action had been taken ?

It is easier to remodel systems than men ; it is easier to draw up statutes than to enforce them. Edward's aims and principles are unmistakable, but their working out in practice is another story. How far was his government able to convince the local government official that the newly defined standards of character and conduct could not be disregarded with impunity ? Undoubtedly, the most effective argument would be a thoroughgoing judicial investigation into the charges preferred by the hundred jurors of 1274–5.

No general time limit had been fixed when these jurors had been invited to report all cases of misconduct within their knowledge, but references in two of the articles to the battle of Evesham and the Statute of Marlborough suggest that the post-war period was chiefly in mind. The returns, however, cover a much wider period, going back into the forties and fifties, and even if these pre-war charges are eliminated, some thousands of officials were implicated in the returns. To take the statistics of a few counties : the numbers of those accused in Essex are 210, in Cambridgeshire 92, in Suffolk 327, and in Norfolk 343. To deal with such an array of charges judicially would tax the existing machinery to the uttermost. In the ordinary way, the Exchequer was the place for dealing with official misconduct, but cases were also heard by the justices *coram rege*. At some date between 1276 and 1278 the council arranged that travelling justices should also be given power to hear and determine charges brought against officials for offences committed within the last twenty-five years, including charges made in the inquests of 1274–5, and also of later offences, including intimidation of the jurors of those inquests. This order of the Council, traditionally known as the Statute of Ragman, does not appear to have been carried out until November 1278, when the first eyres ' for all pleas ' of Edward I's reign began. The justices who then set out on their travels had more extensive powers than any before them. Their commission authorized them to hear and determine pleas of liberties, to hear and redress all complaints of trespasses committed either by the king's bailiffs or by those of other men, according to the law and custom of the realm, the new ordinance (of Ragman), the new statutes, and the articles delivered to them. These articles were alarmingly lengthy. Not only the old chapters of the eyre, sixty-nine in number by now, were to be administered to the eyre juries, but also thirty-nine of the articles of October 11th 1274 and thirty-three new articles, based on the statutes of April and October 1275. The sworn men of the hundred, confronted by these 140 questions, were driven again and again to the reply, ' We do not know,' if the verdicts still surviving are typical. But they had to be on their guard lest they contradicted the statements made in 1274–5. The sheriffs seem to have been ordered to empanel the same men who had served on the previous occasion, and the marks on the eyre rolls show that the names were checked.[1] The judges, it will be remembered, had the Ragman rolls with them—the returns themselves—and their annotations show how frequently they referred to them.

Though, as we have seen, some of the rolls of 1274–5 were lost on the circuit, and many later, we possess enough annotated rolls to get some rough impression of the way the justices followed up the charges made by the ' Ragman jurors '. Good examples of such notes are to be found in the returns for Lincolnshire, Derbyshire, Nottinghamshire, Gloucestershire, Norfolk, and Suffolk.

William de Saham and his fellow-justices reached Nottingham in November 1280, after spending some fifteen months over the eyre of Yorkshire. There are six wapentakes in Nottinghamshire. In Bassetlaw charges had been brought against six wapentake bailiffs and ten of their sub-bedels. In 1280 it was found that two of the bailiffs were dead and one sub-bedel was not available, but eight of the sixteen were brought to book. Against one bailiff fifteen charges had been made in 1275 ; in 1280 it is noted

---

[1] e.g., R.H., I, 249, 276.

'He cannot deny this.'[1] In the wapentake of Thurgarton and Lye a sheriff is brought to judgement for an unjust amercement, all the bailiffs save one are amerced for fining brewsters wrongfully, and one bailiff is acquitted of malicious arrest.[2] In Broxton wapentake the sub-bailiff's exaction of sixpence from five men in 1272 that they might be let off a summons is annotated, 'A small offence'—too small, presumably, for the justices to trouble about. Four offenders, it is noted, have been dealt with elsewhere—it may be in the Exchequer—and two have died.[3] In Bingham wapentake it had been alleged that the sheriff had failed to arrest persons indicted at his tourn in 1274; now in 1280 he demands the names of those who had been seen at large after being indicted, and as none can name them he goes free. He is also acquitted of having raised the farm of the wapentake.[4] An under-sheriff is also acquitted of having refused to give a receipt for an Exchequer debt.[5]

If Nottinghamshire is a typical county, the proceedings against the accused officials were fairly business-like. Lincolnshire was larger, more densely peopled, more heavily staffed. The justices reached Lincoln in June 1281, and their notes on the Hundred Rolls show that a good deal of time was spent on these charges. Some of the most unpopular bailiffs are dead, like Ralph of Ingham in Morley wapentake, who had been accused of twenty-three offences; Robert Turre of Aswardthurn, against whom thirty charges had been made; and Peter de Bures of the same wapentake, charged with sixty-eight offences.[6] Various other bailiffs, coroners, escheators, and sheriffs have died. But there are notes of another sort: one bailiff has been hanged; several officials pay a fine; one compounds 'for all trespasses in the Ragmans', that is, for at least twenty-six alleged offences; one sheriff produces a pardon from the king for failure to execute a writ; in several instances the accused is let off because the trespass is so small or happened so long ago—1266, in fact; and again there are some who have been punished already. The entry, 'He is convicted' or 'He cannot deny this', occurs once

---

[1] *R.H.*, II, 306. [2] Ibid., II, 312. [3] Ibid., II, 315.
[4] Ibid., II, 329. [5] Ibid., II, 320. [6] Ibid., I, 340, 246–7.

or twice ; but more often he is acquitted and goes free.   One man proves that he never was a bailiff, and as no one prosecutes the complaint he goes free.   There are a good many entries to the effect that as no one sues nothing arises from this charge ; once, where the principal offender in a case of alleged false imprisonment has died, it is noted that the injured parties can, if they like, sue by way of complaint (*querela*).

The Cambridgeshire rolls also refer to this method of individual complaint, the alternative to the joint presentment of a jury. Some of the charges made against the officials were such that the crown did not care to prosecute, and left the initiative to the injured party, having made it clear that he could use the simpler and cheaper procedure of the complaint of ' bill ' rather than the more formal and expensive method of the writ.

For some unknown reason general eyres were suspended during the years 1282 and 1283, and the records of the later eyres are less illuminating.   In the few annotated Hundred Rolls for Cambridgeshire (1286), Norfolk and Suffolk (1286), and Gloucestershire (1287), there is, as we should expect, a higher proportion of intervening deaths and a lower of punishments of officials, but there is no doubt that they are being called upon to reply in 1286–7 to charges which had been made in 1274–5.   For Norfolk, with its record number of peccant officials, only one annotated return is extant, that for Mitford hundred.   Here four of the eight bailiffs charged were dead by 1286, and eight of the twenty-six victims.[1]

The process of conviction and punishment seems slow and incomplete in modern eyes, but judged by thirteenth-century standards it was efficient if not rapid work.   It is noteworthy that the country-side was not always vindicated : actual acquittals are recorded.   We may fairly assume that of those whose trial is not recorded a proportion had been dealt with by the Exchequer and the King's Bench.   But it is only fair also to recall the pessimistic statement of the Dunstable annalist : ' The king sent his commissioners everywhere to inquire how his sheriffs and bailiffs had conducted themselves ;   but no good came of it.'

[1] *R.H.*, I, 498–500.

CHAPTER XIV

THE *QUO WARRANTO* PLEAS

HOW about the other aspect of the inquest, the usurpation of franchises ?

No action, it would seem, was taken upon the evidence on the liberties for more than three years. Possibly Edward's Welsh wars were making it unwise for the king to risk antagonizing his military tenants. But in August 1278, when a general eyre was determined upon in Council at Gloucester, and a new, more sweeping commission drawn up for the justices, their instructions empowered them to follow up not only reports of official misdeeds but also reports of unwarranted liberties. By the first of the statutes issued at Gloucester [1] it was provided that all those enjoying liberties might continue to exercise them until the coming of the justices in eyre into their county, but when that should happen the sheriffs were to make proclamation, with the customary forty days' notice, that all who claimed such liberties, whether by charter or otherwise, should appear before the justices to state what liberties precisely they claimed, and show by what warrant—*quo warranto*—they claimed them. If they failed to appear on the set day their liberties would be taken into the king's hands ; but if they appeared, the court would then proceed to examine the warrant or title whereby they claimed.

On the first eyres under these new conditions, which began on November 3rd 1278, the justices were accompanied by pleaders—King's Counsel, as we should call them to-day—to plead the king's cause against all those who claimed liberties. Their arguments are recorded at length on the eyre rolls, long extracts from which are printed in the Record Commission volume entitled *Placita Quo Warranto* ; in geographical, not chronological, order, it should be noted. It was a heavy task ;

[1] *Stat. Realm*, I, 45–61.

only two sets of justices were appointed, and all the counties of England had not yet been visited by 1293.

This wholesale questioning of privileges so ancient and well established provoked again the protest which the clergy had made in 1257, when Edward's father had followed up the inquests of 1255 with a demand that holders of liberties should show their titles. In 1257 the clergy had tried to make Magna Carta cover their grievance ; the liberties of the Church, they declared, had been secured to them by Henry's repeated confirmations of it, and now he was trying to take their liberties away by picking holes in their charters and declaring long-established usage no good warrant. In the storms of 1258 to 1267 this particular grievance had been lost to sight ; there had been no serious challenge to the position of the franchise-holders. Now, in 1278, the first protest comes from the laity. According to the chronicler Walter of Hemingburgh, it was Earl Warenne who led the resistance, who, brandishing a rusty sword, declared that their ancestors had won their lands by the sword and held them by the sword. If such a plea was really put forward (and the only version of the story that we have cannot be earlier than 1304, and may well be later) it would not secure much bearing in a court of law. ' My good sir,' Justice Reigate might reply, ' we are not asking you by what warrant you hold your lands ; it is the liberties which you exercise in those lands that are in question. What do you claim, and what is your warrant for claiming it ? According to these rolls we have with us, which our clerks in their humorous way call the Ragman rolls, you hold nine hundreds in the rape of Lewes ; you claim to hear pleas of *vee de naam* in your court of Lewes ; you claim wreck of the sea in all your demesne manors ; you claim rights of warren and chase through-out the barony, and imprison those who hunt hares and other wild animals at your will.[1] We note, by the way, that it was alleged in 1274 that you had failed on several occasions to execute the king's writs, but that is another story. What you have to do now is formally to claim these liberties, and we can then proceed to business.'

[1] *R.H.*, II, 208.

So the justices might have spoken ; in fact, we have record that they did so. According to the rolls of the eyre of Sussex, June 1279, Earl Warenne said that he did *not* claim *vee de naam*, but he did claim a prison, gallows, pillory and tumbril, assize of bread and ale, view of frank-pledge, and thief-hanging in all his Sussex lands, and produced his warrant, and the eyre jury found that he and his ancestors had had these rights from time immemorial, and that was the end of it.[1] The only touch of romance is in his assertion that John had granted to his ancestors rights of chase and warren in all his lands because their name was Warenne. Neither counsel, jurors, nor judges seem to have troubled themselves with this plea ; they were satisfied that there had been no such usurpation of King Henry III's royal rights of the chase as the jurors of 1274 had alleged.

As a matter of fact, in so far as a stand had been made against this *quo warranto* campaign it had been made before the justices reached Sussex and by a greater magnate even than Earl Warenne —by Gilbert of Clare, the king-maker of Evesham, the future husband of Edward's baby daughter, Joan of Acre. Scarcely had the decree been issued as to the claiming of liberties when the Earl of Gloucester put forward his petition, possibly in the parliament at Gloucester itself, protesting against the disturbance of his liberties and asking for a guarantee of peaceful possession.[2] As a result, the Council at once turned on the experts to draft a writ of liberties. The Clare liberties were not confined to the honour of Clare ; they extended into almost every county of England, and came in question in the very first eyre opened by the justices, at Hertford, on November 3rd 1278.[3] The plea was, however, adjourned to the Kentish eyre, and it was at Canterbury, in January 1279, that Gilbert's lawyers maintained that he was not bound to answer to the writ that commanded him to show by what warrant he held the hundreds of Washling-stone and Littlefield in Kent.[4] The earl's attorney takes the line that this is a newfangled and inadequate sort of writ ; who

---

[1] *Plac. Quo War.*, p. 750–1.
[3] *Plac. Quo War.*, p. 278.
[2] *Rot. Parl.*, I, 8.
[4] Ibid., p. 337.

is claiming these hundreds from the earl ? No name is mentioned, why should he answer it ?

Gilbert of Clare was raising a fundamental question, whether he knew it or not, and the matter was referred to the king's council. With the backing of the justices, they declared that there was nothing new about the writ. The old plea rolls in the Exchequer showed clearly that writs as to the holding of private hundreds had long been in use. Here the records bear them out ; the rolls of the eyre of Devon in 1238 abound in claims to hold hundreds, clearly in response to some challenge. As to the more technical objection, that no party was named in the writ, they called on the judges for a ruling, and a statement was drawn up, signed by ten justices of the two Benches, which was to guide the justices in eyre throughout the campaign. To name the king as party in a plea of *quo warranto* would be unnecessary they say, and, indeed, dangerous. If the formula used stated that the liberty claimed belonged to the crown, it would imply that some liberties did not belong to the crown ; whereas every liberty was royal in origin and belonged either to the crown or to him who had sufficient warrant, either by charter or from time immemorial.[1]

This ruling having reached Canterbury, the king's counsel pressed the argument home. The earl must answer, and he must show either immemorial tenure or a royal grant. Earl Gilbert withdrew his opposition and produced his warrant ; but it was neither charter nor time out of mind. Somewhere between 1216 and 1230 his grandfather had persuaded one Gilbert le Smale-writere, who held the hundreds at farm from the sheriff of Kent, to make them over to him, and the Clares had held them ever since. The fact that there had been two minorities in the intervening period, during which the crown had held the hundreds, and after which they had restored them to the Clares, was good evidence against usurpation, and though the liberties were taken into the king's hands, final judgement was reserved. But later history shows that this is one of the few instances when the king retained a liberty so confiscated ; the Clares never had the two

---

[1] *Parliamentary Writs*, I, 383–4.

hundreds again. On the particular ground where Gilbert of Gloucester had taken his stand he was routed ; he had been compelled to show his warrant, and it was adjudged insufficient, and the judgement stood.

Official history, then, does not back up the chronicler's sensational story of a stout and successful baronial resistance. Instead we see the most independent and mighty of the English earls raising the fundamental issue of vested interests versus royal supremacy, and being defeated by the authority of the Bench. Bracton's doctrine had been vindicated in practice ; the doctrine that liberties are regalities, that no title to them is valid save that which the king has sanctioned by charter or by immemorial acquiescence, and that the king has a right to put the question, ' By what warrant ? ' to any subject claiming regalian rights.

No doubt many incidents took place that are not enrolled on the legal record. Walter of Hemingburgh has another story of the nobles' sons who lived in the king's household as pages amusing themselves by singing songs while their fathers were counselling the king in his parliament :

> The king he wants to get our gold,
> The queen would like our lands to hold,
> And the writ *Quo Warranto*
> Will give us all enough to do ! [1]

It certainly gave the judges and lawyers enough to do. Even the 840 pages of *Quo Warranto* Pleas printed in 1818 only contain a part of the legal proceedings set going by the Statute of Gloucester. Not even all the Eyre Rolls are printed, and numerous cases were transferred to the central courts and must be sought for on the unprinted Exchequer or *Coram Rege* Rolls. There are signs that the judges themselves thought some of this work unnecessary. Extraordinary claims were put forward by the king's counsel on his behalf : in those days any ambitious young lawyer might take it on himself to be the king's advocate, and might use arguments for which a royal justice would not accept responsibility.[2] Thus all kinds of issues might be raised—amongst others, how far the memory of man extended ; and

---

[1] *Hemingburgh*, II, 7 (York Powell). [2] For Serjeant, see Plate VI

the settlement of cases was postponed unduly because the justices
felt bound to refer to the king.   In 1290 a supplementary statute
was passed, which provided that time immemorial ended at 1190,
the date of Richard I's coronation, and bound the king to recognize and confirm to their holders all liberties which a jury should
find has been enjoyed from that date.[1]

Had Edward by this statute of 1290 admitted defeat ?   So it
used to be thought.[2]   He did, in fact, bind himself to accept a
well-established convention (legal memory for some other purposes had in 1275 been fixed at 1190) which before that date he
had been free to override ; but it is difficult to trace any change
in his practice.   After, as before, 1290 the pleaders produce
outrageous arguments on behalf of the crown ; after, as before,
1290 the judgement of the court is reserved, and one suspects
that the case was settled out of court.   No change in policy is
traceable.   If we look for results we find that forfeiture of a
liberty is most unusual.   Almost all the liberties reported in the
Hundred Rolls seem still to be held by the same lords at the end
of Edward's reign.   If the object of the inquiry was to take the
liberties away from their holders he certainly did not succeed.
But why should he have wanted to do so ?   From the Hundred
Rolls it is pretty clear that government ran on much the same
lines within liberties as without.   The bailiffs of the Earl Marshal
or the Abbot of Glastonbury are not accused of more oppression
or injustice than those of the sheriff of Norfolk or Somerset,
bailiffs appointed by the sheriff and responsible only to him and
the king.   The work done is the same, whether done by seignorial
or royal officials, whether the profits and perquisites go to the
king's exchequer or to the abbot's, by way of sheriff or of seneschal.
The only difference is, it would seem, that when things go wrong
the check or spur may be applied more promptly to a royal than
to a seignorial official, and even this depends on the attitude of
the lord of the liberty.   An abbot zealous for the good repute of
his liberty might be more effective, from the point of view of the
man in the street, than a sheriff who had a habit of losing or

---

[1] *Stat. Realm*, I, 107.
[2] See Maitland, *Select Pleas in Manorial Courts*, pp. xx i lxxvii.

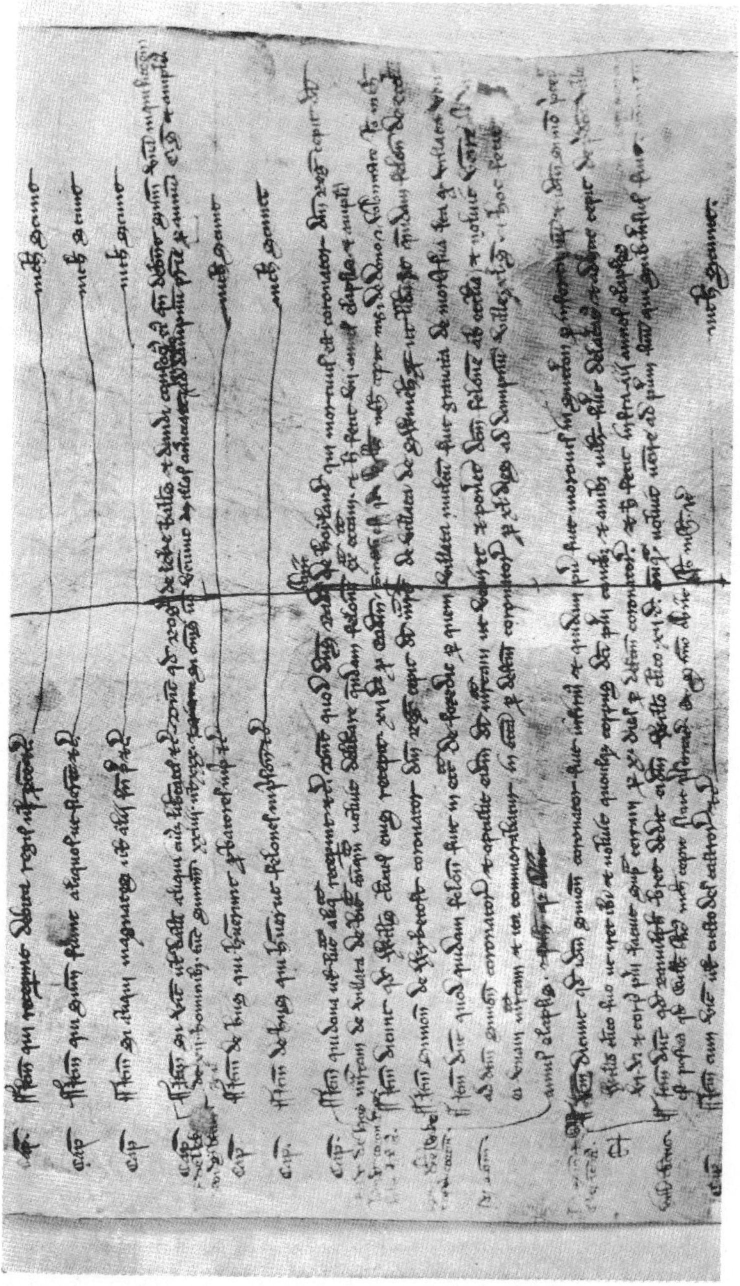

HUNDRED ROLL WITH ANNOTATIONS

PLATE VIII

forgetting royal writs.   And the lord of the liberty, if recalcitrant, could soon be taught that he was, in fact, a royal agent, differing only from the sheriff in holding his governmental powers during good conduct while the sheriff held his during the king's good pleasure.

There was no reason, then, for Edward to expropriate the franchise holders on a large scale.   On the other hand, if he really meant to enforce standards of good government it was all important to fix the responsibility.   The liberties must be set down in black and white, not only to teach the magnate his place in the order of things, not only to prevent quiet usurpation in the future, but also to provide data for checking a defaulting official.   If a sheriff alleged that the lord of a hundred had return of writs, and that it was not his fault therefore that such and such a writ had not been executed, the justices must be able to turn up an up-to-date list of those who had this liberty, so that they could check the validity of the excuse.   So with the hanging of thieves, the escape of felons, and a dozen other important governmental functions.   The returns of 1274–5, as checked by the *quo warranto* pleadings, were as useful departmentally as they were valuable politically.   We cannot doubt that king and ministers alike were well satisfied with their results.

Edward I was not a revolutionary ; in many respects he was strictly conventional.   He believed in monarchy as the form of government, and in law as the basis of government, but he never dreamt of rejecting feudalism as part of the fabric of administration, as of social ethics, even while his work was accelerating its decline.   Disraeli's dictum on feudalism, ' Its main principle was that tenure of property should be the fulfillment of duty ', would have been entirely after Edward's heart, and if he drove home the principle against a Bishop of Durham who had failed to fulfil his duty, he was himself ready in his turn to accept the retention of privilege by those who were performing their great and continuous task of government well and efficiently.

CHAPTER XV

CONCLUSION

*S*ED *nullum commodum inde venit.* Are we to accept the judgement of the monk of Dunstable ? Did the inquests of 1274–5, the statutes, the eyres, have any effect in raising the general standard of official conduct, or in teaching the lords of liberties their place in the scheme of national government ? In answering this question we are in effect seeking to pass judgement on the life's work of Edward I.

Of all the kings of medieval England, Edward appears the completest bureaucrat. In the long array of his legislative and administrative reforms we see the evidence of a passion for law, order, seemliness, and subordination unequalled in any who came before or after him. The rules laid down for the judges in settling difficult points of land law, for sheriffs and bailiffs in governing shire and hundred, for merchants in making business contracts, for coroners and escheators in managing their departments, for Exchequer officials in keeping the revenue accounts, the codification of the police and military rules, the scheme for the government of Wales—all these reflect the personality of an autocrat who is also a martinet. Alongside the regulations go the government inspections ; the inquest of 1274–5 is followed by the survey of 1279, the eyres from 1278 on, the Exchequer inquest of 1284–5, the Winchester articles, the State trials of 1290–93, the Trailbaston commissions of 1304–5. Truly, as Maitland said, this England of the thirteenth century is a ' much governed England ', familiar with red tape and blue books, strangely incongruous with that romantic and misty period of ' strong passions, enormous crimes, profound superstitions ' which the young Disraeli chose for the background of his medieval tragedy. Yet at the end of it all, when the old king dies at Burgh-upon-Sands with this vast accretion of statute law and governmental machinery to his credit, we feel that this is only half the story, and the achievement is less solid than it seems. As Professor Tout has taught us, it was not entirely the fault of his unlawyer-like and unbusiness-like son that the royal power was thwarted by an irresponsible baronage in the next reign. If Edward II reaped the whirlwind, his father had sown the wind : his policy was, even in his lifetime, foredoomed to failure or at best to incomplete fruition.

A general survey of Edward I's reign forces on us the conviction that he was not, in fact, able to keep up the pace he had set in his opening years. He was, it seems, nursing incompatible ideals. Efficiency and order could not be pursued with whole-hearted energy together with projects of foreign conquest. Wales, if we have guessed rightly, twice held up his schemes of administrative reform—in 1276–7 and in 1282–3 ; Scotland and France were to prove even more serious obstacles to peace with order. They exhausted the energy, the personnel, the finances of Edward, whilst the old soldier out of a job was to prove a fertile source of trouble to the English country-side for the next hundred years.

This close connexion between the question of good government and overseas affairs became patent in 1289, when the situation of 1274 was in a sense repeated. · From May 1286 to August 1289 Edward had been absent from England, with his cousin Edmund acting as *locum tenens* ; on his return he was greeted with an outburst of complaints against his officials, from the highest to the lowest, and by the news that two of his chief earls were carrying on something like a private war in the Welsh marches. Once again a special commission was appointed. This time it was to sit in London, not tour the country, and it was given authority not only to hear but to determine complaints against the king's ministers—' not only those of his household,' says a chronicler, ' but outsiders, such as justices of the Jews, justices of the forest, foresters, sheriffs, keepers of manors, in fact any one who could be called a bailiff.' [1] The commission sat for over

[1] Wykes (R. S.), p. 322.

three years, and investigated charges against between seven and eight hundred persons. The records of its proceedings have been analysed, though not printed,[1] and they afford some means of judging how far the legislation of 1275–85 was a dead letter.

Whilst the most spectacular offences are those of the great judges, thirteen of them, including the chief justices of both Benches and five of the justices in eyre who had heard the Ragman and *Quo Warranto* Pleas, for the purposes of local government it is the charges against sheriff, bailiff, sub-bailiffs, and constables that interest us most. The jurisdiction of the commissioners only extended to offences committed during the king's absence, and the field is thus much narrower than in 1274. No general complaints are preferred — only specific charges against individuals. In a very large proportion of cases the plaintiff fails to make good his charge and is amerced for a false complaint, or else fails to appear and loses the case by default. On the whole, the records give the impression that the scales are weighted on the side of officialdom ; that the sheriff or bailiff has resources in a court of law which the ordinary subject lacks, and that only when the king's interests were clearly at stake were the probabilities on the side of conviction. In such cases the punishment was ruthless ; the fines inflicted on the great men were of crushing severity, and we share the traditional sympathy of the legal profession for Chief Justice Hengham, fined seven thousand marks, most of which he actually paid, for technical irregularities committed, it was said, in showing mercy to the poor. William de Saham, again, who sat on all the eyres of the north-western circuit from 1278 to 1287, and brought home enough of the Ragman rolls to the Exchequer to earn our gratitude, seems to have been hardly treated. But the lesser fry got off pretty easily. The sheriffs and under-sheriffs may be taken as typical : forty-one men are charged on one hundred and thirty-eight separate counts ; on forty-three they win the case ; on eighty-seven no conclusion is enrolled, on eight only is conviction and punishment recorded. Very similar averages are

[1] Tout and Johnstone, *State Trials of Edward I* (C. S.).

found for the coroners, escheators, hundredors, constables, and sub-bailiffs of every sort, amongst whom a certain number of our old friends of the Hundred Rolls reappear. Gilbert of Clifton, the bailiff of Staincliff wapentake, who had insulted the king's commissioners in 1274, is charged, as ex-sheriff of Lancashire, with ten offences for none of which does he receive any punishment, not even for his refusal to publish in his county court the invitation to all men to bring their complaints before the king's commissioners.[1] Geoffrey Kempe, described as clerk of the castle in the Hundred Rolls, is now keeper of Ipswich Jail, and answers to ten charges, and in Essex, Norfolk, and Suffolk, to go no farther, the same hundred bailiffs are still rousing the indignation of the country-side in 1289 who were there fifteen years before.

The trials of 1290–3 confirm the impression produced by the fragmentary returns to Kirkby's Quest; the local government official has not greatly improved. This is not surprising; the habits of generations are not reformed in fifteen years, and a system cannot be much better than the men who are working it. These trials also show up the defects in the machinery for enforcing the higher standards. Justices in eyre like Solomon of Rochester and Richard of Boyland had been holding Ragman pleas and administering the articles based on the statutes of 1275 for the last twelve years; now they were convicted of extortion and the perversion of justice. The Exchequer, where the peccant sheriff and bailiff ought to answer, was staffed by men like the infamous Adam de Stratton, in whose house was found the vast fortune of £12,650, amassed by crooked means. Was it surprising that under such judges and accountants low standards still held their own in local government?

The story of the sinners is so spectacular that we ought to bear in mind the existence of a substantial body of justices and Exchequer clerks and sheriffs whose names do not appear on these rolls. *Omnia bene* is a short and unexciting record; but even in 1275 there are times when the jurors expressly state that such an one is a good and harmless fellow. The system worked

---

[1] Case 173, p. 133.

on the whole far too well for us to believe that all the officials of England were dishonest. But more serious than the sins of the small men and the corruption of the great is the attitude of the king himself—the fountain of justice, the English Justinian. When we recall that he came back from France owing £107,784 to his Italian bankers, and that the fines taken from the offenders amounted to £15,590, in addition to Stratton's confiscated fortune, and when, on top of this, we observe that most of the convicted ministers, even Stratton himself, were soon holding office again, it is difficult to avoid the conclusion that Edward was subordinating justice to gain : acting, in fact, exactly like those sheriffs who had been shown up in 1274. If the new ideals of upright government were being pursued half-heartedly, in the last resort the blame lies with Edward himself. *Quis custodiet ipsos custodes ?*

Along another line there is evidence that Edward's struggle to enforce law and order was, if not a defeat, a drawn battle. Since 1277 he had been supplementing the normal shire machinery described above by new devices for dealing with local disorder and enforcing the king's peace. As the sheriff's powers were being more and more strictly defined and limited it became necessary to devise new means of dealing with those burglars and highway robbers who broke into houses and attacked the innocent way-farer. In 1277 the sheriffs of twenty-nine counties were ordered to have elected in the county court a powerful and upright man as keeper of the peace to assist the sheriff in preserving order during the king's absence in Wales, with power to inquire into crime and to arrest the unruly.[1] How long these *custodes pacis* continued to act is not known, but the Statute of Winchester in 1285 opens with the admission that from day to day robberies, murders, and arson are more generally committed than they used to be, and felons cannot be attainted by the oath of jurors. This statute penalized the collusion of hundred juries : if they failed to present criminals, the whole hundred had to pay. The old system of watch and ward was tightened up, and measures dictated for making the roads safer for travellers. In spite of the

[1] *Engl. Hist. Rev.*, XL, 413.

insistence on local responsibility, in spite of the appointment of justices to inquire into the keeping of the statute, in spite of the appointment of new *custodes pacis* when the king goes to France in 1286, the gangs of robbers still flourish. Reinforced doubtless by soldiers returned from the wars to which both king and country-side so gladly dispatched the most troublesome and least diligent citizens, the gangs of clubmen, or ' trailbastons ',[1] who beat, maimed, and wounded the traveller, had become by 1304 such an infliction that king and council determined to send out justices with a commission almost as imposing as that of the justices in eyre to deal with the malefactors and disturbers of the peace, the depredators, homicides, and incendiaries, who black-mailed the country-side, intimidated the juries, and corrupted the officials who should have arrested them.

By appointing local keepers of the peace with power to inquire and arrest, and visiting justices with powers to try and punish these violent criminals, Edward was preparing the way for that official who more than any other was destined to supersede the sheriff. The *custos pacis* was the forerunner of the J.P.[2] Under Edward's grandson he was to acquire powers not merely of inquiry and detention but of trial and judgement. But the multiplication of local justices was not to prove an effective check on local disorders for a long time yet. It can hardly be maintained that Edward's descendants were more successful than he had been in upholding the standards of order, purity, and efficiency in government laid down by him in 1275 but more and more lost to view as he fought a losing battle with disorder at home, distracted between the fear of bankruptcy and the determination to assert his rights against the Scottish rebels and his insolent French overlord.

In his contest with the feudal baronage, again, no clear-cut victory can be reckoned to Edward. The crisis of 1297 showed how little the principle of public obligation weighed with them as compared with class privilege. But here also the king succeeded in securing a compromise and in escaping a surrender. The tussle between Bractonian feudalism and caste

[1] See p. 180. [2] B. H. Putnam, *Trans. R. Hist. Soc.* for 1929, pp. 19–48.

feudalism was to last for another century ; Richard II conducted the campaign on lines that his ancestor would have heartily approved when he tried to build up an official aristocracy to counter the aristocracy of blood and iron. But the final victory in this, as in the administrative field, was reserved for the Tudors.

In admitting that Edward failed to realize his ideals of government it would be wrong to end on the note of failure. When all is said and done, not only his ideals but his methods and achievements are worthy of respect. But for him the principles laid down by Bracton might have remained academic. Napoleon and Justinian live by their codes rather than by their conquests ; the English Justinian, by building on the foundations laid in his father's reign, did succeed in establishing a system that was remarkably tough and long-lived. The law he framed is barely obsolete to-day ; the liberties that he worked into his system of administration still determine the forms of local government to-day ; the keepers of the peace and the constables whom he set alongside the sheriff were destined to rule the English country-side for five hundred years. On the ideas which he took over from the servants and the opponents of his father and developed into a logical working system English local government was to subsist until the days of Bentham. And if he failed to translate into practice his dream of the rule of law ; if civil war under Edward II, speculative militarism under Edward III, oligarchic intrigue under Richard II and the Henrys were to undermine the Edwardian system of discipline and justice ; if the much-governed England of the thirteenth century was to decline into the lawless England of the Paston Letters, when it could be said that the law served for naught else but to do wrong, and of many Acts of Parliament that few were kept with true intent, and when justice, poisoned at the fountain head, was more weak, more corrupt, more inert than Ralph Hengham could ever have conceived, the whirligig of time was to bring its revenges. The law which Henry of Bracton, Simon de Montfort, and Edward Plantagenet had built up in their different ways was so deeply rooted in the national consciousness that the most revolutionary of all English despots felt bound to take it as his ally when he broke the bonds of Rome, and the Stuart antiquaries, though they reshaped them strangely, found the weapons they needed for their fight in the armouries of the Middle Ages.

APPENDIX I

THE ARTICLES OF OCT. 11, 1274, IN LATIN AND ENGLISH

Articuli ad Inquirendum

1. Quot et que dominica maneria rex habet in manu sua in singulis comitatibus, tam scilicet de antiquis dominicis corone quam de escaetis et perquisitis.

2. Que eciam maneria esse solent in manibus regum predecessorum regis, et qui ea tenent nunc, et quo waranto et a quo tempore et per quem et quomodo fuerint alienata.

3. De feodis eciam domini regis et tenentibus ejus : qui ea modo teneant de ipso in capite, et quot feoda singuli ipsorum teneant, et que feoda tenere solent de rege in capite, et nunc tenentur per medium, et per quem medium, et a quo tempore alienata fuerint, et qualiter et per quos.

4. De terris eciam tenencium de antiquo dominico corone, tam liberorum sokemannorum quam bondorum : utrum per ballivos aut per eosdem tenentes, et per quos ballivos et per quos tenentes, et a quibus alienate fuerint, qualiter, et a quo tempore.

5. Simili modo inquiratur de firmis hundredorum, wappentakiorum et trythingorum, civitatum, burgorum et aliorum reddituum quorumcunque, et a quo tempore.

6. Quot eciam hundreda, wapentakia et trythinga sint nunc in manu domini regis, et quot et que in manibus aliorum, et a quo tempore et quo waranto, et quantum valeat quodlibet hundredum per annum.

7. De sectis antiquis, consuetudinibus, serviciis et aliis rebus domino regi et antecessoribus suis subtractis ; qui ea subtraxerint, et a quo tempore, et qui hujusmodi secta, consuetudines, servicia et alia ad dominum regem pertinentia et consueta sibi ipsis appropriaverint, et a quo tempore et quo waranto.

8. Qui eciam alii a rege clamant habere returnum vel extracta brevium, et qui tenent placita de vetito namio, et qui clament habere wreccum maris, quo waranto, et alias libertates regias ut furcas, assisas panis et cervisie, et alia que ad coronam pertinent, et a quo tempore.

9. De hiis eciam qui habent libertates per reges Anglie concessas et eas aliter usi fuerint quam facere debuissent : qualiter, a quo tempore, et quomodo.

10. Item de libertatibus concessis qui impediunt communem justiciam et regiam potestatem subvertunt, et a quo concesse fuerint, et a quo tempore.

THE ARTICLES OF THE INQUEST

1. How many and what demesne manors the king has in his hand in every county, that is, both of the ancient demesnes of the crown, and of escheats and purchases.

2. What manors, moreover, used to be in the hands of the kings who were the king's predecessors, and who hold them, by what warrant and since when, and by whom and how they were alienated.

3. Also concerning the lord king's fees and tenants; who hold them now from him in chief, how many fees each of them holds; what fees used to be held in chief of the king and now are held through a mesne lord, and by what mesne, and from what time they have been alienated, how and by whom.

4. Also concerning the lands of tenants of the ancient demesne of the crown, whether free sokemen or serfs: whether held by deputies or by the tenants themselves, and by what deputies or tenants, and by whom they have been alienated, how and from what time.

5. Likewise inquiry shall be made concerning the farms of hundreds, wapentakes, ridings, cities and boroughs and of all other rents whatsoever and from what time.

6. Also how many hundreds, wapentakes and ridings are now in the lord king's hand, and how many and which are in the hands of others, from what time and by what warrant, and how much a year every hundred is worth.

7. Concerning ancient suits, customs, services and other things withdrawn from the lord king and from his ancestors; who withdrew them, and from what time; and who have appropriated to themselves such suits, customs, services and other things belonging of established custom to the lord king, from what time, and by what warrant.

8. Also, what other persons claim from the king to have return or estreats of writs, who hold pleas of *vee de naam*, who claim to have wreck of sea, and by what warrant, and other royal liberties such as gallows, the assizes of bread and ale and other things which belong to the crown; and from what time.

9. Also concerning those who have liberties granted to them by kings of England and have made use of them otherwise than they should have done; how, from what time and in what way.

10. Again concerning liberties which obstruct common justice and overturn the king's power, and by whom they were granted and since when.

11. Qui insuper de novo appropriaverint sibi chacias liberas vel warennas sine waranto, et similiter qui ab antiquo hujusmodi chacias et warennas ex concessione regis habuerint et fines et metas eorum excesserint, et a quo tempore.

12. Qui eciam, domini aut eorum senescalli seu ballivi quicumque, seu eciam domini regis ministri, non sustinuerint execucionem mandatorum domini regis fieri, aut eciam facere contempserint, vel aliquo modo ea fieri impedierint, a tempore constitucionum factarum apud Marleberwe anno regni domini regis Henrici patris regis nunc quinquagesimo secundo.

13. Item de omnibus purpresturis quibuscunque factis super regem vel regalem dignitatem : per quos facte fuerint, qualiter, et a quo tempore.

14. De feodis militaribus cujuscumque feodi et terris aut tenementis datis vel venditis religiosis vel aliis in prejudicium regis, et per quos, et a quo tempore.

15. De vicecomitibus capientibus munera ut consenciant ad concelandas felonias factas in ballivis suis, vel qui neglegentes extiterint ad felones hujusmodi attachiandos quocumque favore, tam infra libertates quam extra. Simili modo de clericis et aliis ballivis vicecomitum, de coronatoribus et eorum clericis et ballivis quibuscunque ; qui ita fecerint tempore domini Henrici regis post bellum de Evesham, et qui tempore domini regis nunc.

16. De vicecomitibus et ballivis quibuscunque capientibus munera pro recognitoribus removendis de assisis et juratis, et quo tempore.

17. Item de vicecomitibus et aliis ballivis quibuscunque qui amerciaverint illos qui summoniti fuerint ad inquisiciones factas per preceptum domini regis pro defalta cum per eandem summonicionem persone venerint sufficientes ad inquisiciones hujusmodi faciendas, et quantum et a quibus ceperint occasione predicta, et quo tempore.

18. Item de vicecomitibus qui tradiderint ballivis extorsoribus populum gravantibus supra modum hundreda wappentakia vel trithinga ad altas firmas ut sic suas firmas levarent, et qui fuerint illi ballivi, et quibus fuerint hujusmodi dampna illata, et quo tempore.

19. Item, cum vicecomites non debeant facere turnum suum nisi bis in anno, qui pluries fecerint in anno turnum suum, et a quo tempore.

20. Item cum fines pro redisseisinis aut purpresturis factis per terram vel equam, pro occultacione thesauri et aliis hujusmodi ad dominum regem pertineant et ad vicecomites hujusmodi attachiare, qui ceperint fines hujusmodi et a quibus et quantum.

21. Item qui potestate officii sui aliquos maliciose occasionaverint et per hoc extorserint terras, redditus aut alias prestaciones, et a quo tempore.

11. Who, moreover, have recently appropriated to themselves free chases or warrens without warrant, and likewise who have had such chases and warrens from old time by the king's grant and have gone beyond their bounds and landmarks, and since when.

12. What persons also, whether lords or their seneschals or bailiffs of any kind or even the lord king's officials, have not upheld the execution of the lord king's commands or have even scorned to carry them out, or have hindered the doing of them in any way, since the time when the constitutions were made at Marlborough in the fifty-second year of the reign of the lord king Henry, father of the king that now is.

13. Again concerning all encroachments whatsoever upon the king or upon the royal dignity : by whom they have been made, how and from what time.

14. Concerning knights' fees, of whomsoever held, and lands or holdings given or sold to monks or to other persons to the king's prejudice, by whom and from what time.

15. Concerning sheriffs who take gifts to consent to the concealment of felonies committed in their bailiwicks, or who neglect to attach such felons for favour to anyone, both within liberties and without. In like manner, concerning the clerks and other bailiffs of the sheriffs, concerning coroners and all their clerks and bailiffs : who have acted thus in the time of the lord king Henry since the battle of Evesham, and who in the time of the present lord king.

16. Concerning sheriffs and all manner of bailiffs who take gifts to remove recognitors from assizes and juries, and at what time.

17. Again, concerning sheriffs and all other manner of bailiffs who have amerced for default men summoned to make inquests by the lord king's command, when a sufficient number of persons had responded to the summons to make the inquest ; how much and from whom they have taken on this pretext, and since when.

18. Again, concerning sheriffs who have handed over to extortionate bailiffs, oppressing the people beyond measure, hundreds, wapentakes or ridings at high farms, so that they may thus raise their own farms ; who those bailiffs were, on whom they have inflicted such losses, and at what time.

19. Again, whereas sheriffs ought not to hold their tourn more than twice a year, who has held his tourn more often, and from what time.

20. Again, when fines for redisseisins or for encroachments by land or sea, for concealment of treasure and such like matters belong to the lord king and sheriffs ought to attach them, what persons have taken such fines, and from whom and how much.

21. Again who have by the power of their office troubled any maliciously and thus have extorted lands, rents or any other contributions, and from what time.

22. Qui receperint mandatum domini Regis ut ejus debita solverent et a creditoribus receperint aliquam porcionem ut eis residuum solverent, et nichilominus totum sibi allocari fecerint in scaccario vel alibi, et a quo tempore.

23. Qui receperint debita regis vel partem debitorum, et debitores illos non acquietaverint, tam tempore domini regis Henrici quam tempore domini regis nunc.

24. Item qui summonierint aliquos ut fierent milites et pro respectu habendo ab eis lucra receperint, et quantum, et quo tempore. Et si aliqui magnates vel alii sine precepto regis aliquos distrinxerint ad arma suscipienda et quo tempore.

25. Item si vicecomites aut ballivi aliqui cujuscunque libertatis non fecerint summonitiones debito modo secundum formam brevis domini regis vel aliter fraudulenter seu minus sufficienter executi fuerint precepta regia, prece, precio, vel favore, et quo tempore.

26. Item de hiis qui habuerint probatores imprisonatos et fecerint eos appellare fideles et innocentes causa lucri, et quandocumque eos impedierint ne culpabiles appellarent, et a quo tempore.

27. Item qui habuerint felones imprisonatos et eos pro pecunia abire et a prisone evadere permiserint liberos et impune ; et qui pecuniam extorserint pro prisone dimittenda per plevinam ; cum sint replegiati et a quo tempore.

28. Item qui dona vel lucra aliqua receperint pro officiis suis exercendis vel non exercendis vel exequendis, vel aliter executi fuerint seu excesserint fines mandati Regis aliter quam ad officium suum pertinuit, et a quo tempore.

Et omnia ista inquirantur tam de vicecomitibus, coronatoribus, eorum clericis et ballivis quibuscunque quam de dominis et ballivis libertatum quarumcunque.

29. Item qui Vicecomites vel custodes castrorum vel maneriorum domini regis quorumcumque vel eciam qui visores huiusmodi operacionum ubicunque factorum per preceptum Regis magis conputaverint in eisdem quam rationabiliter apposuerint et super hoc falsas allocaciones sibi fieri procuraverint. Et similiter qui petram, maeremium vel alia ad hujusmodi operaciones empta seu provisa ad opus suum retinuerint seu amoverint, et quid et quantum dampnum dominus rex inde habuerit et quo tempore.

30. De escaetoribus et subescaetoribus in seisina domini regis facientibus vastum vel destruccionem in boscis, parcis, vivariis, warennis, infra custodias sibi commissas per dominum regem : quantum et de quibus, et quo modo, et quo tempore.

31. Item de eisdem : si occasione hujusmodi seisine ceperint bona defunctorum vel heredum in manum domini regis injuste donec redimerentur ab eisdem, et quod et quantum ita ceperint pro hujusmodi

22. Who have received the command of the lord king to pay his debts, and have received part of the money from the creditors for paying the rest to them, and yet have had the whole sum allowed them in the Exchequer or elsewhere, and from what time.

23. Who have received monies owed to the king, or a part of them, and have not given the debtors quittance, both in the time of the lord king Henry and in the time of the lord king who now is.

24. Again, who have summoned any to be knighted, and have taken bribes from them to have respite; how much and from what time. And if any magnates or others have distrained any to take up arms without the king's command, and from what time.

25. Again, if sheriffs or any bailiffs of any liberty whatsoever have not made summons in due manner, according to the form of the lord king's writ, or in any other way have fraudulently or inadequately executed the King's commands for prayer, for bribe or for favour, and from what time.

26. Again, concerning those who have approvers in prison and have made them appeal honest and innocent persons for the sake of gain, and have sometimes hindered them from appealing guilty persons, and from what time.

27. Again, who have had felons in prison and have allowed them, for money, to get away and escape from prison free and unpunished; and who have extorted money for letting men out of prison on bail; when they have been bailed, and from what time.

28. Again, who have received any gifts or bribes for exercising or for not exercising or executing their offices, or have executed them or exceeded the bounds of the king's commands otherwise than belonged to their office, and from what date.

All these inquiries shall be made not only concerning sheriffs, coroners and their clerks, but also concerning the lords and bailiffs of all liberties whatsoever.

29. Again, what sheriffs or keepers of any of the lord king's castles or manors, or also what surveyors of such works wherever carried out by the king's command, have accounted for larger sums than they have rightly spent on them and have thereupon procured false allowances to be made to them. And likewise, who have retained or removed for their own use stone, timber or other things bought or provided for such works, and what and how much loss the lord king has thus suffered, and from what time.

30. Concerning escheators and subescheators occupying lands for the lord king who do waste and destruction in woods, parks, fishponds or warrens within the wardships committed to them by the lord king; how much, and in whose lands, and how and when.

31. Again concerning the same : if by occasion of such occupation

redempcione, et quid ad opus suum proprium inde retinuerint, et quo tempore.

32. Item de eisdem qui ceperint munera a quibuscumque pro officio suo exercendo vel non exercendo ; quantum, et a quibus, et quo tempore.

33. Item de eisdem qui minus sufficienter extenderint terras alicujus in favore ejusdem vel alicujus cui custodia illarum terrarum dari vendi vel concedi debuerat in deceptionem domini Regis ; et ubi et quomodo, et siquid pro inde ceperint et quantum et quo tempore.

[*Here the list of articles, as entered on the Patent Roll, ends, but articles 34–39 were also administered to the jurors in every county for which returns are extant.*]

34. Item de eisdem qui prece, precio, vel favore, consenserint vel consulerint quod custodie domini regis venderentur pro minori precio quam vendi debuerant secundum verum valorem, vel maritagia heredum tenentium de rege in capite, vel maritagia viduarum dominarum maritarum sine licencia domini regis, et quid propter hoc ceperunt, et quantum, et quandocumque, et a quo tempore.

35. Item de eisdem qui procuraverint et consenserint quod juratores inquisicionum factorum de etate heredum dicerent ipsos heredes fuisse plene etatis, cum non essent, unde dominus rex per hoc amittat maritagium et custodiam hujusmodi heredum.

36. Item de eisdem qui reservaverint ad opus suum proprium custodias vel maritagia per leve precium vel per concelamentum factum domino regi et cujusmodi dampnum dominus rex inde percepit et a quo tempore.

37. Item cujusmodi terras seisierint et per quantum tempus eos in manu domini regis tenuerint.

38. Item de terris captis in manum domini regis que capi non deberent et postea restitutis per preceptum domini regis eum perceptis ; utrum percepta restituerunt ad mandata domini regis vel non.

39. Item de hiis qui durante discordia inter dominum regem et comitissam Flandrensem, contra inhibicionem et defencionem regis defuncti vel nunc, duxerint vel ducere fecerint lanas aliquas ultra mare ; quantum, et ad quem portum, et quo waranto.

[*The following article was administered on five Circuits.*]

40. De collectoribus vicesimi denarii vel de communibus amerciamentis et tallagiis factis in villis et burgis ad opus domini regis.

[*Articles 41–45 were administered on the Lincolnshire Circuit.*]

41. Qui levaverunt paagia pro defectu pontis vel causey contra consuetudines regni.

42. De vicecomitibus, senescallis dominis, et ballivis quibuscumque qui ceperunt redempcionem de hominibus pro veredictis coram justiciariis.

they have unjustly taken the goods of the deceased or of the heirs into the lord king's hand till redeemed by them, and what and how much they have taken by way of such redemption, and what of it they have kept for themselves and at what time.

32. Again, concerning the same who have taken gifts from any for exercising or not exercising their office : how much, from whom, and at what time.

33. Again, concerning the same who have made inadequate valuations of any person's lands in favour of himself or of some other person to whom the custody of those lands ought to be given, sold or granted, thus deceiving the lord king ; where, and how, and if they have received anything for doing this, and how much and when.

34. Again, concerning the same who for prayer, for bribe or for favour have agreed or advised that the lord king's wardships should be sold at a lesser price than they should be, by their true value, or marriages of the heirs of tenants-in-chief, or marriages of widow ladies, married without the lord king's leave ; what they have taken for this, how much, when, and wince what time.

35. Again, concerning the same who have procured or permitted jurors of inquests into the age of heirs to declare that the heirs were of full age when they were not, whereby the lord king has lost the marriage and wardship of such heirs.

36. Again, concerning the same who have reserved for their own use wardships or marriages at a trifling price or by concealment from the lord king ; what loss the lord king has thereby suffered, and since when.

37. Again, what sort of lands they have occupied, and for how long they have kept them in the hands of the lord king.

38. Again, concerning lands taken into the lord king's hands which ought not to have been taken, and afterwards restored, with their takings, by the lord king's command ; whether they have restored the takings at the lord king's command or no.

39. Again, concerning those persons who, during the dispute between the lord king and the countess of Flanders, against the prohibition and veto of the late king or the present king, have conveyed or caused to be conveyed wool over seas ; how much and at what port.

40. Concerning the collectors of the twentieth penny, or common amercements and tallages imposed in towns and boroughs for the lord king's profit.

41. Who have levied payments for the breakdown of bridges or causeways contrary to the custom of the realm.

42. Concerning sheriffs, lords' seneschals or any manner of bailiffs

43. Item de magnatibus et eorum ballivis quibuscumque qui fecerunt districciones extra feoda sua et pro hujusmodi districcionibus fecerunt redempciones et ceperunt, et quid inde ceperunt, et quantum, et a quibus, et a quo tempore.

44. Qui fecerunt rescussum ballivis domini regis ad impedimentum in districcionibus faciendis.

45. De viris religiosis et aliis qui appropriaverunt sibi advocaciones ecclesiarum que solent esse in advocacionem domini regis et debent, et a quo tempore.

[*Articles 46–50 were administered on the Yorkshire circuit.*]

46. De civitatibus et burgis et dominicis domini regis dimissis ad firmam.

47. De tolnetis antiquis, qui ea augmentaverunt.

48. De muragiis et pontagiis concessis.

49. De mensuris et ponderibus.

50. De judicibus ecclesiasticis.

[*Article 51 was administered on the Gloucestershire circuit.*]

51. De falsonariis et retonsoribus monete.

who have extorted payment from men because of verdicts given before the justices.

43. Again ; concerning magnates and their bailiffs who have taken distresses outside their fees, and have imposed and taken ransoms for such distresses ; what they have taken, how much, from whom, and from what time.

44. Who have made rescues from the lord king's bailiffs and thus hindered them when taking distresses.

45. Concerning monks and others who have appropriated to themselves advowsons of churches which were wont and ought to be in the lord king's advowson, and from what time.

46. Concerning cities and boroughs and demesnes of the lord king that have been let to farm.

47. Concerning ancient tolls ; who have increased them.

48. Concerning murages and pontages that have been granted.

49. Concerning weights and measures.

50. Concerning ecclesiastical judges.

51. Concerning forgers and clippers of coin.

APPENDIX II

THE COMMISSIONERS OF 1274 AND THEIR CIRCUITS

(Where there is no certain evidence, the probable arrangement is indicated with a query.)

1. Salop, Staffordshire, and Cheshire	Osbert de Bereford and Richard de Fukeram *or* Roger Lestrange
2. London, Middlesex, Kent, Surrey, and Sussex . .	Bartholomew de Bryaunzon and James de St. Vigor
3. Oxfordshire, Berkshire, Hampshire, and Wiltshire . .	William de Brayboef, Guy de Taunton, and William Gerberd
4. Somerset, Dorset, Devon, and Cornwall	Bartholomew le Jeune and Roger de Chenne
5. Lincolnshire, Rutland, and Northants	William de St. Omer and Warin de Chalcumbe
6. Yorkshire	Thomas de Boulton, William de Pereton, and William de Chatterton
7. Herts, Essex (?), Suffolk, and Norfolk	Robert de Ufford and Ralph de Sandwich
8. Leicestershire (?), Warwickshire (?), Notts, and Derbyshire	Richard de Crepping and Thomas de Leuknor
9. Bucks, Cambridgeshire, Hunts, and Bedfordshire . . .	Sampson Foliot and Edmund de Caldecote
10. Northumberland, Cumberland (?), Lancashire (?), and Westmorland (?)	Geoffrey Aguillon and Philip de Willoughby
11. Gloucestershire (?), Worcestershire (?), and Herefordshire(?)	

APPENDIX III

HUNDRED ROLLS OF 1274-5 NOT PRINTED IN THE RECORD COMMISSION EDITION

COUNTY	HUNDRED	NOTES
Buckingham .	Cottesloe .	1 membrane
Cambridge .	Chilford. .	2 membranes
	Papworth .	3 do.
	Wetherley .	2 do.
	Whittlesford .	1 membrane
Derby . .	Repton . .	Fragmentary; discovered in 1928
	.Litchurch .	Do.
Essex . .	Rochford .	1 membrane
	Thurstable .	1 Do.
Gloucester .	Cheltenham .	1 membrane
Hereford .	Webtree. .	2 membranes, one not printed
Kent . .	Axton .	Membranes 14 and 15 of one large
	Blackheath .	roll
Lincoln . .	Corringham .	1 membrane
Nottingham .	Bassetlaw .	m. 7, discovered in 1928, fills the gap noted on *R.H.*, II, 308
Stafford. .	Totmonslow .	2 membranes; translation printed in *William Salt Historical Collections*, V, i, pp. 117–21
Suffolk . .	Carlford .	3 membranes
Sussex . .	Longbridge .	1 membrane

Extract Hundred Roll No. 4 (*De Ministris*), covering the Counties of Norfolk, Suffolk, Essex, Herts, Dorset, Northumberland, is not included in the printed volumes; the part covering Northumberland has, however, been printed in *Archaeologia Aeliana*, 3rd Ser., III, 187–90.

APPENDIX IV

THE HUNDREDS OF ENGLAND AND THEIR LORDS, 1274

COUNTY	NAME OF HUNDRED		LORD OF HUNDRED, 1274 [1]
	In 13th cent.	*Modern form*	
Bedford .	Bereford . .	Barford . .	King
	Bikleswad .	Biggleswade .	Do.
	Clifton . .	Clifton . .	Do.
	Flitt . .	Flitt . .	Isabel de Mohun
	Mannesheved	Manshead .	King
	½ H. Stanbrugg	Do. . .	Do.
	Radburnestoke	Redbornestoke	Do.
	Stodden . .	Stodden . .	Do.
	Wylye . .	Willey . .	Do.
	½ H. Botlowe .	Do. .	Do.
	Wyxcomestrei .	Wixamtree .	Do.
Berkshire .	Benerste . .	Beynhurst .	King
	Bray . .	Bray . .	Do.
	Charledone .	Charlton . .	Do.
	Compton .	Compton .	Prioress of Kington
	Cogham . .	Cookham .	King
	Rogeburugh .	Faircross .	Do.
	Burghildebyr' .	Do. .	Do.
	Gossetefeld .	Do. .	Do.
	Farindon . .	Farringdon .	Abbot of Beaulieu
	Gamenefeld .	Ganfield . .	Fulk fitz Warin
	Hornmere .	Hormer . .	Abbot of Abingdon
	Kennetbyr' .	Kintbury Eagle	King
	Eggele . .	Do. .	Do.
	Lamburn' (or Hungerford)	Lambourn .	John Tregoz and William de Plukenet

[1] Square brackets indicate that direct evidence for 1274 is lacking.

COUNTY	NAME OF HUNDRED		LORD OF HUNDRED, 1274
	In 13th cent.	*Modern form*	
Berkshire —*cont.*	Morton (or Blebury)	Moreton . .	King
	Sloteford .	Do. .	Do.
	Oke . .	Ock . .	Do.
	Sutton . .	Do. .	Do.
	Radding . .	Reading . .	Abbot of Reading
	Rippesmere .	Ripplesmere .	King
	Ildeslewe . .	Shrivenham .	William de Valence,
	Scrivenham .	Do. .	Giles de Clifford, & heirs of Thomas de Hauterive
	Suninges .	Sonning . .	Bishop of Salisbury
	La Thele .	Theale . .	Abbot of Reading
	Waneting .	Wantage .	Fulk fitz Warin
	Weregrave .	Wargrave .	Bishop of Winchester
Buckinghamshire .	Essedon . .	Ashendon .	King
	Brehull (or Hukeshull)	Do. .	Do.
	Wattesdon . .	Do. .	Do.
	Eylesbyr' .	Aylesbury .	Do.
	Ryseburgh .	Do. .	Do.
	Stanes . .	Do. .	Do.
	Mucha . .	Buckingham .	Do.
	Rolowe . .	Do. .	Do.
	Stodfeld . .	Do. .	Do.
	Burnham .	Burnham .	Do.
	Coteslowe .	Cottesloe .	Do.
	Erle . .	Do. .	Do.
	Muresleye .	Do. .	Do.
	Dustebir' .	Desborough .	Do.
	Bonestowe .	Newport . .	Do.
	Melsho . .	Do. .	Do.
	Seggelawe .	Do. .	Do.
	Stock . .	Stoke . .	Do.

COUNTY	NAME OF HUNDRED		LORD OF HUNDRED, 1274
	In 13th cent.	*Modern form*	
Cambridge-shire	Aringford .	Armingford .	King
	Cestreton .	Chesterton .	Do.
	Chavele . .	Cheveley .	Do.
	Chilford . .	Chilford . .	Do.
	Flemedich .	Flendish .	Do.
	Stowe . .	Longstow .	Do.
	Northstowe .	Northstow .	Do.
	Pappesworth .	Papworth .	Do.
	Radefeld .	Radfield .	Do.
	Stan' . .	Staine . .	Do.
	Stapilho . .	Staploe . .	Do.
	Trippelowe .	Thriplow .	Do.
	Wereslai . .	Wetherley .	Do.
	Wittlisford .	Whittlesford .	Do.
	Wisbech . .	Wisbeach .	Bishop of Ely
	Wichford .	Witchford .	Do.
Cheshire .	Brexton . .	Broxton . .	King
	Buchelawe .	Bucklow . .	Do.
	Edisbur' . .	Eddisbury .	Do.
	Makelesfeld .	Macclesfield .	Do.
	Wich Malbanc'	Nantwich .	Do.
	Nortwich .	Northwich .	Do.
	Wirhale . .	Wirrall . .	Do.
Cornwall .	Estweuelsyre .	East . .	King
	Kerrier . .	Kerrier . .	Do.
	Lisnelwyth .	Lesnewth .	Do.
	Penwid . .	Penwith .	⅓ King, ⅔ John of Arundel
	Poudresyr .	Powder . .	King
	Pidre . .	Pyder . .	Do.
	Strattone .	Stratton .	Do.
	Trygersire .	Trigg . .	Do.
	Westweuelesyre	West . .	Do.
Derby . .	Apeltre . .	Appletree .	Edmund, E. of Lancaster

COUNTY	NAME OF HUNDRED		LORD OF HUNDRED, 1274
	In 13th cent.	*Modern form*	
Derby—*cont.*	Alt' Pekk .	High Peak .	King
	Morleyston and Ludchirche	Morleston and Litchurch	Do.
	Repindon and Greseley	Repton and Gresley . .	½ Ed. of Lancaster, ½ heirs of E. of Chester
	Skarvesdal .	Scarsdale .	Nicholas Wake
	Wyrkesworth .	Wirksworth .	King and Ed., E. of Lancaster
Devon . .	Axeministr' .	Axminster .	Abbot of Newnham
	Axemue .	Do. . .	and Abbot of Montebourg
	Baunton . .	Bampton . .	John de Kogan
	Blaktoriton .	Black Torring-ton	Thomas de Win-ford
	Brantune .	Braunton .	Abbot of Cleeve
	Buddeleg .	Budleigh . .	King
	Clifton . .	Cliston . .	Guy de Novant
	Cole . .	Coleridge .	Matthew fitz John
	Coliton . .	Colyton . .	Thomas de Sand-ford and Hugh de Courtenay
	Cridiaton .	Crediton . .	Bishop of Exeter
	Ermigtone .	Ermington .	John Peverel
	Exministr' .	Exminster .	Amicia (dowager), Countess of Devon
	Fremington .	Fremington .	Matilda and Geof-frey de Kaumvile
	Hauberton .	Halberton .	William du Bois, of Earl of Gloucester, of King
	Hertiland .	Hartland . .	Oliver de Dinham
	Harrig' . .	Hayridge .	Amicia, Countess of Devon
	Haytorr' .	Haytor .	Roger de Molys
	Hemyok . .	Hemyock .	John of Hydon, of Countess of Devon

COUNTY	NAME OF HUNDRED		LORD OF HUNDRED, 1274
	In 13th cent.	*Modern form*	
Devon— cont.	Lifton . .	Lifton . .	Edmund, E. of Cornwall
	Plympton .	Plympton .	Isabel, Countess of Albemarle
	Rouburg' .	Roborough .	Amicia, Countess of Devon, of Countess of Albemarle
	Schefbeare .	Shebbear .	King
	Syrewill . .	Sherwill . .	Richard de Beaumont, of Hugh of Courtenay
	Sudmolton .	South Molton .	Nicholas fitz Martin, of E. of Gloucester
	Stanburg . .	Stanborough .	Roger de Molys
	Tavistok' .	Tavistock .	Abbot of Tavistock
	Nortaveton .	Tawton . .	John de Valletorte
	Teyngebrugg' .	Teignbridge .	½ Robert Burden, ½ guardians of Theobald Bussel
	Tyverton .	Tiverton .	Amicia, Countess of Devon, of Countess of Albemarle
	Wynkelegh .	Winkley . .	Roger de Keynges, of E. of Gloucester
	Wytherugg .	Witheridge .	Roger le Marchant, of Robert fitz Paine
	Wonford .	Wonford .	Amicia, Countess of Devon, of Countess of Albemarle
Dorset .	Baddebur' .	Badbury . .	Henry Lacy, E. of Lincoln
	Beministr' .	Beaminster .	Bishop of Salisbury
	Bere . .	Bere Regis .	[½ Abbess of Tarrant] [½ John de Turberville]

COUNTY	NAME OF HUNDRED		LORD OF HUNDRED, 1274
	In 13th cent.	*Modern form*	
Dorset—*cont.*	Broneshull .	Brownshall .	King
	Do. .	Buckland Newton	Abbot of Glaston- bury
	Totcumb and Motbergh	Cerne, Tot- cumbe and Modbury	Abbot of Cerne
	Cocdene . .	Cogdean . .	[Maud and John Giffard]
	Cumbesdich .	Coombsditch .	[E. of Gloucester]
	Corf . .	Corfe . .	King
	Craneburne .	Cranborne .	[E. of Gloucester]
	Culfordstre .	Culliford Tree .	[Hugh Poynz, of E. of Gloucester]
	Ekerdon . .	Eggerton . .	King
	St. George .	George . .	Do.
	Gillingham .	Gillingham Liberty	Do.
	Gudrynthorn .	Godderthorne .	Do.
	Haselore .	Hasilor . .	$\frac{1}{3}$ King, $\frac{2}{3}$ E. of Gloucester
	Hundredes- berwe	Hundreds Barrow	Agnes de Vescy
	Knoltone .	Knowlton .	[William de Braose, of E. of Glouces- ter]
	Lessebarewe .	Loosebarrow .	Helen de Vaux
	Pidelton . .	Piddletown .	William de Monta- cute
	Pimperne .	Pimperne .	E. of Gloucester
	La Rydelane .	Redlane . .	King
	Rubir' . .	Rowbarrow .	E. of Gloucester
	Russhemor' .	Rushmore .	Do.
	Shireburn' .	Sherborne .	Bishop of Salisbury
	Sexpenne et Henleye	Sixpenny Handley	Abbess of Shaftes- bury
	Thollereford .	Tollerford .	King
	Huggescombe (*R.H.* II, 223)	Uggscombe .	Do.

COUNTY	NAME OF HUNDRED		LORD OF HUNDRED, 1274
	In 13th cent.	*Modern form*	
Dorset—*cont.*	Up Wimborn .	Upwimborn .	Robert de Plecy [of E. of Gloucester]
	Whytchurch .	Whitchurch .	John de Mandevile
	Wyteweye .	Whiteway .	King
	Winfrod . .	Winfrith . .	John de Newburgh
	Yateministr' .	Yetminster .	Bishop of Salisbury
Essex . .	Berdestapel' (1½)	Barstable .	Gundreda and William Giffard
	Bekentre .	Becontree .	Abbess of Barking
	Chaforde .	Chafford . .	King
	Chelmsford .	Chelmsford .	Do.
	Claveringes (½)	Clavering .	Robert fitz Roger
	Daneseye .	Dengie . .	King
	Dunmauwe .	Dunmow .	Do.
	Froswell (½) .	Freshwell .	Do.
	Herlawe (½) .	Harlow . .	Robert de Bruce
	Hengeford .	Hinckford .	King
	Lexinden .	Lexden . .	William Gernon
	Aungre . .	Ongar . .	John de Rivers
	Rocheford .	Rochford .	King
	Tendringes .	Tendring .	Do.
	Turstapl' . .	Thurstable .	Do.
	East and West Huddeleford	Uttlesford .	Do.
	Wautham (½) .	Waltham (or Epping)	Abbot of Waltham
	Wensetre .	Winstree . .	Prior of Mersea
	Witham (½) .	Witham . .	The Master of the Temple
Gloucester .	Berkeley .	Berkeley . .	Maurice of Berkeley
	Bysleye . .	Bisley . .	Peter Corbet, Theobald Butler, Richard le Heyer
	Blitheslowe .	Blidesloe .	William de Valence and Maud, Countess of Gloucester

COUNTY	NAME OF HUNDRED		LORD OF HUNDRED, 1274
	In 13th cent.	*Modern form*	
Gloucester —cont.	Botlowe .	Botloe . .	King
	Bradileye .	Bradley . .	Abbot of Cirencester
	Bristewalde-barewe	Brightwell's Barrow	Do.
	Chilteham .	Cheltenham .	Abbot of Fécamp
	Cirencestr' .	Cirencester .	Abbot of Cirencester
	Derhurste .	Deerhurst and Westminster .	Prior of Deerhurst and Abbot of Westminster
	Dodestan .	Dudstone and Kings Barton	King
	Grimbaldesesse	Grumbalds Ash	Do.
	Aggemed. .	Do.	Do.
	Hambur' cum Bernetre	Henbury .	Bishop of Worcester
	Kyftesgat' .	Kiftsgate .	King
	Holleford and Gretestan	Do.	Do.
		Do.	Do.
	Berton Regis .	King's Barton (by Bristol) .	Do.
	Langelege Swinesheved	Langley and Swineshead	[Heirs of Fulk fitz King [Warin]
	Langetre .	Longtree .	Abbot of Cirencester
	Pokelechirche .	Pucklechurch .	Bishop of Bath
	Respegate .	Rapsgate .	Abbot of Cirencester
	St. Briavel .	St. Briavells .	King
	Salemonesbirie	Slaughter .	Abbot of Fécamp
	Theokbyr' .	Tewkesbury .	E. of Gloucester
	Tornebiri .	Thornbury .	Do.
	Tedbaldestan .	Tibaldstone .	[King]
	Twyford . .	Westbury .	E. Marshal
	Westbur'. .	Do. .	King
	Wyston . .	Whitstone .	Do.

COUNTY	NAME OF HUNDRED		LORD OF HUNDRED, 1274
	In 13th cent.	*Modern form*	
Hampshire .	Altone . .	Alton . .	Eleanor, Queen Mother
	Andovere .	Andover . .	King
	Bertone . .	Barton Stacy .	Isabel Gascelyn
	Basingestoke .	Basingstoke .	The men of Basingstoke
	Beremundesputte	Bermondspit .	King
	Sutton .	Bishop's Sutton	Bishop of Winchester
	Wautham .	Bishop's Waltham .	Do.
	Bosebergh .	Bosmere . .	King
	Bontesbreche .	Bountisborough	Do.
	Betelsgate .	Buddlesgate .	Bishop of Winchester
	Chertele .	Chuteley .	King
	Holdenhurst *or* Cristeschurche	Christchurch .	Isabel, Countess of Albemarle
	Crundal . .	Crondall . .	Prior of Winchester
	Menes . .	East Meon .	Bishop of Winchester
	Est medina .	East Medina .	Countess of Albemarle
	Evingar . .	Evingar . .	Prior of Winchester
	Farham . .	Fareham .	Bishop of Winchester
	Falele . .	Fawley . .	Do.
	Fynchesdene .	Finchdean .	[Guardian of John fitz Alan]
	Forde . .	Fordingbridge .	John de Rivers
	Holesete .	Holdshott . .	King
	Kyngesclere .	King's Clere .	Do.
	Sumburne .	King's Somborn	Pain de Chaworth
	Maynesburgh .	Mansborough .	R. Daundely
	Manesbregg .	Mansbridge .	King
	Monekestok' .	Meonstoke .	Do.
	Micheldever .	Mitcheldever .	Abbot of Hyde

COUNTY	NAME OF HUNDRED		LORD OF HUNDRED, 1274
	In 13th cent.	*Modern form*	
Hampshire .	Odyham . .	Odiham . .	King
—*cont.*	Overtone. .	Overton .	Bishop of Winchester
	Pachestrow *or* Husseburne	Pastrow . .	King
	Portesdoune .	Portsdown .	Do.
	Redbregg .	Redbridge .	Do.
	Ringwode .	Ringwood .	Do.
	Seleburne .	Selborne . .	Do.
	Thorngate .	Thorngate .	Do.
	Tichefeud .	Titchfield .	Do.
	West medina .	West Medina .	Countess of Albemarle
	Werewelle .	Wherwell .	Abbess of Wherwell
Hereford .	Brachesasse .	Broxash . .	King
	Greytre . .	Greytree . .	Do.
	Grimesworthe .	Grimsworth .	Do.
	Radlowe . .	Radlow . .	Do.
	Stratforde .	Stretford .	Do.
	Wellbetre .	Webtree . .	Do.
	Leominstreforinsec'	Wolphy . .	Abbot of Reading
	Wulfeye .	Do. . .	King
	Wormeleye *or* Irehenefelde	Wormelow .	Do.
Hertford .	Brachinge .	Braughing .	King
	Bradewatre .	Broadwater .	. Do.
	Caysford .	Cashio . .	Abbot of St. Albans
	Dakore . .	Dacorum . .	King
	Edwinestre .	Edwinstree .	King and Bishop of London
	Hertford .	Hertford . .	King
	Hich' . .	Hitchin . .	Do.
	Oddeseye .	Odsey . .	Do.

COUNTY	NAME OF HUNDRED		LORD OF HUNDRED, 1274
	In 13th cent.	*Modern form*	
Huntingdon .	Hirstingstan .	Hurstingstone .	Abbot of Ramsey
	Lectonestan .	Leightonstone .	King
	Normancros .	Normancross .	Abbot of Thorney
	Touleslond .	Toseland .	King
Kent . .	Alolvesbrigg .	Aloesbridge .	King and Abp.
	Acstane . .	Axton . .	King
	Badekeley .	Barclay .	Do.
	Bernefeld (in two lathes)	Barnefield	Do.
	Bircholte (in two lathes)	Bircholt	Abp. and William de Valence
	Blakeburne .	Blackbourne .	King
	Blakehethe .	Blackheath .	Do.
	Blengate .	Bleangate .	Abp. and Abbot of St. Augustine
	Bocton Episcopi	Boughton .	Abp.
	Brenchesle .	Brenchley .	King
	Bregge and Petham .	Bridge and Petham .	Do. Abp.
	Bromley . .	Bromley . .	King and Bishop of Rochester
	Bewesberwe .	Bewsborough .	King and Abp.
	Kalehulle .	Colehill . .	Abp.
	Cherst and Langebregg .	Chart and Longbridge .	Abp. and King Abp., King, Abbot of Battle
	Chatham .	Chatham and Gillingham	King and Abp.
	Godesheth .	Codsheath .	Abp.
	Quernilo . .	Cornilo .	Prior of Christchurch, Prior of Dover and Abbot of St. Augustine
	Cranebrok .	Cranbrooke .	King

COUNTY	NAME OF HUNDRED		LORD OF HUNDRED, 1274
	In 13th cent.	*Modern form*	
Kent—*cont.* .	Dunhamford .	Downhamford .	Abp., Abbot of St. Augustine & King
	Estri . .	Eastry . .	Prior of Christchurch and King
	Eyhorne . .	Eyhorne . .	King
	Faversham .	Faversham .	Abbot of Faversham
	Feleburghe .	Felborough .	Isabel and Alexander of Balliol, and King
	Folkestan .	Folkestone .	John of Sandwich and Bertram de Crioll
	Hamme . .	Ham . .	½ King, ½ Abp.
	Hean . .	Hayne . .	Abp.
	Ho . .	Hoo . .	H. Poynz, Abbot of Reading, and H. Gray
	Kynghamford	Kinghamford .	⅔ Abp., ⅓ Alexander of Balliol
	Langeport .	Langport .	King and Abp.
	Laverkesfeld .	Larkfield .	King
	Litlelye . .	Lessness .	Do.
	Littlefeld .	Littlefield .	E. of Gloucester
	Loneburegh .	Loningborough	½ Abp., ½ William de Leyburn
	Maydenestan .	Maidstone .	Abp.
	Merdune . .	Marden . .	King
	Middeltun .	Middleton or Milton	Do.
	Nywecherich .	Newchurch .	½ King, ½ Abp. and Prior of Christchurch
	Oxene . .	Oxney . .	King
	Preston . .	Preston . .	William of Leyburne
	Ringeslo . .	Ringslow . .	Abp. and Abbot of St. Augustine's

COUNTY	NAME OF HUNDRED		LORD OF HUNDRED, 1274
	In 13th cent.	*Modern form*	
Kent—*cont.* . .	Rulynden .	Rolvenden .	King
	Rokesleye .	Ruxley .	⅓ Abp., ⅔ King
	St. Martin .	St. Martin .	Abp.
	Sellbrightind' .	Selbrittenden .	King
	Schamele .	Shamwell .	John of Cobham and Master of Temple
	Sumerdenn .	Somerden .	⅔ Abp., ⅓ King
	Stuting . .	Stouting .	Guardians of Emma Haringod
	Strete . .	Street . .	Abp. and King
	Tenham .	Teynham .	Abp.
	Tenterden .	Tenterden .	King
	Toltyntre .	Toltentrough .	Abp.
	Twyford .	Twyford . .	Abp. and King
	Wethelestan .	Washlingstone .	E. of Gloucester
	Westerham .	Westerham .	Robert de Caunvil
	Westgate .	Westgate .	Abp.
	Wystapel .	Whitstable .	Alex. of Balliol
	Winghan .	Wingham .	Abp.
	Worth . .	Worth . .	½ King, ¼ Abp., ⅛ Master of God's House, Dover ; $\frac{1}{12}$ Master of God's House, Ospring
	Wroteham .	Wrotham .	Abp. and King
	Wye . .	Wye . .	Abbot of Battle
Lancashire .	Augmonderness	Amounderness	Edmund of Lancaster
	Blakeburnesyre	Blackburn .	Henry Lacy, E. of Lincoln
	Leilandsir' .	Leyland .	Edmund of Lan-
	Lonesdale .	Lonsdale .	Do. [caster
	Salfordesyre .	Salford . .	Do.
	Derbisire .	West Derby .	Do.
Leicestershire	Framelund .	Framland .	King
	Gertre . .	Gartree . .	William de Beyvill

COUNTY	NAME OF HUNDRED		LORD OF HUNDRED, 1274
	In 13th cent.	*Modern form*	
Leicestershire —*cont.*	Gosecot . .	Goscote (East and West)	Nicholas de Segrave
	Guthlaston .	Guthlaxton (and Sparkenhoe)	King
Lincoln .	Aslachoue .	Aslacoe . .	King
	Asewardthyrne	Aswardhurn .	Do.
	Avelund . .	Aveland . .	Do.
	Beltislawe .	Beltisloe . .	Do.
	Boby . .	Boothby Graffo	Do.
	Graffou . .	Do. . .	Do.
	Bradele . .	Bradley-Haverstoe	Do.
	Hawardeshou .	Do. . .	Do.
	Bulingbroc .	Bolingbroke .	E. of Lincoln
	Calsewath .	Calceworth .	King
	Candelshou .	Candleshoe .	Do.
	Coringham .	Corringham .	Do.
	Ellowe . .	Elloe . .	Do.
	Flaxwell .	Flaxwell . .	Do.
	Gayrtre . .	Gartree . .	Do.
	Hille . .	Hill . .	Do.
	Hornecastre .	Horncastle .	Do.
	Kirketone .	Kirton . .	Do.
	Langhou .	Langoe . .	Do.
	Lawris . .	Lawress . .	Do.
	Luthesk . .	Loutheske .	Do.
	Lovedon . .	Loveden . .	Do.
	Ludburg' .	Ludborough .	Do.
	Manlee . .	Manley . .	Do.
	Nesse . .	Ness . .	Do.
	Skirbec . .	Skirbeck . .	Do.
	Walscros .	Walshcroft .	Do.
	Welle . .	Well . .	Bishop of Lincoln
	Wymbrigg' and Threhow	Winnibriggs and Threo	King

COUNTY	NAME OF HUNDRED		LORD OF HUNDRED, 1274
	In 13th cent.	*Modern form*	
Lincoln —cont.	Wraghou . .	Wraggoe . .	King
	Jordeburg .	Yarborough .	Do.
Middlesex .	Eddelmeton .	Edmonton .	King
	Elethorn .	Elthorne .	Do.
	Gore .	Gore .	Do.
	Isteluurth .	Isleworth .	Do.
	Osolveste .	Ossulstone .	Do.
	Spelethorn .	Spelthorne .	Do.
Norfolk .	Blafeud . .	Blofield . .	William de St. Omer
	Brothercros .	Brothercross .	John de Warenne, E. of Surrey
	Clakelose . .	Clackclose .	Abbot of Ramsey
	Knaverynge .	Clavering .	King
	Depwade . .	Depwade . .	Do.
	Disce . .	Diss . .	Roger, Earl Marshal
	Ersham . .	Earsham . .	Roger Bigod, E. of
	Est Fleg' . .	East Flegg .	King [Norfolk
	Eynisford .	Eynesford .	⅔ Elizabeth Marshal, ⅓ John of Brittany
	Fourhove .	Forehoe . .	⅔ King (as guardian of John Marshal) ⅓ John of Brittany
	Frethebregg .	Freebridge .	Robert de Tattershall
	Galehoge .	Gallow . .	John de Warenne, C. of Surrey
	Gyldecros .	Guiltcross .	Isabel (dowager), C'tess. of Arundel
	Grimeshowe .	Grimshoe . .	William de St
	Happing .	Happing . .	King [Omer
	Henstede .	Henstead . .	Do.
	Holt . .	Holt . .	Do.

COUNTY	NAME OF HUNDRED		LORD OF HUNDRED, 1274
	In 13th cent.	*Modern form*	
Norfolk —cont.	Humylerd .	Humbleyard .	William de St. Omer
	Laundiz . .	Launditch .	John Lestrange, of heirs of John fitz
	Lodenynges .	Loddon . .	King [Alan
	Mitford (1½) .	Mitford . .	Bishop of Ely
	Northerping- ham	North Erping- ham	King
	Northgrenehow	North Greenhoe	Do.
	Sropham .	Shropham .	Robert de Tatter- shall
	Smesdon .	Smithdon .	Isabel, Countess of Arundel
	Sutherpingham	South Erping- ham	King
	Suthgrenehowe	South Greenhoe	John Lestrange, of heirs of John fitz Alan
	Thaverham .	Taversham .	William de St. Omer
	Tunsted . .	Tunstead .	Abbot of St. Benet of Hulme
	Walsham .	Walsham .	William de St.
	Waylund .	Wayland .	Do. [Omer
	Westfleg' . .	West Flegg .	King
Northampton	Warden . .	Chipping Warden	William le Latimer
	Cleyele . .	Cleley . .	[Walter de Wyd- ville]
	Coreby . .	Corby . .	William and John le Latimer
	Faluwesle .	Fawsley .	Thomas de Kapes
	Norton . .	Greens Norton	[Reginald de Gray, as guardian of John Marshal]
	Gildeburg' .	Guilsborough .	King

COUNTY	NAME OF HUNDRED		LORD OF HUNDRED, 1274
	In 13th cent.	*Modern form*	
Northampton —cont.	Andefordesho .	Hamfordshoe .	Guardian of John of Hastings
	Hegham . .	Higham Ferrers	Margaret (dowager) C'tess of Derby
	Hokeslawe .	Huxloe . .	Abbot of Peterborough
	Sutton . .	King's Sutton .	Emmeline Longsword, Countess of Ulster
	Nassus Burgi .	Nassaburgh .	Abbot of Peter-
	Navesforde .	Navisford .	Do. [borough
	Neubotlegrave	Nobottlegrove .	[Hugh de Chan-
	Orleberg' . .	Orlingbury .	King [ceaux
	Polebrok .	Polebrook .	Abbot of Peterborough
	Rowell . .	Rothwell .	E. of Gloucester
	Stotfolde .	Do. .	Do.
	Spelho . .	Spelhoe . .	Eleanor, Queen Consort
	Touecestr' .	Towcester .	[William de Munc-
	Wylebrok .	Willybrook .	King [hensy
	Wymerle .	Wymersley .	Guardian of John of Hastings
Nottingham	Bersetelawe (1½)	Bassetlaw .	King and heirs of Henry of Hastings
	Byngham .	Bingham .	King
	Brokholestowe	Broxtow . .	Do.
	Neuwark (½) .	Newark . .	Bishop of Lincoln
	Ryseclive (½) .	Rushcliffe .	King
	Thurgarton and	Thurgarton .	Do.
	Lye (1½) .	Do.	Do.
Oxford .	Baunton .	Bampton .	William de Valence
	Bannebyr' .	Banbury .	Bishop of Lincoln
	Benefeld .	Binfield . .	Edmund of Cornwall

COUNTY	NAME OF HUNDRED		LORD OF HUNDRED, 1274
	In 13th cent.	*Modern form*	
Oxford —cont.	Blokesham .	Bloxham .	Almaric de St. Amand
	Bulingdene .	Bullington .	Hugh de Plessy
	Chadelington .	Chadlington .	E. of Gloucester
	Dorkecestr' .	Dorchester .	Bishop of Lincoln
	Ewelm' .	Ewelme . .	Edmund, E. of
	Langetre .	Langtree .	Do. [Cornwall
	Leukenore .	Lewknor .	Do.
	Piriton . .	Pirton . .	Do.
	Pouwedelowe .	Ploughley .	King
	Thame . .	Thame . .	Bishop of Lincoln
	Wotton . .	Wootton .	King
Rutland .	Anastoue .	Alstoe . .	Edmund, E. of
	Est hundred' .	East . .	Do. [Cornwall
	Martinsle .	Martinsley .	Do.
	Wrangedik .	Wrandike .	William, E. of Warwick
Salop . .	Bradford .	Bradford (N. & S.)	[Walter de Pedwardin]
	Brimestr' .	Brimstrey .	[King]
	Chirbur' . .	Chirbury .	King
	Conedouere .	Condover .	Do.
	Forde . .	Ford . .	Do.
	Munselawe .	Munslow .	Do.
	Overes ($\frac{1}{2}$) .	Overs . .	Do.
	Pemenhul .	Pimhill . .	Do.
	Pusselowe .	Purslow . .	[Guardian of John fitz Alan]
	Stottesdon .	Stottesdon .	King
Somerset .	Bolestan et Abedyk	Abdick and Bulstone	Henry de Lorty
	Andredesfeld .	Andersfield .	King
	Baton' forinsec' de la Berton	Bath Forum .	Prior of Bath

COUNTY	NAME OF HUNDRED		LORD OF HUNDRED, 1274
	In 13th cent.	*Modern form*	
Somerset —cont.	Bemastan	Bempstone	Dean and Chapter of Wells
	Brente	Brent and Wrington	Abbot of Glastonbury
	Briweton	Bruton	Prior of Bruton
	Kanington	Cannington	Robert Waleraund
	Karampton	Carhampton	John de Mohun
	Cattesasse	Catsash	King
	Chyw	Chew	Bishop of Bath and Wells
	Chyuton	Chewton	[Heirs of Hugh de Vivonia]
	Koker	Cocker or	John de Mandeville
	Hundesberwe	Houndsborough	Prior of Montacute
	Cruk'	Crewkerne	[Hugh of Courtenay]
	Frome	Frome	Joan Braunche
	Glaston'	Glaston Twelve Hides	Abbot of Glastonbury
	Hareclive et Bedministr'	Hartcliffe and Bedminster	Maurice of Berkeley
	La Horethurne	Horethorne	King
	Hunespill	Huntspill and Puriton	John de Cogan
	Keynesham	Keynsham	Abbot of Keynsham
	Kynemersdon	Kilmersdon	Emeric de Roche Chouard (wrongly)
	Kyngesbyr'	Kingsbury	Bishop of Bath
	Milverton	Milverton	[Heirs of George de Cantelow]
	Northcury	North Curry	Dean and Chapter of Wells
	North Perton	N. Petherton	Philip de Erlegh
	Norton	Norton Ferris	John de Musegros
	Porbury	Portbury	Maurice of Berkeley
	Somerton Forum	Somerton	Eleanor Queen Consort
	Suthperton	S. Petherton	Ralph Daubeny

COUNTY	NAME OF HUNDRED		LORD OF HUNDRED, 1274
	In 13th cent.	*Modern form*	
Somerset	La Stane .	Stone . .	King
—*cont.*	Tantone . .	Taunton Dean	Bishop of Winchester
	Tyntehulle .	Tintinhull .	Prior of Montacute
	Welewe . .	Wellow . .	H. de Montfort, of E. of Gloucester
	Forinsecum de Welles	Wells Forum .	Dean and Chapter of Wells
	Wyteleg' .	Whitley . .	Abbot of Glaston-
	Wytston .	Whitstone .	Do. [bury
	Wyleton . .	Williton . .	King
	Winterstoke .	Winterstoke .	Bishop of Bath
	Jacton . .	Yatton . .	Do.
Stafford .	Cuthulfestan .	Cuttlestone .	King
	Offelowe . .	Offlow . .	William de Parles
	Pirhull . .	Pirehill . .	[Geoffrey Griffin]
	Seisdon . .	Seisdon . .	King
	Tatemoneslowe	Totmonslow .	William de Kaverswelle
Suffolk .	Balberg (2) .	Baburgh . .	Abbot of Bury St.
	Blakeburne (2)	Blackbourne .	Do. [Edmund
	Blythyng' .	Blithing . .	King
	Bosemere and Cleydun (1⅔)	Bosmere and Claydon	Do.
	Carlesford .	Carlford .	Prior of Ely
	Colneise . .	Colneis . .	Prior of Ely
	Corsford (½) .	Cosford . .	Abbot of Bury St. Edmund
	Exning . .	Exning . .	King
	Hertismere .	Hartismere .	Do.
	Hoxene . .	Hoxne . .	Bishop of Norwich
	Lacford . .	Lackford .	Abbot of Bury St. Edmund
	Lose . .	Loes . .	Roger Bigod, E. of Norfolk, of Prior of Ely

COUNTY	NAME OF HUNDRED		LORD OF HUNDRED, 1274
	In 13th cent.	*Modern form*	
Suffolk —cont.	Luthynglond ($\frac{1}{2}$)	Lothingland .	Devorguilla Balliol
	Mutteford ($\frac{1}{2}$) .	Mutford . .	Edmund de Hem-
	Plumesgate ($1\frac{1}{2}$)	Plomesgate .	Prior of Ely [grave
	Risebrig . .	Risbridge .	Abbot of Bury St. Edmund
	Saunford ($1\frac{1}{2}$) .	Samford . .	Ralph de Ufford
	Stowe . .	Stow . .	King
	Thedwardistre	Thedwastry .	Abbot of Bury St.
	Thinghowe .	Thingoe . .	Do. [Edmund
	Thirdlinge ($\frac{1}{3}$) .	Thredling .	Prior of Ely
	Wayneford .	Wangford .	$\frac{3}{4}$ King ; $\frac{1}{4}$ Bishop of Norwich
	Wyleford .	Wilford . .	Prior of Ely
Surrey .	Blakehetfelde .	Blackheath .	King
	Bryxiston .	Brixton . .	Do.
	Coppedethorne.	Copthorne .	Do.
	Effyngham .	Effingham .	Do.
	Emelebrig' .	Elmbridge .	Men of Kingston
	Farnham. .	Farnham .	Bishop of Win- chester
	Godelmingges .	Godalming .	Bishop of Salisbury
	Godele . .	Godley . .	Abbot of Chertsey
	Kyngestone .	Kingston. .	Men of Kingston
	Reygate . .	Reigate . .	King
	Tanerigg' .	Tandridge .	Do.
	Waletone .	Wallington .	Do.
	Wocking .	Woking . .	Do.
	Wodeton .	Wotton .	Do.
Sussex .	Aylsiston .	Alciston . .	[Abbot of Battle ?]
	Pageham. .	Aldwick . .	Abp. of Canterbury
	Avesford .	Avisford . .	[Guardian of John fitz Alan]
	Baldeslawe .	Baldslow .	John of Brittany
	Berecamp .	Barcomb .	John de Warenne, E. of Surrey

COUNTY	NAME OF HUNDRED		LORD OF HUNDRED, 1274
	In 13th cent.	*Modern form*	
Sussex—*cont.*	La Bataile .	Battle . .	Abbot of Battle
	Bixle . .	Bexhill . .	Bishop of Chichester
	Boseham .	Bosham . .	Roger Bigod, E. of Norfolk
	Boxe and Stocbrugge	Box and Stockbridge	[Guardian of John fitz Alan]
	Bretford . .	Brightford .	William de Braose
	Burgebeche .	Burbeach .	Do.
	Bury . .	Bury . .	Abbot of Fécamp
	Boltynghull .	Buttinghill .	E. of Surrey
	Thille . .	Dill . .	Eleanor Queen Mother
	Dumesford .	Dumpford .	Henry Husee
	Eseburn . .	Easebourne .	Maud and Richard de Amundevile
	Burne . .	Eastbourne .	Queen Mother
	Est grenestede	East Grinstead .	Do.
	Eswryth . .	East Easwrith .	William de Braose
	Fysseresgate .	Fishergate .	Do.
		(in Bramber)$\frac{1}{2}$	Do.
		(in Lewes) $\frac{1}{2}$.	E. of Surrey
	Foxherle .	Foxearle . .	John of Brittany
	Faxberwe .	Flexborough .	Queen Mother
	Colespore .	Goldspur .	John of Brittany
	Gosetrewe .	Gostrow . .	Abbot of Fécamp
	Gestlyng .	Guestling .	John of Brittany
	Hertefeud .	Hartfield .	Queen Mother
	Haukesberg .	Hawkesborough	John of Brittany
	Hennehurst .	Henhurst .	Do.
	Holmestrouhe .	Holmstrow .	E. of Surrey
	Langbrigge .	Longbridge .	Queen Mother
	Lokkefeud .	Loxfield . .	Abp.
	Manewode .	Manhood . .	Bishop of Chichester
	Neddrefeld .	Netherfield .	Do.
	Newinefeld .	Ninfield . .	John of Brittany

COUNTY	NAME OF HUNDRED		LORD OF HUNDRED, 1274
	In 13th cent.	*Modern form*	
Sussex —cont.	Palynges .	Poling . .	King as guardian of John fitz Alan
	Ponynges .	Poynings .	E. of Surrey
	Rutherebregg .	Rotherbridge .	Maud and Richard de Amundevile
	Rytherefeud .	Rotherfield .	E. of Gloucester
	Ryston . .	Rushmonden .	Queen Mother
	Denne . .	Do. .	Laurence de Seinmor and Roger de Leuknor
	Schepelake .	Shiplake . .	Queen Mother
	Shoewell . .	Shoyswell .	John of Brittany
	Sengelton .	Singleton .	[Guardian of John fitz Alan]
	Stapele . .	Staple . .	John of Brittany
	Stenyng . .	Steyning .	William de Braose
	Strete . .	Street . .	E. of Surrey
	Swanberghe .	Swanborough .	Do.
	Typenhok .	Tipnoak . .	Bishop of Chichester
	Tottenore .	Totnore . .	Queen Mother
	Burn . .	Westbourne .	Isabel Daubeny
	Eswryth . .	West Easwrith .	Maud and Richard de Amundevil
	West Grensted	West Grinstead	William de Braose
	Walesbone .	Whalesbone .	$\frac{1}{4}$ Bishop of Chichester, $\frac{3}{4}$ E. of Surrey
	Willindon .	Willingdon .	Queen Mother
	Wyndeham .	Windham .	William de Braose
	Ywonesmere .	Younsmere .	E. of Surrey
Warwickshire	Barlichweye .	Barlichway .	King
	Patlaw . .	Do. .	Bp. of Worcester
	Humelingforth	Hemlingford .	King
	Kinton . .	Kineton . .	Do.
	Knythelowe .	Knightlow .	Do.

COUNTY	NAME OF HUNDRED		LORD OF HUNDRED, 1274
	In 13th cent.	*Modern form*	
Wiltshire .	Alwarbyr' .	Alderbury .	Maud and John Giffard
	Ambresbir' .	Amesbury .	[Maud and John Giffard]
	Bradeford .	Bradford .	Abbess of Shaftes-
	Brenchesberewe	Branch and	King [bury
	Dolesfeud .	Dole . .	Do.
	Calne . .	Calne . .	Millicent and Yvo La Zuche
	Caudon	Cawden and	King
	Cadewith	Cadworth .	Do.
	Chalk . .	Chalk . .	Abbess of Wilton
	Cyppeham .	Chippenham .	Joan and Geoffrey Wascelin
	Crikkelade .	Cricklade .	Isabel, Countess of Albemarle
	Domerham .	Damerham (N. and S.)	Abbot of Glaston- bury
	Dunton and Knowel	Downton . .	Bishop of Win- chester
	Donewurth .	Dunworth .	King
	Ellestubbe .	Elstub and Everley	Prior of Winchester
	Furstefeld .	Frustfield .	King
	Hettredesbur' .	Heytesbury .	Parnel and John de la Mare
	Wurth . .	Highworth .	Isabel, Countess of Albemarle
	Blakingrove .	Kingsbridge .	King
	Kinbrig . .	Do.	Do.
	Thornhulle .	Do.	Do.
	Kynewardston	Kinwardstone .	Eleanor, Countess of Leicester
	Melkesham .	Melksham .	Prioress of Ames- bury
	Mere . .	Mere . .	[Edmund, E. of Cornwall]

COUNTY	NAME OF HUNDRED		LORD OF HUNDRED, 1274
	In 13th cent.	*Modern form*	
Wiltshire —*cont.*	Rughebergh Caninges	Potterne and Cannings	Bishop of Salisbury Do.
	Remmesbir' .	Ramsbury .	Do.
	Selkele . .	Selkley . .	Queen Mother
	Stapelee . .	Staple . .	Robert de Keynes, Hugh Peverel and John Paynel
	Sterkele .	Malmesbury .	Abbot of Malmes-
	Malmesbur' .	Do. .	Do. [bury
	Cheggelewe .	Do. .	Do.
	Swaneber' .	Swanborough .	King
	Stodfolde .	Do. .	Do.
	Wonderdich .	Underditch .	Bishop of Salisbury
	Werministre .	Warminster .	Joan Mauduit
	Westbyry .	Westbury .	Reginald de Pavely
	Wervollesdone	Whorwelsdon .	Abbess of Romsey
Worcester- shire	Blakehurst .	Blackenhurst .	Abbot of Evesham
	Dodintr' . .	Doddingtree .	King
	Domidius Cimi- tatus	Halfshire . .	Do.
	Oswaldesle .	Oswaldslaw .	Bp. of Worcester
	Persore . .	Pershore .	⅓ Abbot of Per- shore, ⅔ Abbot of Westminster
Yorkshire .	Aggebrigg .	Agbrigg .	King
	Alvertonshire .	Allertonshire .	Bishop of Durham
	Aynesty .	Ainsty . .	Mayor and Bur- gesses of York
	Barkeston .	Barkstone-Ash .	King
	Buccros . .	Buckrose .	Do.
	Bulmer . .	Bulmer .	Do.
	Brudford . .	Birdforth .	Do.
	Clarhou . .	Claro .	Do.
	Dykering [P., . R.H., I, 115]	Dickering .	Do.

COUNTY	NAME OF HUNDRED		LORD OF HUNDRED, 1274
	In 13th cent.	*Modern form*	
Yorkshire —*cont.*	Ywcros . .	Ewcross . .	King
	Gilling . .	Gilling (East and West)	John of Brittany
	Halikeld . .	Hallikeld . .	Do.
	Hange . .	Hang (East and West)	Do.
	Herthille .	Harthill . .	[King]
	Holdernesse	Holderness .	In escheator's hands, by death of Countess of Lancaster
	Houedenshyr' .	Howdenshire .	Bishop of Durham
	Langeberge .	Langbaurgh .	Walter de Faukeberg and Marmaduke de Tweng
	Morley . .	Morley . .	King
	Osgotecros .	Osgoldcross .	[Henry Lacy, E. of Lincoln]
	Use and Derwent	Ouse and Derwent	King
	Pykering .	Pickering .	Edmund of Lan-
	Rydal . .	Ryedale . .	King [caster
	Schyrayk .	Skyrack . .	Do.
	Stayncliff .	Staincliffe .	Henry Lacy, E. of
	Stayncros .	Staincross .	Do. [Lincoln
	Strafford .	Strafforth and .	King
	Tykehull .	Tickhill . .	Do.

APPENDIX V

HUNDRED COURT ROLLS OF A DATE PREVIOUS TO 1307

COUNTY	HUNDRED	PERIOD COVERED BY ROLLS	WHERE PRESERVED
Cambridge (Isle of Ely)	Wisbeach	1302–7	Ely, Diocesan Registry
Derby	Appletree	1292–3 ; 1304 ?	P.R.O., Duchy of Lancaster Court Rolls, 43/482, 488
	Gresley	1302	Do., 43/484
	Wirksworth	1281	Do., 43/485
Gloucestershire	Longtree (?)	1273	P.R.O., Court Rolls, 175/79
Hampshire	Crondall	1281–1307	MSS. of Dean and Chapter of Winchester. (First roll printed in Baigent) *Crondal Records*, pp. 142–8
Kent	Hoo	1289–90	Middleton MSS. (Hist. M. Comm., p. 285)
	Larkfield	1305–6	Do.
	Middleton or Milton	1289–92	P.R.O. Court Rolls, 181/74–76
	Wye	1284–1304	Do., 182/1–7
Norfolk	Clackclose	1282, 1284	P.R.O. Court Rolls, 192/67, 68. (Printed in part, in Ault, *Court Rolls of Ramsey Abbey*, pp. 147–69)
Wiltshire	Chalk	1283–4	Brit. Mus. Add. R. 6269
	Highworth	1275–1287 [1]	P.R.O. Court Rolls, 208/83–93
	Kinwardstone	1262	Do., 209/6
	Whorwelsdon	1261–2	P.R.O. Court Rolls, 208/1. (Printed Maitland, *Select Pleas in Manorial Courts*, pp. 178–82)

[1] These rolls cover the period when Adam de Stratton, Chamberlain of the Exchequer, was lord of Highworth Hundred ; he forfeited the hundred, with other possessions, for offences disclosed in the State Trials of 1289–93.

INDEX

The following abbreviations are used throughout : H. = Hundred ; W. = Wapentake; S. = Sheriff ; E. = Earl. References to Appendix IV are not included ; a complete list of hundreds will be found there, arranged alphabetically by counties.

Abdick H., Som., 145
Abingdon, Inquest at, 41
Adams, G. B., cited, 17, 207
Affeerors, 117, 185
Agmead H., Gloucs., 149
Ainsty W., Yorks, 217
Albemarle, E. of, 22
Albemarle, Isabella, Countess of, 57, 140, 163, 168, 264, 268 f., 283
Alderbury H., Wilts., 57, 176
Aloesbridge H., Kent, 178
Alton H., Hants, 142
Amesbury H., Wilts., 57
Amounderness W., Lancs., 6 f., 145 f., 154, 169
Ancient demesne. *See* Crown
Andersfield H., Som., 145
Appeal, 67, 70, 114, 179, 228
Appleton W., Derb., 145, 169, 173, 180 f., 184 f., 193, 286
Approvers, 67, 70–2, 179, 228
Armingford H., Cambs., 123, 149, 172
Arrest, 67 ff.
Articuli super Cartas, 61
Arundel H., Suss., 168
Assize, justices of, 31, 95, 228 f.
    of arms (1181), 188 ; (1242), 189
    of bread and ale, 56, 185, 203, 205, 209 ff., 235
Assized rents, 90 f., 127, 142, 162, 164, 166
Assizes, the possessory, 6, 14, 66, 78, 79, 158, 222
Aswardby W., Lincs., 171
Attorneys (proxies), 173, 184
Austage, 165
Avelund W., Lincs., 159
Averpenny, 216
Axminster H., Devon, 144
Aylesbury, inquest at (1274), 40

Babergh H., Suffolk, 155, 157
Bachelery, the, of 1259, 24 f., 34, 85
Bail, 73

Bailiff, of borough, 56 f., 68, 99, 102,
    of hundred. *See* Hundred bailiff
    of last, 136
    of lathe, 91
    of liberty, 73 f., 76, 78, 86, 113, 133 f., 136
    of lord, 68, 69, 87, 120
    of rape, 136, 149
    of riding, 136
    of sheriff. *See* Sheriff's Staff
    See also Master bailiff, Sub-bailiff
Bailiff errant, 75, 135 f., 138, 154
Banbury H., Oxon., 91
Banlieu of a liberty, 206
Barclay H., Kent, 179
Barford H., Beds., 126
Barnwell, Canon of (*Liber Memorandorum*), cited, 80, 110
Barrow H., Som., 145
Barstable H., Ess., 140, 159
Bassetlaw H., Notts., 154, 230, 259
Bath H., Som., 145, 151
Battle Abbey, Liberty of, 206, 280 f.
Beaminster H., Dorset, 145
Beauver, 142
Bedel, the, 83, 106, 133, 153 f., 156, 158, 160, 223
Bedfordshire : crown lands in, 197
    hundreds of, 137, 157
    in 1274–5, 167
Bempstone H., Som., 123, 145
Bereford, William, Chief Justice, 111
Bereford, Osbert of (H. R. Commissioner), 97
Berkeley H., Gloucs., 147, 179 *n.*
Berkeley, Giles of, S. of Heref., 65
Berkshire : crown lands in, 196
    hundreds of, 9, 141, 149
    sheriff of, 2, 100
Beupleder fine, 91, 117 f., 122
Beynherst H., Berks., 149
Bingham W., Notts., 73, 231
Bishop's Rouburgh H., Wilts. (Modern Potterne), 56
Blackbourne H., Suff., 146, 153, 174

287

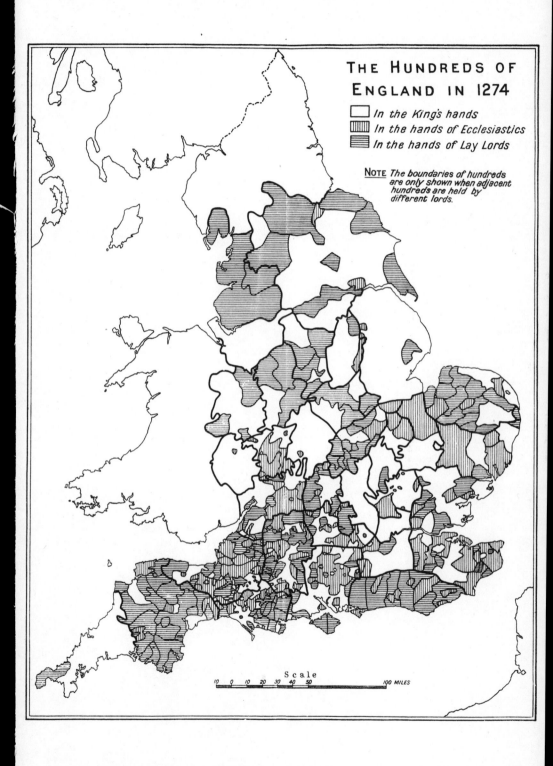

THE HUNDREDS OF
ENGLAND IN 1274

☐ In the King's hands
▥ In the hands of Ecclesiastics
▤ In the hands of Lay Lords

NOTE The boundaries of hundreds
are only shown when adjacent
hundreds are held by
different lords.

Scale

10   0   10   20   30   40   50   100 MILES